DARK STATE

www.richardmoorenorth.com
www.richardmoorebooks.com

Dark State
Copyright 2021 by Richard Moore

Cover design by Lisa Moore

Portions of this book first appeared in similar form in *The Lakeland Times*, and some passages written by Richard Moore appeared in Our View editorials.

Back cover photo: Copy of a record released on August 15, 2020, to *The Lakeland Times* by Oneida County (Wisconsin) board chairman David Hintz, responding to an open records request made nearly three months earlier.

First edition

ISBN 978-0-9906593-3-4

DARK STATE

How citizens can open the doors to Wisconsin's closed government

RICHARD MOORE

HIGHLAND HOUSE PRESS
Woodruff, Wisconsin

ALSO BY RICHARD MOORE

NONFICTION

How the DNR Stole Wisconsin

January Thaw

The Clarity of Clay

Journeys of Lightheartedness

The New Bossism

The Reform of State Legislatures (contributing author)

BOOKLETS

Peace of Mind

What's a Woman's Work Worth?

Rocking Chair Country

COMING IN 2021

How to Write What You Want to Read

Mapping the Close Years

ACKNOWLEDGMENT

It should go without saying that Gregg Walker, the publisher of *The Lakeland Times* and *Northwoods River News*, has an unsurpassed commitment to open government, and his passion for opening if not crashing through closed government doors is legendary. Without Gregg, this book would not have been possible. It's not just that the newspaper he owns and runs has the resources; sure it does. But many newspapers have such resources and do not use them so aggressively to champion and preserve the transparency in government that is so vital to our democratic republic.

In writing this book, I have become aware of how important a role *The Lakeland Times* has played in the shaping of today's transparency landscape—far more than I realized when the actual battles were being waged—preserving it to a far greater extent than it would have been otherwise and in some cases expanding openness into places we never thought we would see. More than that, Gregg knows when to press a fight and when to fold it, and possesses a vision that allows him to see the implications in a violation—sometimes being far greater than it would seem at first glance.

Most people in Wisconsin will never know just how much they owe what open government we have left to Gregg Walker. Suffice it to say I am proud to have had a career working for him at *The Lakeland Times*. There's no other place I would have rather been, and no more important task to have pursued.

Contents

Preamble

A Call for Action

Aside from being the burial place of football's great John Heisman, and the home of its not-so-cuddly-but-still-lovable Hodag, the city of Rhinelander in northern Wisconsin isn't known much for its celebrity. Not that the namesake of football's highest award isn't significant or that the Hodag isn't cool.

They are.

And Rhinelander is a decent working-class town full of decent people. It just hasn't had all that much opportunity to shine, even in tourism, in the remote winter-bitten Northwoods.

Until late 2019, that is. On a gray November day—November 21, to be precise—the sun broke through. Not literally, of course. It was only 39 degrees, the skies overcast, with a light breeze flinging occasional snow flurries about the city.

The falling snow was down to no more than a smattering as deputies of the Oneida County Sheriff's Office, which was commanded by sheriff Grady Hartman, pulled up to city hall. Taking crisp steps and wearing sober faces, law enforcement officials, assisted by officers from three other agencies, swiftly executed search warrants against the Rhinelander city administrator at the time.

These were not just any search warrants. The execution of warrants at a city hall would be dramatic any time it happens, but it was even more noteworthy because of the reason for the warrants—a potential violation of the state's open government laws.

Officers did not execute those warrants to find evidence of mid-management embezzlement. They did not enter the building to find a politician engaged in contract fraud or in dealing or buying drugs or who was committing election crimes. Rather, they entered the building to protect the people's right to access information that the people already owned, and to be confident that that information had not been altered.

Specifically, the search warrants were for misconduct in public office, and they were executed based on an open records complaint by the *Northwoods River News*. (Full disclosure: I write for the newspaper.)

As far as I can tell, it was the first time in Wisconsin that a law-enforcement agency had raided a government building based upon an open records complaint. It was at least the first time in my 25 years as a reporter in the state that such a thing had occurred. At long last someone in the justice system had taken a stand for open government. Hartman and the entire sheriff's department had stood up for the people's right to know, for their right to run their own government.

None of which was to pronounce judgment on the city administrator, who deserved his day in court and who appears likely not to be convicted of anything (the case is ongoing as of this writing), in part because the state's open records and misconduct in public office laws are so weak. So weak that flagrant conduct—and there was flagrant conduct—and even statutory violations are virtually impossible to prosecute as serious transparency crimes. More about that later. For now, what was important was, when presented with probable cause that transparency laws were broken, the sheriff acted.

That Hartman did so is exceptional in an age when just about everyone in the justice system treats open government laws as second-class citizens, or worse, as illegitimate bindlestiffs trespassing on the proper terrain of state law. These days, it is rare for a district attorney to prosecute an open meetings or public records violation, or to exact any consequences even when guilt is found. In Wisconsin, open government laws haven't been taken seriously.

On November 21, 2019, that narrative changed significantly. Oneida County sheriff Grady Hartman not only executed warrants but in so doing served notice to all local government officials that his department would not look the other way when there was probable cause to think those laws had been broken, the law's weakness notwithstanding. The sheriff's actions were commendable.

To be sure, Oneida County is but one of 72 in the state. And, while the events in Rhinelander could represent a sea change in official thinking, it's possible, if not probable, it could become an isolated event, an outlier and anomaly, unless citizens follow up with their own demands for openness. That's especially so given a law so weak it is virtually impossible to charge those purposely evading the law—and there are many—with any serious crime.

The truth is, as we head into 2021, Wisconsin is a Dark State, its citizens intentionally kept in the dark about what their government is doing. And, with the notable exception of that day when the sun broke through in Oneida County and of a few other patches of sunlight spattered about, things are getting darker.

And so this call for action. For those reading this book outside Wisconsin, please read on. For while this may be a case study of one state, the same trends are occurring in every state and nationally. They may be clothed slightly differently, but everywhere the thieves of transparency are at work, and I hope this book can not only lead to their capture in your state but offer helpful policy prescriptions.

—

Over the past several decades, the open government movement has become a powerful force both across the country and in Wisconsin. Not many speeches escape a politician's mouth without mention of just how transparent the politician is. Every public official these days, both Right and Left, is committed to "letting the sun shine in."

If you don't believe it, just ask them.

The truth is, though, the open government movement is in serious trouble. Indeed, as this book will show, this is one of the darkest moments in "letting the sun shine in" that we have endured since the movement itself became a popular force in the 1970s and 1980s. That's true in the United States, and it's true in Wisconsin. It's as if government officials had stripped Lady Justice of her blindfold and are trying to put it instead on all the citizens of the state. And, over the past decade, they have been quite successful in masking our ability to see into certain areas of government activity.

To cite just one example, once upon a time Wisconsin had become one of the first states in which the state Supreme Court conducted deliberations and discussed broad administrative and policy matters in open session. In 2012, they ditched that "experiment," as one justice later described it, and went behind closed doors except when discussing changes to the court's formal rules. Then, in 2017, they voted to go behind closed doors on even more important matters, such as ethics policies. The important point here is that, where once the high court struck a progressive blow for openness, in the last decade it has headed in the other direction, taping over the court's transparent windows a little at a time, which is the trend overall in the state today.

"It is time for us to return to how a court actually operates," then justice Michael Gableman was reported as saying by the *Milwaukee Journal Sentinel*, in arguing in 2017 for more closed administrative sessions.

In other words, in Gableman's view, a court is supposed to operate in the dark, behind closed doors. Apparently a majority of justices over the past decade has agreed. The only problem is, not one of them has ever made a cogent argument why that should be so.

Then, too, in a stunning 2014 decision, a state appeals court ruled that when a government authority says a requested record belongs to a class of records exempt from access under the law, then it is exempt, no matter whether the record is authentic or forged, and that even a judge does not have the right to review those records to see if the government entity is telling the truth.

In other words, so-called exempt records are exempt any time officials say they are, even if those officials fabricated the documents, and no scrutiny or exposure is allowed, paving the way for officials to manufacture administrative fantasies and citizenry nightmares. It was a breath-taking decision inviting all sorts of corruption, and it took place without much notice in progressive Wisconsin. Now, state and local governments are places where bureaucratic dreams can indeed come true, one way or another.

Not that there haven't been some very notable open government achievements. As the Wisconsin Supreme Court declared in a 2010 case, "If Wisconsin were not known as the Dairy State, it could be known, and rightfully so, as the Sunshine State." That's an extremely arguable point—and this book does argue it—but in the past 40 years, before its terrible turn in the last decade or so, the state did make strides in opening the doors and filing cabinets and computers of government.

Fees for open records must be kept to actual costs, for example; a citizen can bypass a prosecutor and take an open records complaint straight to court, with the state acting as plaintiff on the citizen's behalf; with a notable exception, government entities and their agencies must keep records for specified periods of time, usually seven years, and the records, with certain exemptions, are presumed to be accessible; closed investigative files are public records, too, and records requesters don't have to reveal their identities or reasons for the records they are seeking.

Also important, denials of records requests must list the statutory exception being used to deny the records. Likewise, government meetings are expected to be open, with agendas specific as to the topics to be discussed and acted upon, and the burden is on government actors to demonstrate why any meeting should be closed.

In sum, the state's open meetings and open records laws presume openness, and the codified requirements for records access and open meetings are considered foundational. They were among the strongest in the country.

But, in the past decade especially, there have been colossal setbacks. The history of open government is always one of give-and-take, one step forward and a half-step back or more. Always there will be obstructionist government bureaucrats and elected officials who seek to find loopholes in the law, or to interpret them in secretive fashion. The truth is, many who crow about their commitment to transparency are not actually committed to transparency, often enough just the opposite. That's just life, as it is in many arenas of public policy.

In recent years, however, this natural tension between transparency and secrecy has given way to aggressive new threats against openness as those in power seek not merely to bend and exploit the law where they can but to rewrite and repeal the law altogether. In every branch of government, forces for secrecy have amassed not to obstruct the law but to destroy it, and the efforts have been successful far more so than most imagine.

One could say that the open government movement is a victim of its own success. Because of the actual gains made through the years (even if the most important ones were in the early years); because of universal commitments to transparency by politicians everywhere, evidencing the popularity of transparency as a cause; because of the burgeoning open-data movement, where governments open public portals into vast amounts of government-collected data; because of the annual celebrations of Sunshine Week—because of all those things open government is often treated these days as a given.

The more astute observers among us know it is not. Counterintuitively, not only is the fight for transparency not won, it is being lost, and lost at a furious pace. Most average citizens don't see it, either, precisely because of the camouflage of the past successes: the political proclamations, the open-data portals, the celebrations.

Perhaps it's more accurate to say that the open government movement is not so much a victim of its own success as it is a victim of its perceived success. We're so busy going gaga over our storied history and everybody's self-proclaimed commitment to transparency that we aren't paying attention to the warplanes gathering in the sky above us.

So, then, just what are the threats to our cherished openness?

The first is the law itself. Now there's no question that Wisconsin once was a leader in letting the sun shine into state and local government, and the open meetings law, enacted in 1975, and the modern open records law, enacted in 1982, reflect that progressivism. To be clear, the laws were foundational, ahead of their time, and they are still progressive compared to some states.

But that was 40 years ago, light years ago in technological time. Put simply, the laws are outdated. Back then, records were largely paper records, and no one contemplated the complexities that would accompany digital formats: whether the metadata was part of the record, not to mention the issue of interactive public participation and access posed not only by government meetings but by accompanying emails, texts, and other digital communications between government officials. Back then, too, a meeting was a meeting, people gathered in a room, and so no one really contemplated walking quorums and negative quorums, or, for that matter, attending meetings by Zoom.

It was a time when the statutory definition of government business was understood by everybody to be a quorum of a government entity discussing business over which it had jurisdiction. That is not necessarily the case anymore.

The second threat is the open government movement's neglect of the right-to-privacy movement, which also involves technology. Those advances, for better or worse, have enabled government to see ever more into the private lives of citizens and to collect data about them and about virtually anything. Government data can tell you how much your neighbors' homes sold for, and what permits they have taken out, and government records can tell you who is tax delinquent.

That's just the tip of the iceberg. The problem is, as government makes more and more use of technology to collect reams of personal data for various aspects of policymaking, the transparency movement presses ever harder for all that data to be open, thus jeopardizing the right to privacy, at least in the view of many privacy advocates.

Opponents of open government see that collision course between the two as a logical contradiction, and argue that privacy, in moral equation as well as in constitutional doctrine, trumps open government. This is a red herring—even the open government laws of the 1970s and 1980s are flexible enough to resolve the contradiction satisfactorily, but privacy itself is a movement of particular potency in the modern age, and open government opponents have seized upon it to crusade for secrecy, which, ironically, would likely sacrifice privacy even more.

This book argues that the right to open government and the right to privacy should be two sides of the same coin, not opposing currencies, and that it is vital that the transparency movement make this so.

The third biggest threat to the open government movement, and it seems strange to say it, is, well, the open government movement itself. That is to say, for decades the open government movement was a unary campaign, otherwise known as the freedom-of-information (FOIA) movement, a movement concerned with processes, such as open meetings, and disclosures through public records of the actions of government officials.

In recent times, though, a second distinct and parallel campaign has emerged within the open government movement, transforming it into a binary construction—the open government data movement. Simply put, the open data movement seeks to have all or most of the information government compiles universally accessible, where the public can use, share, and redistribute it freely and collaboratively.

But strains have emerged between the two sides, and there are questions about the impact of the latter on the former, and what the competition for scarce resources means for both. This book will explore that competitive nature in detail.

Suffice it to say up front that the traditionalists—the FOIA supporters—believe the open data movement is draining precious resources away from FOIA efforts that are critical to keeping government and business leaders accountable on a daily basis. It is further argued that government officials now release reams of technical data through web portals—data that oftentimes average citizens lack the expertise or time to make use of and analyze—as a way to justify their refusal to fulfill mundane yet more revealing and understandable records requests detailing the public's business.

As a result, at least in this view, the terrain of 'open data' becomes largely surrendered to experts—more often than not biased partisans—who analyze and spin the data, leaving the public to take in the data through ideological filters.

The fourth dire threat to the open government movement is posed by our state elected officials, principally the position of governor and the elected representatives and senators of the state Legislature. Anyone who follows *The Lakeland Times's* annual Sunshine Grades knows that the governor of the state and the entire Legislature as a body get the worst grades of all.

That's right, the governor and the Legislature—the people who make our laws and enforce them—are the biggest proponents of the Dark State, the biggest enemies of openness. Just how could this have possibly happened, and what does it mean for open government?

To be sure, the Legislature has for years now consistently opposed transparency and not just passively. It exempts itself from records retention laws, which effectively exempts that body from the open records law; it thwarts open records requests any way it can; and it generally refuses to release investigative records about its members and staff.

When both the state's legislative and executive branches are so entrenched in hole-and-corner conduct—and if anything unites the two political parties, it's that conduct because Republicans and Democrats are all equally guilty here—two nightmarish scenarios are likely to play out.

First, sooner or later, they will gut the open government laws completely. That's just what lawmakers and then Gov. Scott Walker tried to do in 2015. Back then, they did it so brazenly and radically—it was a virtual repeal of the open records statutes—that they provoked a rebellion among the populace and backed down.

Their failure has not stopped them from trying, though, and so instead the Legislature and the current governor, Tony Evers, chip away here and there, trying to deliver death by a thousand cuts. There are always lawmakers poised to take away online court records, to expand records exemptions in general, and to increase costs for citizens seeking records—records they have already paid for with their taxes.

The second ramification of having such opposition in the Legislature and in the governor's office is the bad message it sends to local officials. If the Legislature isn't going to follow the law, if the governor isn't going to follow the law, why should anyone else? Our statewide elected officials set a tone, after all, and it's not a pleasing one that emanates from Madison these days.

The fifth major threat to open government comes from the state's judiciary, which has stacked so many bad decisions upon bad decisions that case law resembles a Dagwood sandwich. There are some decent court rulings, to be sure—to cite just one recent example, an appeals court determined that requesters have the right to receive digital records when requested in that format, if they exist, and that's a huge cost saver for those requesting records—but there are a slew of bad decisions to overcompensate for the good ones.

What's most concerning about the judicial trend is that, in the bad decisions, judges are actively rewriting the law, and not for the better. Later we will take a look at a very recent case, now on appeal, in which Oneida County judge Michael Bloom attempts to allow government bodies to meet in secret to discuss almost any topic they want, except in one narrow instance, but courts across the state, including the state Supreme Court, are engaged in the same kind of legislating.

For instance, the Supreme Court allowed officials to withhold records of those who had voted midway through a three-week union election when the union requested them because, according to the court, union officials might have used those records to pressure those who had not yet voted. That decision effectively rewrites the statute because it allows the motivations, or potential motivations, of requesters to be considered in an open records request, contrary to the plain language of the law, namely, that an open record is open to anyone and for any reason.

Of course, the Legislature could take action by passing new language that would underscore its true intent and render such court decisions null and void, but, given the hostility to transparency in the Legislature, that is not going to happen anytime soon.

Finally, perhaps the most important threat to open government is the lack of consequences for breaking the open meetings or open records laws. Right now, an open meetings violation is simply a forfeiture of between $25 and $300. A public records infraction may involve criminal penalties for destruction, damage, removal, or concealment of public records with intent to injure or defraud, or for altering or falsifying public records, but all other infractions involve civil forfeitures, not to exceed $1,000 against a legal custodian. Damages and legal fees may also have to be paid, but taxpayers pick up the tab for all of those.

In many cases, district attorneys, when they don't ignore complaints completely, merely admonish the guilty parties without issuing citations. And when they do, what are the consequences? Many times the open meetings fines are $25, or a scolding (Don't do that again!), or a demand that the guilty take an hour of open government training, which of course is next to impossible to find.

The problem is, when a prosecutor loudly announces that he or she doesn't consider open meetings or open records violations serious enough to cite or serious enough to impose even the statutory penalty for those violations, he or she is announcing to the world that it is okay for others to break that law.

Any law for which there is no consequence for breaking is in effect no law at all. It's a mirage, always seemingly there in the distance, teasing you with thirst-quenching protection, but never quite materializing when you need it. Even worse, the lack of teeth is an open invitation to break the law, the equivalent of a legal shrug of the shoulders.

If no one is ever going to be punished for breaking those laws, if the justice system is always going to look the other way, why bother following them anyway?

To be sure, a raft of studies indicates that the certainty of punishment rather than the severity of it is a more effective deterrent to lawbreaking. But that is only true when the certain punishment carries with it some significant exactment. In the case of open government laws, there has been neither certainty nor severity, and that has led to brazen defiance by local officials as they close government from the public.

Dark State will explore each of these obstacles to openness, but proposals and activism that would once again let the sun shine in will be plumbed as well.

Indeed, none of this is to argue there is no hope. Just the opposite, there is the bright glimmer in Rhinelander, witnessed like the Northern star, a beacon now for all law enforcement and district attorneys to follow. Then, too, important institutions have emerged to fight secrecy, groups such as the Wisconsin Institute for Law & Liberty and the Wisconsin Transparency Project, which are fighting in the trenches alongside age-old allies in openness.

Most important, as this book will recount, in the past several years citizens in small towns across the state, from Lafayette County in southwestern Wisconsin to Boulder Junction in northern Wisconsin, have fought against government secrecy and corruption and won. These average citizens, keen to be engaged, point to a path for victory. But all of us must listen to what they have to say.

For the moment, it is enough to say that now is the time to focus our attention on openness as a foundational principle, a principle to be elevated and fought for in every political campaign and in every movement for advocacy. For without it, no cause—liberal or conservative, libertarian or collectivist, statist or individualist—no cause at all can truly be authenticated and debated and decided in the public square, for the public square will not be in the arena of decision-making. Important decisions will be made in dark government back alleys, the reasons for which will be elusive, barricaded as they are from public view and inquiry.

Such decisions can only serve one cause, the cause of the power of those making them, not of any true merit or democratic constituency.

In an 1804 letter to John Tyler, Thomas Jefferson summed it up:

"No experiment can be more interesting than that we are now trying, and which we trust will end in establishing the fact, that man may be governed by reason and truth. Our first object should therefore be, to leave open to him all the avenues to truth."

Jefferson was specifically talking about the freedom of the press, the first to be "shut up by those who fear the investigation of their actions," as he put it. The press may still be first in line to be shut up, but all of us who would question decisions and investigate closed government actions leading to those decisions are in line not far behind. Rest assured, government officials seeking secrecy won't stop with the press.

Then, too, they have their mammoth corporate allies, the big oil and chemical, telecommunications, and technology industries that have come to dominate so much of our lives. They limit our freedoms and choices, they rob us of our prosperity, and more and more they take away our ability to protest their actions and petition our government with our grievances. Sadly, too often secretive government agencies are their gatekeepers and guardians. To say it bluntly, and it seems incredible to believe in the United States, but it is true, we are being oppressed by these special interest coalitions. Our constitution and our civil liberties are not merely being overthrown, they are being imprisoned as things that can no longer be tolerated.

We must surrender to corporate judgements about what we can see and hear to protect us from misinformation, Facebook and Twitter tell us. We must relinquish our freedom to assemble and travel so the government can keep us safe, government officials decree. We must agree to let government act in secrecy, so the experts can concentrate on keeping us healthy without fear of distraction or of disagreement with their science.

Censorship and secrecy are the foundations of this new coalition; open government and freedom of speech are its enemies.

Without question, open government, the freedoms of speech and religion and assembly, the freedom to petition our government and protest, and, not least, the freedom to think are on the line. Open government and civil liberties are the weapons we have, and they must be foundational, core principles as we go forward, for it is hard to argue that core democratic rights are not essential to the hopes of all sides of the political divide.

An old protest sung once cautioned us that "freedom doesn't come like a bird on the wing; it doesn't come down like the summer rain; Freedom,

freedom is a hard-won thing; you've got to work for it, fight for it, day and night for it, and every generation has to win it again."

It is time for our generations to fight and win it again. That is no less important in Wisconsin than it is on the national and international stages. In Wisconsin, as this book will show, transparency and thus fundamental liberties are being attacked and they are being attacked by Democrats and Republicans alike. To beat back that assault, it will take a powerful force of a citizenry united in the critical cause of freedom to fight for our liberties.

It will take Republicans and Democrats alike to fight together—and to fight together now—for the most important cause of transparency.

Chapter 1

Wisconsin: Sunshine State, or Dark State?

This past year, the Wisconsin Freedom of Information Council, a reliable and steadfast organization when it comes to standing up for open government, was glowing in its praise of retiring state Supreme Court justice Shirley Abrahamson, bestowing upon her its Political Openness Award for a lifetime of standing up for open government.

To be sure, Abrahamson had her share of decisive rulings in support of transparency. She even wrote a lead opinion in 2010 from which I have already quoted: "If Wisconsin were not known as the Dairy State it could be known, and rightfully so, as the Sunshine State. All branches of Wisconsin government have, over many years, kept a strong commitment to transparent government."

Ironically, though, those words were written in a terrible decision that, with Abrahamson's support, effectively rewrote the public records statute to create a new exemption for documents, such as emails, that were created on government computers for personal rather than public purposes.

The case involved a request for all emails sent by teachers on work computers. The teachers did not mind turning over work emails but balked at turning over personal emails sent on those computers, and so they went to court to block the school district from releasing them.

Before the ruling, all documents on government computers were considered public records that must be released; after the court's 5-2 decision, government workers no longer have to turn over personal communications composed on those computers.

That might seem reasonable, but, as the dissenting justices on the court pointed out, that means taking the word of those employees that the records were actually for personal use. After all, who knows if the records are truly personal if they don't have to be released.

It was a decision of subterfuge that mocked and subverted Abrahamson's claim that Wisconsin was the Sunshine State, and it is a shining example of a court using a decision to rewrite and restrict Wisconsin's open government laws. Though Abrahamson celebrated the triumph of transparency, she embedded her words in a court decision that itself undermined the claim.

The seminal case is worth a recap because it quintessentially underscores all the moving parts of our transport to darkness: a vague law that the high court exploits to rewrite in a way that undermines openness; the interplay between the right to privacy and the right to transparency; and the refusal of the Legislature to correct a bad decision. We'll explore each of those elements separately but this case classically demonstrates their interplay and complexity.

The case also cleanly captures the three dominant schools of thoughts on the modern landscape of open government: those who want to wall off ever more activities of government as none of the public's business; those who believe open government is beginning to trample privacy rights; and those who actually believe in transparency.

In the opinion, there were four separate summations: the lead opinion joined by two other justices; two concurring analyses; and a dissent joined by one other justice. All totaled, a majority of four justices concluded that personal emails on government computers were in fact public records, while a different majority of five determined such emails should not be disclosed. Despite the lack of compatibility in the opinions, one thing was clear: The emails of government employees are no longer open for inspection merely because they are written and stored on a government computer or because they were composed and sent during work hours.

Three distinct views emerged, and their reasoning provides a worthy summation of each line of thought.

Abrahamson, then the chief justice, and justices Patrick Crooks and David Prosser found that the emails did not qualify as public records because of their purely personal nature. Therefore, they wrote, they should not be disclosed. These were the believers in secrecy.

Justices Ann Walsh Bradley and Michael Gableman believed the emails were public records but that the public's interest in nondisclosure of personal emails that do not violate law or policy always outweighs the public's interest in disclosure. These were believers in open government, but believers who believed more in privacy than in transparency.

Justices Patience Roggensack and Annette Ziegler said the emails were clearly public records that required release. These were the truly committed to the principles of openness.

The latter opinion was shared by attorney and open records expert Robert Dreps, who had filed a nonparty brief on behalf of the Wisconsin Freedom of Information Council, the Wisconsin Broadcasters Association, the Wisconsin Newspaper Association, the *Milwaukee Journal Sentinel*, Journal Broadcast Group, Inc., and the Associated Press.

However, the Wisconsin Education Association Council (WEAC), whose attorney had represented the interests of the large teachers' union and had filed a brief for five teachers whose emails were implicated in the case, praised the ruling.

"The decision supports the intent of Wisconsin's public records law, which clearly states that it does not benefit the public interest to require that any public employee's miscellaneous personal emails that have nothing to do with government business be released," Mary Bell, WEAC president at the time, said.

The case began in 2007 when a citizen, Don Bubolz, sent the Wisconsin Rapids school district an open records request for all emails from the teachers' school computers for the period March 1, 2007, through April 13, 2007.

The school district subsequently notified the teachers it would release the emails. The teachers filed suit in circuit court, saying the contested emails were personal and thus could not be construed as public records under the statute. The school district acknowledged that those messages were private in nature but the teachers nonetheless lost in circuit court.

On April 30, 2009, the court of appeals certified the case to the Supreme Court "to determine if the employees' personal emails are public records and if they are, whether public policy reasons outweigh the public's interest in disclosure."

In the court's lead opinion, Abrahamson said the content of a document was determinative, not when or where it was written.

The justices, she wrote, had reviewed all possible interpretations of the open records law to determine what was and what was not a record: the text of the statute; the Legislature's statement of intent; the statutory history and case law interpretations of prior versions of the statute; executive branch interpretations of the definition of records, especially the opinions of the attorney general; as well as practices and laws in other states.

"All these avenues of interpretation lead to one conclusion: In determining whether a document is a record under (the public records law), the focus is on the content of the document," Abrahamson wrote. "To be a record under (the law), the content of the document must have a connection to a government function."

As for the emails at hand, she continued, no one contested their personal nature. What's more, no one had asked the circuit court or the Supreme Court to examine the contents of the emails to determine whether they were indeed personal or related to government business or were a mixture of the two.

Abrahamson said the school district's policy allowed the teachers to use school computers to write personal emails, and such a policy could be a good thing, while a lack of privacy—there's that word again—could impede productivity and personnel recruitment. And when workers use such email for personal purposes, those emails are private, she concluded.

"The personal contents of these emails are not subject to release to a record requester merely because they are sent or received using the government employers' email systems and then stored and maintained on those systems," Abrahamson wrote.

In separate concurring opinions, Bradley and Gableman agreed with the lead opinion in part and disagreed in part. While they thought the emails were public records under the law, they both concluded there was no public interest in disclosure.

In examining the statutory definition of 'record,' Bradley stated, she believed the language clearly placed the emails in the public realm, both by definition and by the lack of any specific exemptions for them. Nothing in the definition distinguished between content that was personal and content that was work-related when that content was prepared by an originator and in the possession of the custodian, she stated.

Indeed, Bradley wrote, the definition of records in the law points to "any material on which written, drawn, printed, spoken, visual, or electromagnetic information or electronically generated or stored data is recorded or preserved, regardless of physical form or characteristics, that has been created or is being kept by an authority," and "includes, but is not limited to, handwritten, typed, or printed pages, maps, charts, photographs, films, recordings, tapes, optical discs, and any other medium on which electronically generated or stored data is recorded or preserved."

To be sure, the justice continued, the definition does not include drafts, notes, or other preliminary documents "prepared for the originator's personal use" or "materials that are purely the personal property of the custodian and have no relation to his or her office," but the teachers' emails were not the personal property of the custodian and the reference to drafts and other preliminary documents clearly referred to items that would ultimately, after editing, become permanent records, such as the minutes of meetings that would be edited and finalized.

More determinative was the assertion that "any material on which [information or data] is recorded and preserved" and that has been created or kept by an authority is a record, with the exception of those preliminary drafts, Bradley asserted. That definition makes clear that it is where the documents are stored rather than the content that is decisive, Bradley argued—it is the material or medium on which the data is recorded and preserved, like a government computer.

"Given this definition and unlike the lead opinion, I conclude that the teachers' personal emails are records," she wrote.

That said, Bradley continued, a records custodian still has an obligation to determine whether the record is purely personal and, once that is resolved, personal records should not be released because "the public interest in nondisclosure will always outweigh the public interest in disclosure."

Her conclusion, she wrote, rested on the open records law's public policy declaration, which is "that all persons are entitled to the greatest possible information regarding the affairs of government and the official acts of those officers and employees who represent them."

In this case, and in the case of other personal emails, the release of the records would not fall within the parameters of meeting that public policy, Bradley concluded.

What's more, the justice stated, there was a public interest in keeping the emails private, because, as the lead opinion argued, allowing private email use can boost productivity and help attract and retain good employees, both of which are in the public interest.

Finally, Bradley said she could find no precedent for releasing the emails.

"In the years since the advent of email and the resulting changes in the way that we communicate, many jurisdictions have been asked to address whether personal emails should be disclosed in response to a records request," she wrote. "Every single one of the jurisdictions has concluded that the policies underlying public records laws do not support the disclosure of purely personal emails that evince no violation of law or policy."

Gableman wrote a separate opinion finding the records to be public but not subject to disclosure, but Roggensack and Ziegler dissented vociferously to allowing the teachers an exception to the law.

"This exception, when combined with the concurring opinions, grants government employees (here, teachers) a broad, blanket exception for emails that the teachers create in school district email accounts, on school district computers, maintained by school district servers, when the teachers characterize their emails as 'personal,'" Roggensack wrote. "This broad exception prevents the public from discovering what public employees are doing during the workday, in the workplace, using equipment purchased with public funds."

In so doing, she continued, the court had contravened Wisconsin's long history of transparency in, and public access to, actions of government employees.

"It is contrary to the letter and the spirit of the public records law and is a disservice to the public's interest in government oversight," she stated.

For one thing, she wrote, the concurring opinion misread the Wisconsin statute in discussing the law's public policy declaration and what Roggensack called the law's clear and unambiguous language stating that there is to be "full access" to records. She quoted the law to make her point: "To that end, ss. 19.32 to 19.37 shall be construed in every instance with a presumption of complete public access, consistent with the conduct of governmental business," the law's public policy objective states. "The denial of public access generally is contrary to the public interest, and only in an exceptional case may access be denied."

Roggensack said the lead opinion ignored that objective, too.

"The legislature's statement that Wis. Stat. 'ss. 19.32 to 19.37 shall be construed in every instance with a presumption of complete public access,' was not followed in the lead opinion," she wrote.

Indeed, Roggensack stated, the lead opinion accorded no presumption of access to the requested emails.

"There is nothing ambiguous in the legislative directive of 'complete public access,'" she wrote. "All emails in the school district's email account should be released, unless there is an exception in (the law). Any exception to the general presumption of complete disclosure must be narrowly construed."

And that exception simply didn't exist in the statutes, she wrote.

Roggensack asked rhetorically why the open records law included a presumption of complete public access in the first place, and she had a ready answer.

"It does so to enable the public to see for itself what is going on in government work places," she wrote. "The lead opinion shuts down this public access whenever public employees characterize their emails as 'personal.' It is not possible to accord public oversight of government employees' activities when those same government employees decide what the public is permitted to see."

Indeed, Roggensack continued, in the case at hand none of the justices had actually seen any of the emails.

"Throughout the lead opinion, it repeats that whether an email is a record within the meaning of the public records law depends on the content of the email," she wrote. "This is a curious position for justices that have never read any of the emails. As stated, the emails are not in the record, so there is no means by which any justice could know the content of the emails."

While other courts in other jurisdictions have applied a content-based analysis to freedom-of-information types of requests, they have made a decision about whether the material should be released only after an in camera review of the emails under consideration, Roggensack wrote.

Roggensack then attacked the lead opinion for using examples of what the emails contained—such as making child care arrangements or social plans—when the justices could not possibly know that.

"The lead opinion errs," she wrote. "No justice has seen any of the emails at issue; they are not in the record. Therefore, there is no way any member of this court can provide examples of what the emails say. Notwithstanding this lack of knowledge, a majority of this court relates what the emails say."

Roggensack also pointed to broader complications. First, she wrote, the decision created a blanket exception for teachers' emails, which runs counter to open government laws that caution against blanket exceptions.

"Here, there is no statutory language excepting any type of email from disclosure," she wrote. "Despite this, the lead opinion creates a broad, blanket exception for all emails in the school district's email account, based solely on the teachers' allegation that the emails are 'personal.' The lead opinion has crafted its exception 'by implication only,' id., when it concludes that for an email to be a 'record' under Wis. Stat. §19.32(2), it must involve the carrying on of governmental business. There is nothing in Wis. Stat. ch. 19 that supports this interpretation. Indeed, claims have been filed against government employees based on the allegation that government computers were being used for purposes other than government business."

Then, too, Bubholz alleged that the teachers were attempting to preclude him from reviewing the extent and quality of use of school district computers and email services during the workday.

"He explains that he 'believes if the teachers' emails, sent or received, discussed school board members, school board proceedings, school board candidates or organizations supporting or opposing school board members or candidates,' he should be able to learn of it," she wrote. "The school district agrees that if the emails demonstrate 'excessive personal usage' of district email accounts during the workday 'the public's interest may then be implicated.'"

Roggensack said she agreed with Bubholz.

"While one could assert that those types of emails are personal in nature because the teachers are doing things outside of their jobs duties, one could also assert that it is not proper for teachers to be campaigning for school board candidates or members using school district email accounts and computers during the workday," she wrote. "However, there is no way of knowing what is going on here because the lead opinion prevents the public from learning the content of the teachers' emails and how often they are using school district email accounts and computers for non-job related tasks."

In this, one of her very best decisions, Roggensack was working on all cylinders, and, as she suggested, the implications of the majority decision were broad. First, as Roggensack observed, it created a broad blanket exception for emails that the statutes don't countenance. Second, that exception can be employed based solely on the word of government officials whose records—and thus conduct—are the subject of requests. As this book will explore, that distressing conclusion has been buttressed in a later ruling by an appeals court that if a government authority says a record is exempt, it is exempt, and that's that.

Roggensack was absolutely right that the decision was a terrible one, one that has set off a spectacular display of judicial hostility to transparency, exploding for a decade now in the political skies around us, like a Fourth of July fireworks show. With a sweep of the hand, the court sabotaged the public's ability to peek inside the daily workings of their government.

As Roggensack admonished, when we now request emails, and records' custodians tell us they are withholding some or all of them because they are personal, how do we know the custodian is telling the truth?

Perhaps more often, the custodian will simply be baffled because so many emails will live on the edge of interpretation. If school teachers, to use an example, are campaigning for local school board candidates on school time and on school computers, is that their personal business or is it related to their jobs? Given the court's determination, a custodian might well decide that a person's political activity is purely personal.

Or, hypothetically, would romantic emails from a married senator and candidate for governor, written to a person who is not the senator's spouse, be personal or public? Certainly one's romantic life is a private thing, at least usually. But doesn't the public have a right to know if a candidate is having an affair, and the realm of that affair is being recorded and stored on government computers? Doesn't this go to the question not merely of character but of responsibility and recklessness? Or does it?

And just who gets to make that decision, and will such decisions be made consistently or depending upon the personal views of each records' custodian?

In the same year as the court decision, a gubernatorial campaign in South Carolina provided just such an example. There, then GOP nominee Rep. Nikki Haley walloped her competition in the Republican primary, but right before election day she was accused of cheating on her husband—not once, but twice by two different men who stepped forward to say they had slept with her.

Haley cried foul, the men could not prove their allegations, and she went on to win in a cakewalk. But here's a problem. One accuser said Haley's emails would prove the dalliance. The news media immediately issued open records requests. Unfortunately for them, Haley declined because in South Carolina, as in Wisconsin, legislators have conveniently exempted their communications from that state's open records laws.

So in South Carolina, they never knew for sure what was in those emails. Wisconsin's situation is not exactly analogous because the Legislature is not exempt from the open records law, but it is exempt from the records retention law—almost the same thing but not quite—but the court's decision has actually put the public here in an even worse position.

Now, in a similar situation in Wisconsin, if a legislator is slapped with an open records request about a purported affair, and he or she has kept the emails, the lawmaker can simply decide that the romantic emails are personal and exempt. Nobody can stop them, not even the courts, who would not be entitled to in camera review. Remember, in the Wisconsin Rapids case, no justice had seen the emails they were fighting over. The school district said they were personal and exempt and so they were personal and exempt.

One can see how easily and broadly this blanket exemption can—and is— used, as it was in a 2014 case involving *The Lakeland Times*. We'll explore that case later.

And what about pornography? In 2007, Oneida County suspended a zoning department employee for five days after finding emails containing pictures of adult nudity on his computer, a blatant violation of county policy. The employee had forwarded non-work-related emails to a group of individuals using his county computer; he also received non-work-related emails from the group, which included a town of Minocqua police officer.

All this took place after *The Lakeland Times* issued an open records request, and the public was able, because of the strong fabric of the law, to see what certain employees were up to on work time. Now, even if the county were to find such emails, officials would not have to disclose them if they chose to label them as personal. We'd never know the employee did anything wrong, and perhaps we wouldn't know if the employee had been disciplined, or how.

As it was before the ruling, the public could discover not only misconduct but how officials dealt with that misconduct, which is just as important. Without the threat of disclosure, officials might not exact any discipline at all.

Even for innocuous emails, the public should be able to review records to see how much personal time public employees are spending. Statistical summaries of such time are not adequate because they do not give context. If a group of public employees is spending hours passing along jokes, or scheduling softball games, or discussing where to eat dinner, we have a right to know it.

Practically speaking, say goodbye to that reasoning. In South Carolina, legislators exempted themselves from the open records law; in Wisconsin the Supreme Court has exempted the entire state government from the law.

The bottom line is, the ruling enables the government to block the public from seeing whether public employees are engaged in misconduct, from seeing what that misconduct is and how it is handled, and it enables the government to apply the label of 'personal' to many acts related to serious public business.

All of which brings us to the architect of the decision, the late chief justice Shirley Abrahamson, who wrote the ridiculous lead opinion concluding that personal emails aren't even public records. For Abrahamson, ostensibly, it was all about content, not where or when the emails were written. The chief justice said she looked at other states to see what they had done, and all of them found personal emails to be exempt.

"Several other states have already addressed this issue," she wrote. "... We know of no state that has reached the conclusion that the contents of such personal emails should be released to members of the public."

The key word in that paragraph is 'several.' That's right, a handful of states had done so at the time—five by my count back then—and, in some, lawmakers were crafting laws to correct the bad decisions. In most states, though, the issue of personal emails and open records was not settled. In most states, in fact, open records laws in general are an unsettled matter.

For many years, by contrast, our state had been a national leader in government accountability. Meaning, Abrahamson would have done better just to stay home and look at the laws here. To be sure, in her decision, she says she did get around to that. In doing so, she interpreted the Legislature's statement of intent in the public records law, and concluded that lawmakers believed "public records" must contain content related to the "affairs of government."

In her blistering dissent, in which she macerated the chief justice's baloney like a puppy shreds a roll of toilet paper, Roggensack correctly called Abrahamson out. Interpretation, she pointed out, begins with the statutory language, and, if that language is clear and unambiguous, there is no need to consult "extrinsic sources such as legislative history, to discern the meaning of the statute."

And the statutory definition of a public record, Roggensack continued, was clear: "'Record' means any material on which written, drawn, printed, spoken, visual or electromagnetic information is recorded or preserved, regardless of physical form or characteristics, which has been created or is being kept by an authority."

How clearer can it be? The broad range of information that is recorded or preserved and kept by an authority makes no exception whatsoever for personal information and is irrelevant to determining what is and what is not a record.

In addition, Roggensack chided Abrahamson for asserting as fact things she could not possibly know because, again, none of the justices had ever seen any of the emails in question. Indeed, a read of Abrahamson's lead opinion shows it was part fairy tale and part legal fiction, as if the chief justice had written a bad novel that serious publishers had rejected and she was just trying to use it somewhere, anywhere.

But there was a serious footnote to this case. In the aftermath of that ruling's wreckage, then attorney general J.B. Van Hollen issued a memo to clarify the ruling and he did a service in doing so. The attorney general pointed out that the public could still request statistical records showing how many emails were personal and how many were private, and he said the ruling should not deter people from making open records requests. That was noble, but the court decision undoubtedly has done just that, as more officials claim records to be personal.

The ruling thus demanded a legislative remedy. It demanded that the Legislature reverse by statute what the justices did. It never happened, though, because by 2010 the anti-transparency crowd was firmly in control of the Legislature, and here we can see the major threats to openness converging. First, the high court exploited the law's lack of clear language, then it used the makeup of privacy concerns to powder over the substantive reality that it was rewriting law and adding language to the statute, then the Legislature refused to correct a bad decision.

In this case, to be more precise, the language about what is government business and what is not isn't spelled out as clearly as it should be, perhaps because it was thought at the time that the answer was obvious. Obviously one part of the law was clear, the part Roggensack pointed to that defined 'record' as 'any material' on which information is recorded and preserved and kept by an authority, but the declaration of policy seemed to limit that to "the affairs of government and the official acts" of officials, allowing the majority to broadly interpret that as foreclosing the release of personal emails either because they are not records or because they fall under the ambit of "the affairs of government."

But they are records, and the amount of time spent composing them and even the content, as explained above, can make them highly relevant to the affairs of government and to the actions of public employees (campaigning for school board candidates on school time, spending excessive time on personal matters while at work). And so the decision weakened full public access to legitimate public documents, the very opposite of what Abrahamson said she intended. But the ruling did more. It has helped to inflate the cost of fulfilling public records requests in which personal information must be redacted, driving prices so high as to make records requests too expensive for many people.

For example, in the Wisconsin Rapids case itself, the *Wisconsin Rapids Tribune* reported after the ruling that the district would charge $2,061.34 for the records, as opposed to photocopying charges that would have totaled about $200 before the ruling. According to reporter Adam Wise, the district said the charges were for staff time related to reviewing, copying, and redacting personal information.

Such a disturbing ruling in the "Sunshine State" calls such a noble nickname into question. Perhaps it would not if it was the only such ruling, an outlier, but unfortunately that's not the case over the decade, as this book will show.

In earlier days of the open government movement, the courts systematically upheld the open government laws and its presumptions of full access.

In *Linzmeyer*, for example, the high court found that the public interest in monitoring the behavior of a publicly employed individual, a teacher, was much higher than the public interest in preserving privacy. In *Showers*, the court recognized that members of a governmental body can violate the open meeting law by participating in what is called a 'walking quorum,' or, as it described it, a series of less-than-quorum-sized gatherings among separate groups of members, who agree, implicitly or explicitly, to act and vote in a certain manner in numbers sufficient to reach a quorum. In *Kroeplin*, the court held that closed disciplinary investigatory records are not exempt from disclosure under the law.

There have always been decisions that tilted away from openness, even in the early days, but these days such decisions are the rule rather than the exception, and the question is why. The same question could be asked of the Legislature. These days public officials do not attempt to merely resist the laws in any way they can, they have committed to destroying them.

One wonders whether the 1975 open meetings law and the 1982 open records law could even be passed in today's legislative environment. Indeed, as evidenced in the 2015 attempt to repeal the law, the pressure is in exactly the opposite direction.

—

A little look at history can provide some context to today's bleak situation.

As James Friedman, an attorney with Godfrey & Kahn who is an open records expert and legal counsel for the Wisconsin Newspaper Association, has observed, the very first statutes adopted after the organization of Wisconsin as a state provided for public access to the meetings and records of county government. That was in 1849.

"From that early starting point, the Wisconsin tradition of full public access to the affairs of government has grown steadily," Friedman has written in an

Open Government Guide for the Reporters Committee for Freedom of the Press. "The original statute requiring county constitutional officers to have their records open for examination has survived virtually unchanged."

In 1917, the policy of public access to records was extended to all state, county, city, town, village, school district, and other municipality or district records, Friedman wrote.

In those early days, too, the state's courts were in sync with the desire for openness, as attorney Linda de la Mora pointed out in an excellent 1983 piece on the state's open records law for the *Marquette Law Review*.

In 1856, de la Mora wrote, the state Supreme Court ruled that clerks of court must keep wood for heating and candles for lighting so citizens could comfortably transact business and examine all books and papers required to be kept in the clerk's office. Perhaps disappointingly so, though, the court did not require the clerk to keep a tavern for the public's convenience, de la Mora acknowledged with her tongue firmly in her cheek.

De la Mora, whose article still provides the best overview of the open records law through 1983, also points to an 1887 state Supreme Court ruling in which the court refused to adopt common-law restrictions regarding who should be allowed to examine public records.

"The case involved an individual who wanted to copy public records in order to set up a rival abstract business," de la Mora wrote. "The local register of deeds objected, contending that the right to inspect and copy was confined to one having an interest beyond mere curiosity or pecuniary gain. The court departed from prior common law and ruled that any person may examine and copy public records for any lawful purpose."

And thus was born the heart and soul of today's law, at least today's mission in name.

In 1917, as both de la Mora and Friedman point out, the first unified public records law was passed in Wisconsin, and that law remained virtually unchanged until 1981. The law granted "any person" access to public records, and, curiously, provided for forfeitures of between $25 and $2,000 for violations, much stronger than today's laws.

In that time span of 64 years, de la Mora offered up what she considered were 10 important court decisions, but for my money three were critical.

One was a 1969 decision in which the court found that partnerships, associations, political, and corporate bodies were within the statutory words affording "any person" the right to inspection. In so ruling, the court refused to place strict limits on the statutory right to access. Decisions such as *Newspapers, Inc. v. Breier* in 1979 and *State ex rel. Youmans v. Owens* in 1965 also gave newspapers the same rights as individuals to examine public records, even if its motivation was to publish the material, de la Mora wrote. As we'll see, that right has proven critical in an age when newspapers and other media are among the few entities both financially capable of and committed to the pursuit of government accountability.

In *Youmans v. Owens,* the *Waukesha Freeman* had sought access to an investigatory report by the city attorney to the mayor concerning potential police misconduct. A central question was whether the newspaper had standing to sue, and the court ruled not only that it did but that the publisher's motivation in seeking inspection—even if the motive was to benefit the newspaper and permit it to publish the material—was immaterial.

"The fact that he as a citizen deems it essential that the material contained in the report be made available to the public is sufficient to qualify him as the real party in interest," the court determined.

That ruling—that motive could not be considered in granting access to records—was critical (if a record is public, it is public to anyone, period), and it stood the test of time until a disastrous 2018 state Supreme Court ruling.

In a similar case in 1969, the state Supreme Court reluctantly ruled that a newspaper had to be given access to a decision in a celebrated custody case, even though the judge wrung his hands in worry that ongoing publication of matters pertaining to the case would not only harm the child but complicate enforcement of the court's order.

"The Journal Company is 'any person' within that statutory category. Sec. 990.01 (26) provides that 'person' includes all partnerships, associations and bodies politic and corporate," the court found.

As for the substance of the case—whether court decisions could generally be impounded from public view—the court rejected that thinking: "We are also satisfied that it is contrary to our Anglo-American policies of judicial administration to impound a decision of a court once the determination has been made and filed."

In reading these decisions from the 1960s, one clear fact emerges: In those days judges took the mission statement of the open government laws seriously —that the presumption is one of access, and that laws are to be liberally construed as favoring transparency. The courts worked hard to ensure transparency, and, if anything, the bias was toward openness.

And that was as it should be. In the 1969 *Journal* case, the high court justices underscored a little cited but important passage from a New York decision concluding that no other rule besides public access to court decisions and records was "conceivable in a society nurtured on freedom of discussion of matters of public interest."

The justices went on: "This statement parallels the public and legislative policy of the state of Wisconsin from its early history, and any legislation should be examined with the purpose, if possible, to effectuate that policy and not to defeat it. The courts have been the great repositories of personal liberty, and their obligation is not only to see that the conduct and performance of executive and legislative officials is open to public scrutiny, but to maintain for themselves the high standards that they prescribe for others. It would ill behoove a court of this state to conclude that it has the inherent right to impose its mandates on the parties to an action, but to conceal those mandates from the examination of the public. While we recognize the exemplary purpose behind the trial judge's order herein, we can think of no device more subject to abuse, more conducive to a climate favoring star chamber judgments, and more likely to result in judicial caprice, than a mandate of this court upholding the order impounding this decision."

The justices clearly saw that their sworn duty was to "effectuate" the open government laws of the state, not to defeat them. Sadly, these days, the courts see their roles as just the opposite.

—

Against the backdrop of such court decisions, there was a growing freedom-of-information movement both in the United States and in Wisconsin. The federal Freedom of Information Act was enacted in 1967, and then amended in 1974 in the aftermath of Watergate, as a public still engaged by the passions of the 60s sought ever more accountability from public officials.

There was an equal clamor for stronger laws in Wisconsin, as de la Mora discusses in her 1983 article.

"Attempts to modify the longstanding Wisconsin public records law began in 1977 and continued throughout the 1979 session of the Legislature," she wrote. "These bills proposed substantial procedural and substantive changes to the existing statute."

It's important to note, though, as de la Mora does, that, unlike the serendipitous court decisions of the 1960s, there was substantial opposition in the Legislature to those reform efforts, and no bill was passed in the 1970s. Finally, in 1981, a serious bill gained traction. In its original version, as she reports, there were 17 specific types of materials to which the balancing tests were to be applied, and the bill would have established an Ethics and Open Records Board to provide oversight and accountability. What's more, the bill would have enabled the board to review denial of access to a record.

The bill had a long row to hoe. It would have been dead on arrival, but the bill's authors subsequently deleted the specific list of materials to which the balancing test would be applied and dropped the idea of the Ethics and Open Records Board, giving the attorney general the ability to issue advisory opinions on the application of the law to specific concerns.

Translated, that means the bill was watered down. As former *Lakeland Times* reporter Jonathan Anderson recounted in his 2013 thesis paper (University of Wisconsin-Milwaukee), "Resolving Public Records Disputes in Wisconsin: the Role of the Attorney General's Office," the open records board would have included seven members, including state and local government officials, two representatives of the news media, and two members of the public and would have allowed records requesters to petition the board to review record custodians' disclosure decisions, such as the denial of a records request or imposition of a fee.

Custodians would have been required to comply with the board's decisions.

The deletion of that administrative board was the most significant change, but it fell victim to the politics of the day. The board had to be dropped from the bill, according to Anderson's 2012 interview with one of the bill's chief sponsors, then state Sen. Lynn Adelman. Adelman said then attorney general Bronson La Follette opposed the board. Adelman characterized it as a turf issue, Anderson reported.

Curiously, though, and for whatever reason, as de la Mora reports, the Associated Press also opposed the board. With both the attorney general and a key component of the media opposing the board, it was dead. But there was other opposition to the overall bill within the Legislature. Before it was finally adopted, de la Mora reports, lawmakers offered up 55 amendments to the bill, of which 18 were adopted.

So, while it is easy to say that today's lawmakers are intransigently opposed to transparency, it would not be accurate to say there was a love fest for open government back in 1981. Nonetheless, the bill, which was enacted in 1982 and took effect in 1983, represented a major overhaul and step forward in open government statutory provisions, and its enactment pushed Wisconsin to the top of the list for transparency on the state level.

There were likely two reasons the bill passed. First, there was the willingness of the bill's authors to jettison some of the stronger provisions within it. Second, and most important, lawmakers were happy to support open government so long as it did not apply to them.

That is a traditional legislative template in Wisconsin. Similarly, for example, in the 1960s, lawmakers who wanted to enact shoreland zoning laws to protect water resources ultimately could only win much-needed support from urban lawmakers by exempting cities and villages from it. Hence, today, shoreland zoning applies only in unincorporated areas of the state.

Likewise, open records laws apply to virtually everyone in government except the Legislature. As I have reported, while the Legislature is technically under the law, it did exempt itself from the records retention law, meaning it does not have to keep a public record for any specific length of time. So if you ask a lawmaker for a releasable public record, and the lawmaker has it, he or she must release it. But if that lawmaker has put it through the shredder, you're out of luck, and it's all perfectly legal.

It's an effective if not formal exemption from the public records law, for what lawmakers in their right minds are going to keep records they don't want released? As it turns out, plenty, but that's beside the current point. That point is, despite the high court's warning in *Journal* that all branches of government must "maintain for themselves the high standards that they prescribe for others," lawmakers were all too willing to impose the high standards of the law on others while refusing to prescribe it for themselves.

Malicious? Yes. And yet, there's still something that sets those earlier lawmakers apart from the current crop. While those lawmakers at least sanctioned transparency for most of the government, these days lawmakers have attacked it broadly, trying to obliterate openness at all levels, as the 2015 attempt to repeal the entire law demonstrated. This malignant contempt for the law is shown time and again in ongoing legislative efforts to conceal the records they do retain, in their ongoing efforts to shut down required government noticing in the media, in their attempts to curtail access to online court records, and in their expressed intent over the past few years to impose higher costs on requesters.

That last initiative is both novel and telling. In this view, the cost of fulfilling a records request is not seen as something the government should bear —as an essential function of government that taxpayers have already paid for— but as an additional, discretionary cost that citizens should pay. One legislator has argued that newspapers should accept higher fees for fulfilling records requests as a "cost of doing business," when in fact the government should assume those higher fees as a cost of doing the people's business.

In this worldview, what is truly the people's business is flipped on its head, and open government laws become nonessential to liberty and democracy, mere annoyances to be swatted away. These days the Legislature's growing contempt for transparency is equalled only by the same contempt in an activist judiciary that is rewriting open government laws decision by decision.

Wisconsin can hardly be called the "Sunshine State" in this environment. In reality, it's the Dark State, and only by recognizing that can we citizens begin the arduous task of opening the government's doors and once again letting the sun shine in.

Chapter 2

The Need to Reform the Law's Fundamentals

The starting point to correcting our transparency woes is to overhaul the open records law itself.

The law's flaws and weaknesses are obvious just by viewing what was deleted from the original version of the 1981 bill before it was enacted the following year. De la Mora cited other weaknesses—such as failing to address privacy issues—way back then as well. Through the years, others have shone a light on specific defects that continue to hobble transparency. Among others, in 2008 the nonpartisan Citizen Advocacy Center compiled a list of issues they found in the law as it existed.

For example, the report stated, the lack of firm deadlines to mandate responsiveness to requests allows public bodies to delay the production of those records. Then, too, the center stated, excessive and broad interpretations of records exemptions circumvent transparency, such as the exemptions for drafts, or records "prepared for the originator's personal use or prepared by the originator in the name of a person for whom the originator is working."

"Though pivotal court rulings and attorney general decisions have narrowly construed the draft exemption, custodians regularly claim that draft status extends to any form of a document short of the final version they determine fit for release," the report stated. "As a result, public bodies routinely refuse the production of records disclosable under the [law] which is in contradiction to case law."

High fees also continue to dog records requesters because of a statutory lack of clarity, the analysis stated, while ambiguity about who is covered under the law leaves large loopholes, such as those for quasi-governmental entities like local economic development corporations. Perhaps most important, though, at least in the eyes of the Citizen Advocacy Center, was the lack of an administrative appeals process that forces citizens into litigation as the primary avenue to address nondisclosure.

That omission hearkens back to the deletion of just such an appeals board from the draft of the 1981-82 open records overhaul, as already reported. Instead, district attorneys and the attorney general can prosecute, but their decision leaves no room for administrative appeal. Citizens can bypass and file their own suit if a district attorney fails to prosecute, but they must jump through hoops—strict deadlines, notarized complaints—and can incur substantial costs in pursuing such litigation. Such judicial hurdles often leave those improperly denied records out in the cold.

"Going to court to obtain public information should be the absolute last resort," Terry Pastika, then executive director and community lawyer for the Citizen Advocacy Center, said. "Taxpayers should not have to foot the legal bill every time the state is challenged on a violation, when a simple change to the statute could save Wisconsin precious funds in these tough economic times."

In the 2008 analysis, the advocacy center made a number of recommendations for overhauling and reforming the law, but suffice it to say for the moment no changes have been made by the Legislature, and the problems those statutory weaknesses were causing then are still a headache today.

In 2015, for example, during the same year that Scott Walker and the GOP launched their ill-fated attempt to repeal the open records law, the governor tried other tactics to block the release of records, such as labeling certain records "transitory" so they didn't have to be kept, including text messages between government officials. The governor also tried to withhold records he considered part of a "deliberative process" that would be exempt under the law, such as documents related to the governor's efforts to rewrite the University of Wisconsin System's mission statement known as "the Wisconsin Idea."

That bid failed, too.

The problem is, the law's vagueness about such documents (exempt records include drafts, notes, preliminary computations, and like materials prepared for the originator's personal use) allows officials to undertake endless attempts to define certain records as deliberative or drafts that are exempt. Such language may have been adequate in 1982; it no longer is, if it ever was.

The law's failure to specify time limits in providing records also continues to haunt those seeking transparency. For example, during Democratic Gov. Tony Evers's first year in office, in 2019, the Wisconsin Institute for Law & Liberty (WILL) tracked the Evers' administration's responses to records requests and found the administration woefully lacking, with one out of three of all open records requests either unfulfilled or not recorded properly.

High costs for copying and locating records, another problem that can be traced back to faults in the law itself, continue to plague requesters, and not just average citizens but more well-heeled media outlets as well. The pages of newspapers around the state are filled with the nightmares of requesters who received bill estimates for thousands of dollars—advance payment, please—for asking for quite mundane public records, and at *The Lakeland Times* we have had our share of horror stories. In 2013, for instance, Lakeland Union High School asked the newspaper to pay more than $800 to fill a request for emails —more than $600 of that in location fees—and, ironically and absurdly, cited ancient, inadequate technology as the overriding reason for its inability to fill the request at less cost.

Specifically, the newspaper asked for all emails, letters, and correspondence between an area resident and administration staff from April 22, 2011, to April 22, 2013. The district located 924 pages, which would cost $231 to copy; it also said it took 30.25 hours to locate the records, at an additional cost of $618.01.

The total cost billed was $849.01; that figure included $20.43 an hour in location fees. At the time, the district used a cumbersome and time-consuming process by which requested emails were extracted from zip files, imported into an email client, printed, and redacted. *The Times* could not find another government entity that used such an old and cumbersome process, but, asked about that, then district administrator Todd Kleinhans said simply: "That's the way it is."

In the Dark State, that's too often the way it is.

But perhaps the best example to demonstrate just how far officials and agencies will go to exploit vagueness and weaknesses in the current law is another *Lakeland Times* case, this time a lawsuit stretching out over four years with the Wisconsin Department of Natural Resources. In the end, after tens of thousands of dollars in legal fees and a four-year battle to the state Supreme Court, it came down to protecting fewer than 100 names and less than four pages of text.

In October 2009, following a decision in favor of the newspaper by the Wisconsin Supreme Court that summer, the DNR finally turned over records requested by the newspaper in 2005. On its face, it seemed a simple request and a no-brainer at that. Specifically, *The Times* had asked for the names and salaries for DNR personnel working out of the agency's Rhinelander and Woodruff offices.

The DNR had refused to turn over the names of union members, saying a provision in a collective bargaining agreement ratified by the state Legislature prohibited the disclosure of certain employee details and conditions of employment, including their names. The information had been available under the open records law prior to the agreement's adoption, but the contract provision effectively amended the open records statute, the state argued.

The Times disagreed and joined the *Milwaukee Journal Sentinel* in a similar lawsuit against the state; the *Journal Sentinel* had requested a list of employees no longer allowed to drive state vehicles. A Dane County circuit court judge sided with the newspapers in 2007, but the unions appealed the ruling. Finally, in July 2009, on a 6-1 vote, with chief justice Shirley Abrahamson dissenting, justices affirmed the decision of the circuit court, saying state agencies cannot withhold the names of union workers under the current open records law.

In addition, the court found, the mere ratification of a contract by the Legislature cannot amend state law, even if it contains a provision effectively doing so, without accompanying companion legislation to that express effect.

The records delivered to the newspaper in October contained the names of 95 employees, their 2004 annual salaries and their 2005 hourly rate. Of course, that was a little dated by then, so, with the Supreme Court decision safely in hand, *The Times* issued another open records request, this time for compensation for the DNR's Madison staff.

Having lost in court, the agency delivered the information, but—wait for it —there was a catch, namely, the data was not in an assembled format as before but instead contained employee names and their base pay rate on separate pages of the document collection. Bottom line was, it would have taken a jigsaw puzzle master to put it all together.

Nice folks that they were, though, the agency did provide instructions by which they said the newspaper might glean an approximate though not necessarily actual 2009 base salary.

We were curious enough to dig through the data for a few notable names, though because of the fragmentary information offered by the department, the annual pay was approximate and could be calculated using only hourly base pay, without any potential compensation or salary adjustments.

Hardly what we were looking for. So, our appetites still not satiated, we decided to request another set of employees with their pay, this time for 2008 and this time to be received as collated and assembled pay data. Sure, the agency said, we'll do that, and for the low fee of only between $5,000 and $8,000, you know, for the time officials said it would take their staff to complete the project.

Think about it. All we were asking for were the names of their employees and their salaries—the salaries we all were paying with our taxes. To be sure, officials do not have to compile lists from raw data for open records requests if those lists don't already exist, but does anyone believe a state agency would not have a list of its employees and their pay?

Since then, state and local compensation records have become an open book, so that's progress with a couple of important caveats. The first is, it's a no-brainer that public employee pay should be readily available to the public, a record so obviously essential to open government that it should never have been questioned. So the opening of public payroll information is not so much progress as it is the correction of an almost criminal cover-up by state agencies and unions.

The second caveat is, though requests may not be for the same information, officials and agencies are still using the same tactics of high records costs, fake exemptions, and interminable delays to thwart transparency.

And to do it they are using a law that has outlived its time. A reformed law is needed.

—

Every once in a while, depending upon which way the political winds are blowing, some officials actually promise to finally open the doors of the state's closed government.

Beginning in 2009, as the public's patience was wearing thin with a tyrannical DNR in particular, and with an overgrown bureaucracy in general, there were increasing demands for public paper trails about what state agencies were doing with our tax money (and what they were doing TO some of our citizens), and with those demands there were increasing calls to make state government more open.

There followed a lot of hollow promises from politicians that they would act, but nothing was ever done.

Take Scott Walker, for instance. In his campaign for governor in 2010, Walker might not have made transparency a central focus, but it wasn't an insignificant issue, either. In a 2010 interview with me, Walker stressed how committed to open government he was, making bold promises and pledging to convene an independent commission to study how the state's open government laws could be strengthened.

When I say I believe in government transparency, it's not just a campaign slogan, Walker said right off the bat.

"I don't just say that, I've lived it," he said. "(In Milwaukee County), we have put all government purchases online at no additional cost. Every purchase, everything we enter into our accounting software, automatically in real time goes on a website that tells the public every purchase by department. Not only a journalist but a citizen journalist or anybody else can track it down."

Walker told me he did not favor proposed constraints on access to police 911 tapes or to the state's online circuit court records, and he said he also believed the Legislature itself needed to be more transparent.

"In fact I've even proposed—in terms of the budget process, but it would apply to anything—other things that would help transparency," he said. "I don't think there should be any votes in closed caucus, on any issue. If a county board or school board can't discuss a budget in private, then the state

Legislature certainly should not. There should not be any closed caucuses on the budget."

What's more, Walker said, the budget should only entail budgetary items; there shouldn't be any non-fiscal items in it.

"And I would make it, by statute, that the Legislature can't vote on anything after 10 at night or before 9 in the morning," he said. "They did things this last (budget) at 2 and 3 o'clock in the morning. As I tell my staff, nothing good happens after midnight. But they did it on purpose because not only do they not want average persons to know, they don't want reporters with deadlines to know—after 10 you miss the nightly TV news and you're not in print for the daily newspapers. They push it back on a Saturday, hoping people won't read about things like that."

Critically, Walker said he did not believe the state Legislature should effectively exempt itself from the state's open records law and be able to delete public records at will. In a modern technological age, storage is easy, Walker said, and he pledged to work to end the loophole.

"Why should they be exempt?" Walker asked. "It's just like the Congress. They make laws that apply to everybody else but exempt themselves and that just seems to be fundamentally wrong."

Walker said he would establish a council or committee to look at revamping the open records law, and to look at philosophical and legal issues, as well as the practical, technical side of fulfilling the law's requirements.

None of that ever happened, not in two terms and not in eight years. The party caucuses still meet in private. The state Legislature still votes late at night and in the early morning. There are still non-fiscal policy items in the budget, though the number has been reduced. The Legislature is still exempt from the open records retention law.

On the one hand, none of this is Scott Walker's fault alone. No one person could single-handedly accomplish such an agenda. On the other hand, once in office, with the exception of strengthening some of the state's open-data portals, Walker governed just like most other elected officials—with hostility toward openness.

It's important to mention the politics of all this. I am not, generally speaking, opposed politically to Scott Walker. I voted for him for governor four times, and I am thankful for the many good things he did for the state during his tenure. These days, I know many Democrats who feel the same way about Tony Evers. They generally like him politically but despise his embedded opposition to transparency. So they vote for him.

The reason we advocates of transparency continue to vote for opponents of transparency is that, deep down, we know that all of the candidates will end up being hostile to open government, no matter what they say on the campaign trail. So we vote based on other ideological criteria. That's the way it has been, and that's the way it is.

And that's the way it will continue until the cycle is broken. There is a broad need to depoliticize transparency as a partisan issue, but for now the point is that hostility to transparency is a poison drink enjoyed in large quantities on both sides of the aisle, and the poison must be flushed from the system completely if we are ever to have any reform of what has now become a burdened and frail open government law.

But back to the narrative. After he was elected, Walker pursued none of the things he pledged in that 2010 interview, and finally ended up galloping down the opposite path until his effort to repeal all open government laws—and make no mistake he was right in there in the thick of it with the GOP leadership— crashed and burned in 2015.

That doomed effort might have had a silver lining. For one thing, it focused attention not only on the need to preserve the protections the law affords but on the inadequacies of the statute in the modern age. Then attorney general Brad Schimel even hosted an open-government summit to address those inadequacies, acknowledging that many in the public and media viewed the state's open meetings and public records laws as outdated.

"Our state's open government laws were written before technology changed the way public bodies conduct business and the current law leaves many unanswered questions about the limits of open government," Schimel wrote in a 2016 column about the summit. "This gathering of more than 200 stakeholders, from media representatives to citizen watchdog groups to government records custodians, started the lengthy conversation about reforming and updating our open government laws. We continue this important dialogue with public officials, media representatives, and citizens and look forward to hosting future meetings and discussions."

At the summit, which was held in 2015, the attorney general's description of the event stated, participants mulled how changing technologies, like body cameras, increasing public scrutiny of policing practices, and evolving laws, such as officer involved shooting legislation, had challenged law enforcement in the 21st century. And, it pointed out, statutory procedures pertaining to records requests, including electronic communications, the balancing test, and retention rules, had all been opened to interpretation because of new technology. The question was, did current statutes need to be updated to keep the system honest and effective, and if so, how could the old statutes be altered to fit new mediums?

Participants also pondered the need to develop new records retention schedules to deal with the advent of emails and police body camera videos since the early 1980s. Other questions included whether an electronic version of a record necessarily followed the same disclosure laws as the record itself and whether the copy fee of a scanned and emailed document should be the same as the hardcopy version.

And, as Walker had promised in the 2010 campaign, summit attendees expressed support for convening a committee of stakeholders to comprehensively revisit the law and update it.

There were negative ideas floated at the summit, too. Schimel himself hedged his bets on a rewrite of the law, saying changes could be made to make some records secret so that lawmakers could exchange ideas. That was a revival of Walker's horrible bid to exclude "deliberative" documents from the law.

But the saddest part of the summit was that there was no follow-up on any of the ideas discussed, just as nothing ever happened after Walker's robust campaign promises in 2010. The summit came and went in a day, and the ideas dispersed with the crowd.

To be fair, part of the issue with reforming the law is that some open records advocates, though keenly aware of the statutory problems, are nonetheless wary of opening the door to a rewrite. Their fears were well-founded after what lawmakers and the governor had tried to do that year. The fear was, instead of strengthening the law, they would weaken it or worse.

One might compare it to the concerns of those who oppose a constitutional convention on the grounds that convening a convention to consider a balanced budget amendment might open the barn door to a complete rewrite of the entire document. And such a total remodel would be easier to do with state government laws than it would with the nation's founding charter.

For example, open records attorney Bob Dreps, who handled many open records cases for *The Lakeland Times*, told the *Wisconsin State Journal* that he supported convening a committee to look at updates of the records law, but he said he wanted the results withheld until a new Legislature could be seated.

"I would not present the results of that committee to this Legislature," the *State Journal* quoted him as saying. "I would rather see them face the voters first in 2016 and explain to them if they still want to see these privileges and exceptions and whether they think it's good public policy. As currently structured, I do not trust this Legislature to do the right thing."

Neither did Bill Lueders, the president of the Wisconsin Freedom of Information Council. After Republican lawmakers had withdrawn their bid to gut the law, they promised to form a Legislative Council committee to further study the issue of open records access. That prompted Lueders to tell Wisconsin Public Radio that he was very concerned that that could open up the law to changes, but, Lueders said, there was no evidence any changes were warranted.

"I don't think the case has been made that there's a need for it," Lueders told the network.

Another open records attorney, April Rockstead Barker (who has also litigated open records cases for *The Lakeland Times*), also advised caution.

"Updating Wisconsin's open records law, as Schimel proposes, could help clarify the obligations of public officials with respect to emails and other records that exist in electronic form," Barker wrote in a 'Your Right to Know' column. "But it is critical that any updates be guided by the law's stated and essential purpose: to provide the greatest possible oversight of the actions of government. Public records advocates must be vocal and vigilant to ensure that revisions or guidance have the effect of amplifying access. Otherwise, there is a danger that the process proposed by Schimel could result in less access."

So in the wake of the 2015 controversy, there was simply no momentum coming out of the open government summit to actually attempt to revise and strengthen the law, given fears that a rewrite could end up accomplishing exactly the opposite purpose.

As Schimel said at the summit, "Let's get right to the elephant in the room —messing with open government laws is like touching the third rail."

But that still doesn't mean that changes to strengthen an increasingly impotent law aren't needed. They are.

—

In her novel *The Beet Queen*, one of the writer Louise Erdrich's characters was on her way to a funeral when she began to ponder both the life and the afterlife of the deceased. Life events could be recounted in the memories of others, she knew, but then she wondered what would happen beyond life, not just to the body but to all the intangible intellectual materials of life that were collected and stored in that body over oh so many years.

The character wondered: "Where did it all go? Everything that happened in life, all the things we said and did, where did it go? What was really inside? Were thoughts like tiny bees, insects made of blue electricity, in a colony so fragile that it would scatter at the slightest touch? Who would be able stop them? Who could catch them in their hands?"

Beautiful literary writing, but the same wonder could be applied to many thoughts and ideas about reforming the records laws over the years. All the ideas at the summit, all the campaign promises about strengthening the laws, all the columns urging reform—where did all those ideas go? Have they been like that colony of tiny bees made of blue electricity in Erdrich's novel, so fragile that they scattered at the slightest thought that reform efforts would be futile and perhaps counterproductive?

Apparently so, for in early 2021 there is not so much as a whisper that our foundational laws, upon which all our open government rights rest, are fragile and cracking and crumbling under the weight of the modern age.

But that is exactly what is happening. Right now, this year, that foundation must be repaired and reinforced. That means we have to go out and collect the bees we've let escape for years through the holes in the hive of hollow talk. We have to catch the reforms in our hands, scoop them all up in one package, and present them as a unified collection of reforms to be enacted simultaneously.

How we actually get the Legislature and the governor to pass and enact such legislation is another topic. For now, let's summarize what reforms need to be made to the current law.

In discussing these reforms, I refer for now simply to underlying weaknesses in the original legislation—items that should have been addressed then, including many that were dropped from the original drafts, or language that was just vague or otherwise inadequately written. Because they should have been anticipated even in the 1980s, and because the ensuing years underscore that 'should,' these simple, straightforward, and compelling foundational matters should be addressed immediately, so long overdue they are.

Other important issues such as privacy, open government data and the threat of technology, and court decisions that either need to be codified or overturned will be addressed later.

First, what about the lack of firm deadlines to respond to records requests? In 2016, a *USA TODAY* analysis found that almost 1,300 out of 8,000 record requests took a month or more to fulfill, and approximately 140 requests took more than 100 days. One of the slowest of the departments was also one of the most important when it comes to open records compliance: the Wisconsin Department of Justice. According to the *USA TODAY* analysis, about 7 percent of 600 requests the DOJ filled in 2016 took more than 100 days, double that of any other agency with at least 100 requests. In addition, the DOJ had the second-highest percentage, 23 percent, of requests that took more than a month.

The DOJ is not the only agency that uses delayed responses to thwart the filling of records requests, but it has a track record that dates back years. During a 2011 Department of Justice webinar, for example, then assistant attorney general Mary Burke observed—whether wittingly or not—that the vague language of the statute could be exploited to delay responses, observing that responses to public records requests is required "as soon as practicable and without delay," but, she added, that did not mean immediately.

Not surprisingly, state officials often push back on claims they deliberately delay responses. Despite the *USA TODAY* analysis, then attorney general Brad Schimel, who was elected to the office in 2014, said his department was actually doing better than under his Democratic predecessor. As dismal as the response time was, Schimel said, it was improving.

"In the year before I took office it took DOJ, on average, 53 days to fulfill a public records request," he wrote in a column. "Every year since then, DOJ's average response time has dropped: 32 days in 2015, 23 days in 2016, and now just 5 days in the first quarter of 2017."

Schimel said the decline in response times could be attributed to the Wisconsin Department of Justice's Office of Open Government, which he established in 2015.

But the DOJ's response times began to slide a bit in 2018, when Schimel was still in office, and also during the first six months of 2019, under attorney general Josh Kaul, when it took the department an average of 11 days to respond to a request. Both attorney generals attributed the slower response times to increasing requests: In the first half of 2019, requests increased by about 30 percent.

Other agencies and offices aren't doing nearly so well, as evidenced by WILL's findings during Democratic Gov. Tony Evers's first year in office.

The law contributes directly to this obstructionism. The lack of definitive deadlines for responding to or fulfilling or denying requests, as well as the omission of any penalties for not meeting those deadlines, is like buying a flower whose instructions for care simply direct the caretaker to water the plant, or not, to put it in the sunlight, or not, you know, on a case-by-case basis. Every flower is different.

And so apparently is every interpretation of Wisconsin's open records laws. Yes, the law tells us records must be provided or access denied "as soon as practicable and without delay," but one bureaucrat's practical is another's impossible. The Wisconsin Supreme Court essentially tells us that a reasonable amount of time to respond to a records request is whatever time the government decides is reasonable in any given request. How extensive is the request? Does the agency or local government have the staff to even respond to the request? How many open records requests are on the table at the time? These—and other related considerations, the high court has told us—determine what is a reasonable time for such a response.

Naturally, there's never enough staff to answer promptly. There's always too many requests to get to all at once, and usually the requests are too burdensome. So, just how much time does the government have to fill a request? Well, here's how the DOJ sums up the high court's thinking:

"In short, how long an authority has to respond to a request depends," the DOJ states on its website. "Ten business days may be a reasonable response time for a simple request seeking a limited number of records that are easy to identify. However, as the court has said, sometimes an authority can be swamped with public records requests and may need a substantial time to respond to a request."

So when a person requests a public record in Wisconsin and turns to the law for guidance on how long she or he should wait for an answer, the law tells us: It depends. As one would imagine, as the DOJ added in a rare moment of lucidity, "this leaves room for interpretation."

Other states simply do not allow such nonsense. In Illinois, a public body must generally fulfill the request within five days, or notify the requester of an extension for another five days, as well as give a date certain time for fulfillment. In New Hampshire, if a public body is unable to make a public record available for immediate inspection and copying, it must within five business days of the request make the record available, deny the request in writing with reasons, or furnish written acknowledgement of the request and a statement of the time reasonably necessary to determine whether the request shall be granted or denied.

Specific time frames are absolutely critical to prevent broad interpretations of the law, and date specificity is critical as a first inflection point.

A couple of matters. Governmental bodies should never be given extra time to decide whether to fulfill or deny a request, for it doesn't take months to look at a request and decide whether it falls within the straightforward exemptions of the law. It is reasonable for a government body to decide that such records must be released but that a request is large enough to warrant more time, at which point the agency should be given a short automatic amount of extra time to fulfill the request or decide it needs even more time and advise the requester just when the request would be fulfilled. At that point, however, the requester should have the right to appeal the extended timeframe administratively.

The second point is, if an agency cannot fulfill the request within the timeframe of the automatic extension, it should not be able to charge for the records, either for location fees or copies.

Let's take an example. The state could impose a 10-business-day deadline for an initial response, giving the body 10 days to provide the records, deny the records request with reasons, or to request more time. If more time was needed, the government body could invoke a five- or 10-day automatic extension, which would be unappealable. Or the government body could say it needs even more time and advise the requester of the time it needs. That last action would be appealable administratively, and, if the extended time is granted, the agency would relinquish any claim to costs.

Such a framework would prevent a situation that happened with *The Lakeland Times* a few years back. On October 2, 2009, *The Times* sent the state Department of Natural Resources a request for all documents, emails, correspondence, letters, and records between October 2002 and October 1, 2009, related to the department's shoreland zoning revisions.

It was indeed a hefty request. Even so, the agency never bothered to respond for months, until December in fact. By late December, agency officials and *Times* publisher Gregg Walker had hashed out an agreement about narrowing the scope of the request, and the agency agreed to fulfill it. Ultimately, the DNR charged the newspaper $1,000 for the time it says it took staff to locate the relevant records, and it took the department until May to provide the records, more than seven months after the original request was submitted.

Under the framework suggested above, the agency would have had to contact Walker no later than October 16, not December. Under the situation that unfolded, we should assume that the agency would have insisted it could not meet the automatic two-week calendar extension, and so another time-certain timeframe would have been negotiated with Walker. Would Walker have agreed to another five months (December to May)? Probably not. Would the DNR have won an appeal if it had imposed a May date for delivering the records?

The answer is no. Emails obtained later by *The Times* indicate that the agency did not even ask affected employees for pertinent records for five months after *The Times* made the request. A review of the responses of about 30 percent of those employees shows they spent less than a half hour locating and compiling documents, on average. In other words, the agency actually spent only two months gathering the records, not seven, and even then the amount of time spent gathering the records indicates the compilation could likely have been completed with an automatic extension of two weeks, even for such a hefty request.

So instead of May, the agency likely could have completed the request by the end of October—the end of the automatic time extension—and still charged the newspaper its location and copying costs. One could argue that scanning the documents for redactions would have extended the time the agency needed, but one can also argue that such a date-certain framework—whatever that framework turns out to be, it doesn't have to be what I have suggested here—provides incentives for governmental bodies to fulfill requests rather than sticking them in a drawer somewhere to drag out the records release.

Revising the law to replace the vague 'as soon as practicable and without delay' with time-specific deadlines allowing for time-specific extensions, is absolutely essential.

—

A second major flaw in the law as written pertains to the costs of complying with records requests.

In Wisconsin, a governmental body may charge for copying and location costs. Other charges are allowed but those are the two that generate concern. Under the law, copy fees are limited to the "actual, necessary and direct cost" of reproduction unless a fee is otherwise specifically established or authorized to be established by law. Costs associated with locating records may be charged if they total $50 or more.

The state and most local governments have been pretty good over time about copying costs. Oneida County, for example, lowered its copying costs in 2019, and, on the state level, the Department of Corrections (DOC) did so a few years ago. In 2016, DOC chief legal counsel Winn Collins oversaw an overhaul of the public records process, and one of the first changes made was DOC's adoption of the Wisconsin Department of Justice's public records fee schedule, which dropped per-page costs for paper records and for scanned records by nearly half and eliminated per-page fees for electronic records.

Still, many officials still charge hefty fees for the time spent locating records, sometimes charging thousands of dollars that no one can be reasonably expected to pay. And it goes without saying that many officials know they are overcharging.

In the case cited above when *The Times* asked the DNR for seven years of shoreland zoning documents, not only did agency officials know they were overcharging, they were internally called out for it by a DNR records consultant.

In the case, the consultant, Helen Flores, advised the agency that it should operate transparently and that it could come under fire for inefficient record keeping if it charged excessive fees. Flores also questioned initial agency estimates that it would take 50 hours—one hour per person—for employees to fulfill the request.

In an Oct. 29, 2009, email to multiple agency officials, Flores expressed concern that a significant charge would make the agency appear incompetent. She marked the importance level of the email as 'high.'

"First of all, I am generally opposed to charging for locating records, especially when dealing with the press," Flores wrote. "If it costs DNR so much to collect all relevant records related to NR115 rulemaking, it looks like we don't have effective, efficient record keeping and records handling systems."

That wasn't her only concern. She also questioned the underlying assumptions used to calculate how much time it would take the agency to fulfill the request.

"First of all, will it REALLY take each of 50 employees an hour each just to locate information about NR115? Why? We could provide copies of their emails on a CD or DVD, instead of making copies. We could collect the information and have *Lakeland Times* use an external copy service to make paper copies and pay them directly (a process developed long ago to deal with high volume copy work). Note that we cannot charge for sorting out confidential information from open information."

The DNR should keep its public relations' image in mind in complying with the request, Flores continued.

"DNR needs to be perceived as an agency committed to open, transparent government accountability," she wrote. "Access to information—a basic responsibility for all employees."

Flores then urged agency staff to "consider carefully" the costs and negative implications the DNR could incur for charging location fees. Those included, she wrote, "cost to determine and calculate actual labor costs—can't add a charge for that," "potential fall-out from the press or the public if we have to itemize actual salaries and fringes of DNR employees, a sore point, especially in an economic downturn," "perception that files are not managed efficiently," and "perception that access to information includes obstacles."

Flores attached information about allowable costs for open records from the DNR records management handbook and once again stressed that the DNR could not charge a fee for separating confidential information from public records. Indeed, she cautioned, "we should not be mixing confidential materials with open ones—either in emails or in paper files."

Ultimately, the DNR ignored Flores and charged the newspaper $1,000 anyway for the time it says it took staff to locate relevant records.

—

So overcharging is going on, and it requires a legislative fix. Unfortunately, right now, any legislative "fix" would head in the opposite direction, if the recent words and actions of lawmakers are any indication.

Let's look at the issue of charging for redactions, which would drive the cost of records through the heavens, to make the point.

In 2012, in *Milwaukee Journal Sentinel v. the City of Milwaukee*, the newspaper challenged redaction fees, and, in a unanimous decision, the state Supreme Court ruled that custodians of public records could not charge requesters of records a fee for time spent redacting sensitive and confidential information from those records.

The lawsuit stemmed from an open records request for incident summaries of 2009 police reports related to sexual assaults. The city wanted the newspaper to ante up $3,390 for staff time spent reviewing and redacting the records.

The newspaper refused to pay and sued but lost in circuit court. The paper then appealed directly to the Supreme Court, bypassing the appellate level; the high court agreed to take the case. In the ruling, written by chief justice Shirley Abrahamson, the court said the 1981 open records law did not expressly allow for such charges, and lawmakers had not changed the law to do so, even though the issue had been subsequently raised and had even prompted an attorney general's opinion saying government bodies could not collect a redaction fee.

Abrahamson also said the case went to the core of the public records law: the ability of the public to have reasonable access to public records.

"This case is not about a direct denial of public access to records, but the issue in the present case directly implicates the accessibility of government records," Abrahamson wrote. "The greater the fee imposed on a requester of a public record, the less likely the requester will be willing and able to successfully make a record request. Thus, the imposition of fees limits and may even serve to deny access to government records."

Then attorney general J.B. Van Hollen applauded the ruling.

"This decision provides a straightforward and commonsense interpretation of the public records law," Van Hollen said. "A requestor cannot be required to pay for something unless the statute clearly authorizes a fee. This is the correct decision, and a decision which promotes open government."

Still, the ruling focused only on whether the Legislature had intended to allow for redaction costs in the past, and four justices, in a separate concurring opinion, thought it wise for the Legislature to revisit the question on its own. Justice Patience Roggensack said the court's decision, while the correct one, would likely result in either taxpayers being required to pay for the statutorily required separation of voluminous public records requests, rather than the person who would receive and use the records, or public records requests would go unmet due to a lack of necessary personnel to do the separations.

"Fundamentally, this case implicates public policy choices: whether taxpayers or record requesters should bear the financial burden of statutory record separations, and whether the costs associated with voluminous record requests should be addressed in a manner different from that employed for requests of only a few public records," Roggensack wrote. "Therefore, although I am aware of and concerned for the significant costs and personnel deployments that voluminous record requests can impose on authorities who are subject to public record requests and who may be operating with diminished revenues and personnel, addressing those concerns is a legislative function, not a function properly undertaken by the courts."

Justice David Prosser, joining Roggensack's concurrence, said he, too, had concerns.

"The plain implication of this ruling is that an authority may not charge a fee for an unenumerated 'task,' no matter how costly that task may be," Prosser wrote. "As a result, shrewd requesters will be able to use government resources to obtain valuable information at little or no cost …"

Prosser said there was no doubting that public records requests could be highly salutary and could expose deficiencies and shortcomings in public performance.

"But some public records requests may harass public officials or units of government," he wrote. "This reality is seldom acknowledged. The ability to impose charges reflecting the actual cost of compliance has sometimes served as a brake on malicious, frivolous, or unreasonable requests. To some extent, the court removes this brake. The court's decision changes the dynamics of the public records law. I join justice Roggensack in asking the Legislature to revisit the law to consider the ramifications of the court's decision."

Van Hollen said he saw two practical implications.

"First, this case is a win for requestors," he said. "However, I would encourage requestors to continue to consider and respect the obligations that governmental bodies face when complying with the public records law, and to be patient when trying to obtain information. Complicated requests and redactions do take time and all governmental agencies are facing the challenges of tight budgets and reduced personnel."

Second, he said, the decision made it clear that the Legislature, not the courts, must balance the competing interests under the public records law when determining who should bear the costs of redaction.

Nonetheless, Abrahamson wrote in the lead opinion, the decision bolstered the state's commitment to the open records law.

"Wisconsin's commitment to open, transparent government rings loud and clear in the Public Records Law," she wrote.

The next year, lawmakers responded to the high court's invitation to take up the question, only—wouldn't you know it—it was a push the minority implicitly called for, to overturn the court's decision and allow for redaction fees. The proposed measure was introduced by eight Republicans and one Democrat, fully two years before Republicans tried to jettison the entire public records law. During legislative debate, critics said the proposed law would cause fees for open records requests to balloon and have a chilling impact on the public's access to needed information; proponents said the mounting time and cost of fulfilling records requests had placed an unreasonable burden on taxpayers.

Writing in a *Your Right to Know* column for the Freedom of Information Counsel, Mike Juley of the *Milwaukee Journal Sentinel* pointed to the already high costs of public records requests.

In just a year, he wrote, the *Journal Sentinel* spent more than $22,400 on open records and database searches, while the newspaper had doled out more than $86,000 on public records requests in the previous five years. That's because people already have to pay actual copying costs and also location costs if it takes more than $50 in time spent locating records. And those totals, Juley wrote, didn't include legal fees.

"Adding more fees on top of what already is required in the statute will put many record searches out of the reach of many news organizations, let alone the general public," he wrote.

Another issue, he continued, is that officials often use higher-paid staff to do the redacting, when lower-paid clerks could just as easily accomplish the task. The bottom line was, Juley wrote, people already pay for open records searches through taxes, and allowing additional costs would put public access out of reach for many ordinary citizens.

"Should public records be available only to those who can afford to get them?" he asked. "The public owns and has the right to see the records of its government, with a few reasonable exceptions. Public records do not belong to administrators and bureaucrats—some of whom, experience tells us, would use these proposed redaction fees to hide problems and keep taxpayers and voters from learning about potentially embarrassing or even incriminating documents."

Support for the measure came from several entities that use tax dollars for lobbying, including the Wisconsin Counties Association and the League of Wisconsin Municipalities. In a 2013 memo to the Assembly committee of jurisdiction, the WCA's legislative associate, David Callendar, said his group supported openness but recent Supreme Court decisions and legislative changes had increased the need for counties and other public records custodians to redact information before releasing the records, and that had increased the costs of requests.

"WCA has long supported providing as much public access to public records as possible," Callendar wrote. "However, when the cost of providing those records to individuals imposes a substantial burden to local taxpayers, then those costs should be borne by the requester, as the law already allows for locating, copying and mailing of records. The cost of redacting information from a record is no different—it is part of the cost of providing a record to an individual who requests it."

Callendar called the proposed legislation a common-sense approach to those rising costs.

Ultimately, the court decision stood, yet the legislative activism exposed a subterranean but rising current to allow costs to requesters to increase, not fall. That inclination has only hardened and increased in the intervening years, and some lawmakers have not been shy about saying it. In a 2016 election interview at *The Lakeland Times,* for instance, then state Rep. Mary Felzkowski said she believed in allowing for reasonable costs.

"I have a situation right now in which we are working with a school district in Florence County," she said then. "They had an administrator seven years ago and they are still receiving open records requests about him. First it came from the district that he went to, and then it went to a state association, now it's a national association. The Florence district has racked up $50,000 in costs over this. Why should it be the taxpayers' burden to fulfill open records requests to all of these different entities?"

For newspapers, Felzkowski said, the newspaper should pay reasonable fees as a cost of doing business.

"It should be the cost of that person and the cost of the paper and the reproduction," she said. Felzkowski said her office received tons of requests that asked for years of emails that were broad and not specific.

"Our staff sits for hours upon hours and then you'll get that same request from another person," she said. "We see open records requests that are nuisance requests. You can tell they are nuisance requests. So if there is a fee applied to it, the people that want it and who are genuinely looking for the information will take it and utilize it. A realistic fee to reimburse the taxpayers for information that you are going to utilize in your business, I have no problem with that."

Now this is inverted thinking that shows just how much lawmakers miss that transparency should be considered a core function of democratic government because self-government is impossible without accountability. Somehow Felzkowski missed the fact that taxpayers have already paid reasonable fees for the core functions of government, otherwise known as their taxes, and that open government, as well as the consequent waiving of fees in the public interest, should be seen by officials as the cost of doing the people's business, rather than the other way around.

Instead, Felzkowski wants to place the cost of openness on the backs of average people rather than on a \$76-billion state government, where it would be, and is, a minuscule portion of the tab.

That's what is called having your priorities wrong.

Felzkowski is by no means alone in her abhorrence of transparency, and, sadly, transparency is rarely a campaign issue in her or other incumbents' election campaigns. But openness should be a major issue, and lowering the costs of attaining records should be a major plank in that platform.

Cleary, the law should be amended to prohibit government entities from charging more than the actual costs of paper copies, rather than being able to set fees by law. Most government agencies routinely build into their budgets the actual costs of their internal printing services anyway. As for location costs, the Wisconsin Freedom of Information Council has long advocated updating the threshold for charging those costs. Right now, government entities can charge for location costs only if they exceed \$50, using the hourly rate for the lowest paid worker who can perform the location tasks. These days, that threshold should be increased to \$125, the FOIC asserted a few years back.

I much prefer the viewpoint taken by the DNR consultant Helen Flores, who opposed any charges for locating records. After all, given an avenue of revenue collection, there is always the temptation to inflate the amount of time it takes, as Flores suspected the DNR was doing. And that actual time is almost always not onerous anyway in an age when most records are digital and can be accessed with a few keystrokes.

Compromise? Perhaps. What about a threshold fee of \$125 to charge any locations costs, with a cap of \$500 (or some other reasonable number). All backed up by the ability to appeal administratively if someone feels a fee is too high.

—

Refining the definition of 'a draft' for purposes of open records exemptions is a third critical need, and, in fact, it's another court case waiting to happen if the Legislature does not make it so.

That's because case law and policy are both muddled on the matter, and officials routinely try to thwart openness by proclaiming drafts to be off-limits. Oftentimes, though, such documents, when and if they see the light of day as official versions, are substantially different from the drafts, often suspiciously so.

In the context of this discussion, I am not referring to deliberative documents and the recent controversies swirling around evolving policies and the like, but actual draft records—preliminary rather than evolving versions of records that are then scrutinized for accuracy and completeness before becoming official final documents.

Meeting minutes are the perfect example.

Abuse of the definition is widespread and the question about whether draft minutes of open government meetings are public records has not been clearly resolved within states statutes or in case law, so once again I'll pluck a case from my own backyard to explore the point.

In 2019, the Oneida Vilas Transit Commission became embroiled in several high-profile controversies that raised questions about its transparency, namely, the commission's bid to eliminate county board approval of its budget and to abolish a requirement for an annual financial audit, as well as an open meetings complaint filed against its executive committee by *The Lakeland Times*.

The latter charge raised yet another concern about the commission's transparency—its refusal to turn over draft minutes of its meetings.

As *The Times* reported, the commission refused a request by an Oneida County sheriff's department detective sergeant for the draft minutes of a March 29 meeting the department was investigating in relation to the alleged open meetings law infraction. That refusal came after the commission's secretary told detective sergeant Kelly Moermond she would finish typing the minutes later that day and after transit commission manager Roger Youngren told Moermond she could have them.

He changed his mind, though, saying "he could not release the minutes from the meeting because they had not been approved at the meeting," Moermond wrote in her report of the matter.

Of course, while many governmental entities withhold draft minutes as a result of that murkiness, many others release draft minutes out of a commitment to transparency. Oneida County is one of those counties. In fact, the Oneida County code directs all draft minutes to be posted to its website within 10 days of a meeting.

"Each committee shall keep minutes of each meeting, and within 10 days of a committee or county board meeting provide an electronic copy of the draft minutes, clearly marked 'DRAFT,' to the county webmaster for posting on the county website," the code states.

What's more, the code directs each committee to file approved minutes with the county clerk within 10 days after approval or correction of the minutes by the committee at the following meeting, with an electronic copy of the approved minutes posted on the county website.

A slew of towns, counties, and cities also release draft minutes, as do state agencies such as the Wisconsin Department of Natural Resources.

Still, as *The Times* reported, the transit commission is not an outlier in refusing to release unapproved minutes, even to a law enforcement officer conducting an investigation of the meeting in question, short of a subpoena. And, as the Oneida County website clearly states on its website about the transit commission, "due to this being a joint county commission, the Oneida County code regarding the posting of minutes does not apply."

And so with plenty of precedent behind it, and an exemption from Oneida County posting requirements due to its structure, the commission was able to turn down Moermond on April 17, 2019, 19 days after the March 29 meeting being investigated. In fact, almost six weeks after the meeting, the commission had still not posted any minutes of the meeting, draft or otherwise.

"The minutes for this meeting are not available," the Oneida County clerk's office stated in early May 2019 on the county website. "They have been requested from this commission/committee and will be posted as soon as they are received."

That's not to say withholding draft minutes could survive a court challenge if someone brought one over a refusal to release such minutes. One significant court case, while not ruling specifically on the matter, suggests that draft minutes are releasable public records, and one attorney general's opinion also strongly suggests draft minutes should almost always be released. What's more, in 2011 an assistant attorney general opined in a seminar that draft minutes are generally releasable records.

However, those who say that draft minutes can be withheld point to the exemptions from disclosure in the open records law itself.

That exemption is contained within a portion of a single sentence in the records law: "'Record' does not include drafts, notes, preliminary computations, and like materials prepared for the originator's personal use or prepared by the originator in the name of a person for whom the originator is working…"

Over the years, that exemption for drafts has been subject to an overly broad interpretation; many agencies simply mark documents they don't want released as drafts or use the exemption to delay release by dragging out formal approval, as can be the case with meeting minutes that are sometimes not approved for months after the meeting of a governmental body. Such delays can shield government actions from the public during crucial periods of time.

Again, the courts have not faced the question directly, but at least one major decision did address the question peripherally. In *Fox v Bock*, a 1989 case, the state Supreme Court directly addressed the potential for officials to evade the law by marking documents as drafts, and it also clarified what was meant by 'draft,' saying the intent was to limit the exemption to documents that are prepared expressly for the personal use of the originator of the document.

That latter definition would appear to rule out withholding draft minutes of open meetings, which are certainly not prepared for personal use, unlike the handwritten notes of a meeting that an official might make for himself or herself.

The issue in *Bock* was whether a study conducted by the Institute for Liability Management, which was commissioned by and prepared for the Racine County corporation counsel's office, was a record.

William F. Bock, the corporation counsel, had become concerned about the increasing number of civil claims that were being brought against Racine County and ordered a study of the problem. However, Bock later testified, he had no intention of requesting the study from the institute unless he could be assured that the report, in whatever form it took, would not be subject to inspection by the public.

Later, when the local newspaper got wind of the study and requested a copy, Bock denied them on the grounds that the institute's study was prepared in draft form and did not constitute a record. The trial court agreed with Bock; the state

Supreme Court rejected the interpretation and ruled that it was a releasable record.

The other specifics of that case aside, the court in the course of fashioning its decision did address what was a draft and what was not under the law. Its starting point was that any exceptions to the general rule of disclosure must be narrowly construed. But, citing precedent, the court made a declaration that cuts directly to the issue of whether meeting minutes or any other document must be in final form to be a releasable record. They do not, the justices determined, and, if they did, that would lead to attempts to evade the law.

"Whether the document is in 'preliminary' form and therefore not in final form is not determinative of whether it is a record," the court stated. "The trial court erred when it found that the institute's study was a draft unless and until the final corrections were made on it. If the trial court's rulings were correct, legal custodians of public records could circumvent the effect of [the public records law] by merely claiming that the report is not in final form and further changes must be made in it."

Public policy favoring public disclosure does not allow a custodian of a record to delay or cancel delivery of the "final" report in an attempt to have it qualified as a draft, the court determined.

Next, the justices turned to the fact that the exception for a draft ties it to personal use.

"A determination that a document is a draft prepared for the originator's personal use creates an exception to the general rule of disclosure," the decision stated. "It is a draft if it is prepared for and utilized for the originator's personal use. The institute's study was not created for the personal use of the corporation counsel nor was it so utilized. Under sec. 19.32(2), Stats., a document prepared for something other than the originator's personal use, whether it is in preliminary form or stamped 'draft,' whether recommendations of the document are implemented or not, is by definition a record."

Likewise, minutes of open meetings are not prepared for the personal use of the transit commission or any other governmental body or official; they are by definition prepared to create a public use, to create a public record of the meeting, and, to parallel the justices in the *Bock* decision, it could be argued that a document such as minutes that are not prepared for personal use is a record, whether in preliminary or final form.

Just the year before, in 1988, attorney general Don Hanaway, in an opinion entitled "treatment of drafts under the public records law discussed," also addressed the exemption for drafts, and homed in on the personal use requirement. As with the Supreme Court, Hanaway's starting point was the proposition that exceptions to the public records law should be narrowly construed.

"It follows that exclusion of material prepared for the originator's personal use is to be construed narrowly," Hanaway wrote. "Most typically this exclusion may be invoked properly where a person takes notes for the sole purpose of refreshing his or her recollection at a later time. If the person confers with others for the purpose of verifying the correctness of the notes, but the sole purpose of such verification and retention continues to be to refresh one's recollection at a later time, it is my opinion that the notes continue to fall under the exclusion."

But that's not the case for notes or documents created for the purpose of preserving a record of government activity, Hanaway wrote.

"However, if one's notes are distributed to others for the purpose of communicating information or if notes are retained for the purpose of memorializing agency activity, the notes would go beyond mere personal use and would therefore not be excluded from the definition of a 'record,'" he wrote.

Simply put, an agency secretary's notes—which are prepared as draft minutes for the purpose of memorializing agency activity—would be public records.

Finally, in answering questions submitted during a 2011 Department of Justice webinar, assistant attorney general Mary Burke directly addressed the question. Though it was simply her belief and not an official attorney general's opinion, it nonetheless aligned the DOJ at the time with the earlier court case and Hanaway's opinion that stressed that any draft must be for personal use to qualify for exception, and that personal use needs to be narrowly construed.

Burke specifically addressed two questions—whether a board member's request of a draft of board meeting minutes is in fact a public records request, and whether the minutes are available immediately for public viewing. On the first question, Burke said the answer depended on the specific situation at hand.

"Under some circumstances, a board member's request for a draft of the minutes of a meeting of a board on which the board member serves may be an internal operations matter rather than a request pursuant to the public records law," Burke wrote.

But if a board member—or anybody else—does make a public records request for the draft minutes, then the following considerations would be relevant, Burke asserted.

"First, have the draft minutes been prepared? If not, the public records law does not dictate the timetable for preparation of the draft minutes," she wrote. "The public records law generally applies to records that already exist at the time the request is made."

Second, Burke continued in her analysis, if some draft minutes exist, are they still being revised and finalized by the person preparing them, or are they in the form in which they will be presented to the board for final approval?

"If the person preparing the minutes still is working on revising and finalizing the draft minutes, then they probably are preliminary documents that do not constitute a 'record' as defined [by the statute] for public records law purposes," she wrote. "If the draft minutes have been finalized and are ready for board approval, or have been circulated in pre-meeting materials or otherwise, then they may be 'records' subject to disclosure in response to a public records request from a board member or a member of the public."

However, Burke wrote, response to public records requests is required 'as soon as practicable and without delay,' not immediately.

In the end, Burke wrote, echoing the *Bock* decision, whether or not the draft minutes have received final approval from the board may not be the controlling factor in determining whether they should be disclosed in response to a public records request.

"Other relevant considerations would include the status of their preparation, how they have been circulated, and how they have been used," she concluded.

Applying Burke's analysis to the transit commission, the sheriff's department's request for the minutes of the March 29 meeting would seem, in this particular context, to constitute a public record that should have been released to the department.

To be sure, when Moermond first called the transit commission secretary, the document was not a releasable record because the secretary was still typing and preparing it. However, after she finished it later in the day, and it was ready to be presented to the executive committee for approval, it became a releasable record under Burke's analysis, especially because the minutes were intended to memorialize a public meeting of the transit commission's executive committee and were not created for the originator's personal use, or for the personal use of the committee or Youngren.

The sheriff's department did not press the matter, though, and the question of draft meeting minutes as public records remains a test case waiting to happen.

Before it does, the Legislature should amend the law. While this book will look at so many other changes we need to ensure government transparency, attacking the most basic fundamental flaws of the current law—time delays, fees, drafts—would resolve some of the most common barriers to access that citizens face today.

—

I close this chapter with a current case that underscores just how weak the law is. This book began by recounting how law enforcement finally stood up for open government and for consequential accountability for breaking transparency laws. I reported that the case against the then Rhinelander city administrator, who was charged with felony misconduct in office stemming from the newspaper's open records complaint, was ongoing. It still is.

In the case, the defense is making a number of substantive arguments too complicated to fully recount here. But one of the arguments goes to the very heart of this chapter. Specifically, the city administrator was charged with misconduct in public office for intentionally failing or refusing to perform a known mandatory, non-discretionary, ministerial duty related to the open records complaint. However, the defense maintains that the actual conduct was irrelevant because fulfilling an open records request is not such a duty. Here's how the attorney explains it:

"But an evaluation of [the] alleged conduct is immaterial to the primary dispositive issue before the court, which is whether the duty alleged to have been violated—here, responding to an open records request—is itself a mandatory, non-discretionary, and ministerial duty," the attorney stated in a brief to the court. "This is the issue because the violation of a mandatory, non-discretionary, ministerial duty is an affirmative element of the misconduct in public office crime for which [the administrator] has been charged."

And why aren't fulfilling open records requests a non-discretionary duty? Well, the attorney argues, "the employee responsible for filling the request... must make a number of discretionary judgments," such as whether the request is reasonable, performing a balancing test, and, tellingly, when the request must be fulfilled or denied ("the public records law does not 'define the time' in which a request must be fulfilled in a manner that deprives the public employee of discretion").

Now there's no telling whether that argument will succeed, but it calls painful attention to a couple of things. First, as argued in this chapter, the law is too vague on many points, with Exhibit A being the lack of specific times to fulfill records requests, which the attorney is trying to exploit. Making the law more ministerial internally would remove some of the barriers to exacting consequences for misconduct. For example, mandating specific times would make a failure to fulfill a request a violation of a non-discretionary duty, even if other elements of fulfilling the request do unavoidably involve judgment.

At the very least, no matter the outcome of this case, the interplay between the misconduct in office statute and the open records law needs to be examined to ensure that intentional and flagrant violations of open government laws are classified as felony misconduct in office.

That an attorney can even credibly argue that the public records law is so insignificant that alleged conduct with respect to fulfilling records requests is immaterial when considering a misconduct in office charge is outrageous, and another signal that the law needs to be strengthened to take its rightful place as a core responsibility of government officials.

Chapter 3

The Right to Privacy

Wisconsin's open records law needs a provision clarifying how the law is to be applied to privacy concerns, which are increasingly becoming an issue in the release of information as government collects ever more data on citizens.

Make no mistake, those are legitimate concerns, and, if any roundtable were to be finally convened on the open government laws, the interplay between the two rights should be a central focus. But it should also be said that, once again and unsurprisingly, those whose mission is to obstruct transparency (lawmakers, we are looking at you) have not hesitated to use privacy as an excuse not to release public information.

From the very start, Wisconsin's open records law was weak when it came to the right to privacy, a fact de la Mora pointed out in her 1983 article in the *Marquette Law Review*. That's not really a criticism because the interplay between privacy and openness wasn't on the radar screen of many people back then—it was well before the real life application of the law would send them on a collision course.

But it was on de la Mora's radar screen. She called the right to privacy the open records law's "missing element."

"In striking a balance between the right of the public to know and the competing rights of individuals, the Wisconsin public records law overlooks the right of confidentiality, a right the United States Supreme Court has described as 'the individual interest in avoiding disclosure of personal matters,'" she wrote. "In order to carry on their delegated functions such as education, police protection, dispensing welfare benefits, licensing and taxation, governmental agencies must acquire detailed information on citizens. Much of this information is supplied with the express or implied understanding that it will be kept confidential."

That said, de la Mora continued, Wisconsin had not adequately dealt with privacy problems inherent in information collection and its release, except through separate statutes that dealt only with a specific type of record.

"The Wisconsin public records statute contains no specific exemption dealing with privacy, and the balancing test makes no mention of the privacy concern," she wrote. "The balancing test, as enunciated by the supreme court, weighs the need of the public to be informed against the harm to the public interest rather than harm to any private interest in the release of the record."

What's more, de la Mora wrote, Wisconsin's 1977 privacy statute did not protect the privacy rights of individuals when confidential information was contained in public records.

"The supreme court, referring to the foregoing legislation, has stated, 'individuals have no right of privacy in materials contained in public records that are open to the public generally,'" she wrote. "Thus in both the privacy statute and the public records statute neither the Wisconsin Legislature nor the Wisconsin Supreme Court has confronted the privacy right of an individual regarding confidential information given to a governmental agency."

But, as anyone who has dealt with government knows, there are individuals and then there are individuals. Let's look at the two categories: the privacy rights of public employees, and the privacy rights of the rest of us.

—

In the years following a case referred to as the *Woznicki* decision, the Legislature enacted the so-called Woznicki fix, a response to two calamitous court decisions designed to help protect the privacy interests of government employees but that made it exceedingly difficult to obtain records relating to public officials.

It all started in 1996, in *Woznicki v. Erickson,* when the state's high court determined that a person could contest in court the release of a public record by a district attorney if that release might damage the person's privacy and reputational interests. After all, a person can sue for a decision not to release records, so implicit in that logic is that a subject of a records request can have a court consider the decision to release records.

In 1999, in *Milwaukee Teachers Education Association v. Milwaukee Board of Education,* the court drilled down into that ruling, finding that *Woznicki* gave virtually all public employees a right to contest the release of so-called reputational facts, and, to ensure their right to mount a challenge, the decision created notification-and-review requirements that bogged down the release of all records, to the point of virtually voiding the public records law.

In general, the court decisions gave citizens, and public employees in particular, what many critics called excessive court-granted privacy rights, and the so-called Woznicki fix was enacted in 2003 to curb the extreme tilt toward privacy. Under the 2003 legislation, most notice-and-review requirements for public records were done away with, and Woznicki notifications giving public employees a right to challenge disclosure were only required if the records pertained to disciplinary investigations and records obtained by a subpoena or search warrant.

For department and agency heads, the law granted only a right to be notified and to place a statement in the files.

Notably, the Woznicki fix not only constricted when a public employee could challenge records releases, it provided a timeline for notification, response, and adjudication of those protests, which has helped to stem delays in releasing records. That those timelines have been effective should indicate that specific timelines should be enacted more generally to records responses and releases.

As it turns out, the Woznicki legislation, which was actually a compromise, had its own flaws. The first is, while the law limited what records public employees could challenge, it was precisely those records that are the most important for the public to have—disciplinary records that examine what one does on the job.

As open records attorney Robert Dreps told Rebecca Daugherty, the director of the Freedom of Information Service Center, back then, public employees were limited only to the right to challenge the release of information on the performance of their duties but that was the very area where they should be held accountable for what they do.

A landmark case involving *The Lakeland Times* that resulted in a definitive Supreme Court ruling that closed disciplinary investigation records are releasable illustrates the point. The case was *Kroeplin v Wisconsin DNR*.

In the case, then DNR conservation warden Thomas Kroeplin used *Woznicki* to attempt to block the release of documents relating to his alleged misuse of motor vehicle records. The question was, why? The newspaper knew some things from the public record already. For instance, Kroeplin was heard on a recording asking for license plate particulars just minutes after his nephew had unsuccessfully tried to get that same information. A dispatcher was heard giving him the details after he promised not to tell anybody else.

About a half-hour later, the nephew's former girlfriend, obviously in distress, placed a 9-1-1 call, saying the nephew had just been to her residence and threatened her and her current boyfriend. As it turned out, the car whose plate information Kroeplin was seeking was parked that day at the former girlfriend's house.

The question was, did Kroeplin's unauthorized use of license plate information ultimately lead to the 9-1-1 call and to the alleged threats against the woman and her friend? The newspaper believed the public had a right to know the answer to the question, and that access to the DNR's investigatory findings was a critical step in finding out.

For one thing, if his actions did spark that chain of events, it called for the harshest of consequences, for things could have easily ended tragically. Indeed, as in the case of the late actress Rebecca Schaefer, the misuse of motor vehicle information had ended tragically before, and on a number of occasions.

But the newspaper also felt the public needed to know something else: What was the DNR's attitude toward the possible violation of federal drivers privacy protections by its employees, for it was against federal law for anyone— including law enforcement officials—to access that information without a legitimate government purpose for doing so. Was there a zero-tolerance policy in place? Were there stiff sanctions? Or did the DNR just look the other way?

Simply put, obtaining the DNR's investigatory findings and disciplinary recommendations were necessary both to determine the extent of Kroeplin's culpability as well for understanding the DNR's position on such misconduct. Yet the Woznicki fix allowed Kroeplin to challenge the release of the records.

In the beginning, the DNR had decided to release only a portion of its investigatory findings and a portion of the disciplinary recommendation, and that was a red flag decision in and of itself, but, even worse, Kroeplin went a step further by trying to block the release of all the findings.

So, Dreps worried when the law was passed, the statute allows an employee to challenge the release of information about that person's conduct in carrying out his or her public trust responsibilities, when that's the very conduct the public should have a right to know about and question.

How in the world can there ever be accountability if the law shields what public employees do on the job from the public itself? Of course, Kroeplin's attorney argued that his privacy and reputational interests would be damaged if the documents were disclosed, but how can anyone claim a right of privacy when it comes to alleged wrongdoing, especially a violation occurring while the employee was acting in an official capacity?

The same would go for Kroeplin's reputational interests. If he did nothing wrong, the documents would exonerate him. If he did abuse his public position, if he did break the law, well, then his reputation would deserve to suffer. Such are the consequences of wrongdoing; such is the outcome needed to deter people from doing wrong in the first place.

Another aspect of the equation is that no one was seeking Kroeplin's entire or general personnel record or disciplinary file. The requests focused narrowly on one incident, the knowledge of which was germane to public safety. Disclosure said nothing about the total body of his career work; it would simply made him take his medicine for one act, and to take it publicly.

And that, after all, is exactly what Kroeplin, as a conservation warden, asked the public to do. When people end up in court, accused by a conservation warden or other officer of wrongdoing, their records aren't sealed. They must satisfy the requirements of whatever sanctions are handed down, and they must do so out in the open.

In the *Kroeplin* case, a major victory was secured in that, once and for all, closed disciplinary investigations were considered to be public records. Still, while the Woznicki fix was a step forward, it did not go far enough in remedying the court decision because there's no telling what a future court might do in a similar challenge to the release of specific records.

In the end, the Woznicki legislation left intact for public employees a shield around the records the public needs most. It's a double standard every private citizen should object to because the law should not afford public employees special protection based on their employment or position.

The bottom is, the Woznicki fix needs to be fixed. There is simply no reason that public employees should have a right to notice. Public records should be public records, period, and either exempt under the law or not. Just as the identity of a records requester is irrelevant, so should be the subject of the record, save for certain sensitive and already established exemptions that call for redaction rather than notice.

Back in 2003, when the Woznicki fix was enacted, John Laabs, executive director of the Wisconsin Broadcasters Association, told the *Milwaukee Journal Sentinel* that the new legislation "doesn't go far enough."

"We'd prefer to go back to the days when there was no notice required and all records were considered to be open records," he said.

In an article entitled "Fixing Bad Judicial Rulings with Good Laws," Rebecca Daugherty of the Reporters Committee for Freedom of the Press quoted Laabs's sentiment and summed it up nicely: "So would we."

We still should. The law should wear a blindfold when it comes to the subject of the record.

—

Woznicki aside, government officials still use privacy as a broad brush with which to try and paint away access to public employee records.

To cite one significant example, in 2018 *The Lakeland Times* went to court after the state DOJ attempted to shield wrongdoers in its department from public exposure. The agency had released the disciplinary files of the employees that *The Times* had been seeking, including details of the infractions and the discipline imposed, but, citing privacy, withheld the names of those employees that it claimed were lower-level workers who had committed only minor infractions.

The outcome of the case could have had far-reaching open records implications, said *Times* attorney April Rockstead Barker, because a ruling favoring the DOJ would have shielded many state and other public workers from having their misconduct records tied to them by name. That would allow workers to evade individual accountability, a fundamental tenet of the public records law.

Then attorney general Brad Schimel and the DOJ disagreed, saying there was no public benefit to releasing the names. The DOJ said that, because both the details of the misconduct and of the discipline imposed had been released, the public already has a complete picture of how the Wisconsin Department of Justice managed employee discipline.

The Times filed a motion seeking the removal of redactions to the disciplinary records turned over to the newspaper, primarily for the names of certain DOJ employees the department continued to shield. The department released some of the names but not others.

Ultimately, the newspaper and the department resolved differences pertaining to redactions in a second category of requested records—those containing the names of law enforcement personnel who were disciplined or were accused or suspected of database abuse involving the state's Transaction Information for the Management of Enforcement, or TIME, system between 2013 and 2015. *The Times* received those records.

The outstanding disputes concerned the names of DOJ employees disciplined for the years 2013-2016. As Barker wrote in the newspaper's brief supporting the motion, the DOJ redacted the names of 19 employees from the disciplinary letters. The penalties and offenses ranged from written reprimands for such things as unexcused or excessive absenteeism, insubordination, refusal to carry out written and verbal assignments, and unauthorized and improper use of state resources, to three-day suspensions without pay for, among other things, negligence, inattentiveness and insubordination, and making false and malicious statements about other employees or supervisors.

One employee received a written reprimand for falsifying records or giving false, misleading, or deceptive information to DOJ staff, other state agencies, or private organizations or to employees responsible for record keeping. Another received a five-day suspension without pay for failure to report six instances where the employee entered cyber tips in the DOJ's system.

Still, in court, assistant attorneys general Anne Bensky and Gesina Seilor Carson argued that there was no public benefit to releasing the names.

"[This case] is not about whether the public has a right to public employee disciplinary records: it does, and the DOJ has provided records detailing the work rule violations, the conduct that led to the work rule violations, the procedure provided to the affected employees, and the discipline imposed," they argued. "With disclosure of these records, the public has a complete picture of how the Wisconsin Department of Justice manages employee discipline."

The DOJ argued that *The Times* failed to explain how the public at large would benefit from knowing the names of civil servants subject to workplace discipline, and, what's more, the assistant attorneys general wrote, while there is a presumption of openness, that general statement does not outweigh the significant public harm that would accompany release of employee names.

"Disclosing such information about employees who do not hold significant positions of public trust will do nothing to shed light on the workings of government, but it will brand those employees with a modern-day scarlet letter that can negatively impact their ability to succeed in their current employment and obtain future employment, among many other potential harms that follow someone whose name is forever on the internet in conjunction with their workplace discipline," the DOJ brief stated.

The personal stigma that accompanies persons whose names are on the internet in conjunction with employee discipline could not be understated, the assistant attorneys general argued, and they contended that the implications transcended previous open records cases.

"This goes far beyond concerns over reputational interests expressed 16 years ago in *Linzmeyer* and 12 years ago in *Kroeplin*," the brief stated. "If names of all employees who receive workplace discipline are released, managers responsible for enforcing work rules will be reluctant to investigate and issue discipline at all."

With the public's ability to obtain volumes of records related to public employees and publish them forever on the internet, public servants are at a significant disadvantage in comparison to non-public employees, whose mistakes, lapses in judgment, and occasional tardiness are not broadcast throughout the nation, the assistant attorneys general argued.

"The reality of the world in the social media and internet age necessarily alter the balance of interests; what may have been fleeting moments of embarrassment 15 years ago are now easily accessible, permanent records that can cause far more detriment to public employees now than ever before," the brief stated. "Thus, relying wholly on case law analyzing a public employee's privacy and reputational interests from 10 or more years ago ignores the impact that disclosure can have in contemporary times."

That said, the assistant attorneys general contended, the previous cases cited by *The Times* and Barker were inapplicable to the current situation for a more obvious reason: They involved whether an authority must release any records related to a particular disciplinary investigation.

"Unlike the present case, those cases did not simply seek to keep names confidential," the brief stated. "In *Kroeplin v. DNR,* the plaintiff was a DNR warden with law enforcement powers who was disciplined for running an unlawful license plate check for personal purposes. The DNR agreed to release some records and denied access to others."

In other words, Kroeplin sought to enjoin release of the records, period: "*Kroeplin* was not merely about whether the public was entitled to know Kroeplin's name, it was about whether the public was entitled to records detailing potential misconduct by a law enforcement officer and the manner in which the DNR investigated that misconduct," the brief stated.

Unlike in *Kroeplin*, the assistant attorneys general wrote, the DOJ released the requested records, nearly in full, with only names and other personally identifying information redacted.

"Public disclosure of the employees' names will not provide the public with any additional information about employee misconduct or how that conduct was investigated," the brief stated. "Also unlike in *Kroeplin*, the redacted employee names are not law enforcement officers with significant powers over the public."

The DOJ argued that in another case, *Local 2489, AFSCME, AFL-CIO v. Rock County,* the sheriff released disciplinary records with names and identifying information redacted, and the court observed that that afforded some protection to the employees' privacy and reputational interests.

Neither did the redactions create, nor attempt to create, a blanket exception to public access to personnel records, the DOJ argued, saying that blanket exception occurs when access is denied to a particular category of records regardless of content. In other words, DOJ argued, the law prohibited arbitrary classifications inapplicable to particular records and it disfavored using extrinsic information to determine whether a particular record should or should not be released.

The DOJ avoided those missteps, its attorneys argued.

"DOJ's records custodian reviewed all of the records individually and balanced interests based upon the nature of the allegations and the relative position of public trust that the employee held," the brief stated. "Following the custodian's fact-intensive, record-by-record review, the custodian determined that records containing similar content warranted similar treatment under the balancing test."

That is not unlawful categorization or creation of a blanket exception but rather common sense, the DOJ asserted.

"Review of the documents demonstrate DOJ released all requested records that explain the disciplinary actions DOJ took, the basis upon which they were taken, the procedure afforded to the affected employee, and the discipline issued," the brief stated. "The custodian determined release of the names of certain affected employees is not in the public interest. The employees whose names were redacted did not engage in criminal conduct or serious misconduct, there is a public policy interest in protecting the reputations and privacy interests of public employees, and the employees were not highly placed and therefore had a higher expectation of privacy than those with significant authority (such as appointed officials)."

In her reply brief for *The Times,* Barker argued that there had never been a recognized exception to the public records law allowing custodians to routinely redact employee names from any records, including personnel records, and, by asking the court to condone that practice, the DOJ was in fact asking the court to change the law.

"Moreover, while they argue otherwise, defendants are asking the court to create a new categorical public policy exception," Barker wrote. "Defendants' argument is that the disciplinary records of all employees that a custodian considers to be 'low level' and whose discipline involves what the custodian considers to be 'minor' misconduct are of no interest to the public. This classification would allow custodians to withhold records even when a different result would be compelled by considering all pertinent public policy considerations."

For example, Barker continued, if a so-called low-level employee briefly crossed the center line while driving a state-owned vehicle, an allegedly minor infraction, and caused an automobile accident, injuring others, the public would have an obvious interest in knowing the name of the employee and about the employee's prior track record while driving state vehicles.

"Nonetheless, under defendants' argument, the custodian could withhold the employee's name from all disciplinary records—for that incident and for prior incidents—so that the public would never know if the employee had engaged in similar misconduct in the past, prior to the misconduct that produced serious results," she wrote. "This example is not remote to the circumstances presented in this case, because the records show that in cases in which the department withheld employee names, the discipline imposed followed misconduct that the department characterized as involving significant harm to the agency's interests."

Tellingly, Barker asserted, the DOJ argued that it treats all "similar" records "similarly"—in other words, they did not look at the records individually to see whether any exceptional grounds for nondisclosure were presented. Instead, she continued, they simply used a two-step test: 1) Was the employee "low level," according to their definition; and 2) Was the employee's work rule violation "minor," according to their definition.

"Accepting this approach would create a new categorical exception to disclosure that all government agencies would be using to justify redacting employee names in no time flat," she wrote.

The DOJ also argued that the public only needs to know what discipline was imposed, not who received it, Barker wrote, but the public records law was enacted to allow the public, not government agencies, to decide what information the public needs to know.

"Moreover, defendants' argument ignores the fundamental tenet of the Public Record law that it is not just the agencies, but public officials and employees, individually, who are accountable to the public," she wrote. "The department has previously acknowledged this point, stating in a prior opinion, '[T]he main purpose of the public records law is to enable the citizenry to monitor and evaluate the performance of public officials and employes [*sic*].'"

Barker contended that the DOJ also ignored the fact that there is no such thing as "no public interest" in any public record and that the public interest is especially high where employee misconduct is concerned.

"Moreover, plaintiffs explained in their most recent brief in this case that there are practical reasons why names should not be disclosed," she wrote. "Without names, it is impossible for the public to know if serial offenders who have engaged in misconduct are being transferred and hired and re-hired without public knowledge. What the defendants characterize as 'branding' employees by their misconduct is just defendants' negative spin on the necessary task of providing information that allows the public to fairly judge employees by their past performance."

And that's not all, Barker argued.

"While the department may want to be lenient with certain serial offenders or to provide them with multiple chances, the public is entitled to know that the department is doing so," she wrote. "Similarly, without names, it is impossible to rule out nepotism as a reason for particularly lenient discipline or retaliation as a potential basis for particularly harsh discipline against outspoken employees."

Barker also took issue with the DOJ's claim that in certain previous cases, custodians "did not simply seek to keep names confidential."

"But that was precisely what the defendants attempted to keep confidential under the balancing test, among other reasons, in *Milwaukee Journal Sentinel v. Department of Administration*," she wrote. "As plaintiffs have previously explained, the Wisconsin Supreme Court held that the names had to be released despite the arguments of the employees' union that employees would be subject to harassment if the names were released—the exact argument that defendants are making in this case. The Wisconsin Supreme Court rejected that generally stated concern as a basis for denying access to the employees' names."

The Wisconsin Court of Appeals had also similarly rejected an assertion that publicly identifying information could be redacted from email messages from members of the public to state legislators, in *MacIver v. Erpenbach*, Barker observed.

As for *Local 2489, AFSCME et al v. Rock County*, Barker observed, while the DOJ argued that the court of appeals noted in passing that the employees' names were redacted from disciplinary records, the court was not called upon to decide anything about that point because no one challenged those redactions.

"Even if there were any precedential value that could potentially arise from the court's explanation of the parties' positions in *Local 2489*, the Wisconsin Supreme Court's opinion in *Milwaukee Journal Sentinel v. Dept. of Administration*, issued four years later, establishes that employee names should not be redacted from public records based on generalized arguments about potential harassment," she continued.

The defendants also complained that public employees would be at a disadvantage compared to private-sector employees if their names were released, Barker observed, but she said the Wisconsin Supreme Court had explained that release of public employees' names was a consequence of accepting public employment.

Addressing another DOJ argument, Barker argued that the internet does not make existing authority obsolete: The argument fails because the internet has been around for more than 25 years, she wrote—far before the cases the DOJ said were litigated in a pre-internet environment.

The DOJ argued, too, that managers would not discipline employees if information about employees is released, but Barker observed that the court of appeals in *Kroeplin* rejected that argument, saying that "if public employers know that the investigations they perform are subject to public review, common sense dictates that they will be more diligent in ensuring that charges of potential misconduct are thoroughly investigated, and that the appropriate discipline is imposed, than they would be if they were not held accountable to the public."

Just as important, Barker asserted, the DOJ's arguments were inconsistent with the facts.

"Plaintiffs explained in their prior briefs that the offenses for which the employees were disciplined violated significant work rules and that they are employees who have substantial responsibility in their positions," she wrote. "Defendants have not filed a reply brief and therefore, they have not conceded this point, including all others contained in the plaintiffs' response brief."

Finally, Barker asserted, the DOJ had not established any "exceptional" reasons justifying their nondisclosure of the records.

"Instead, they are requesting that the court recognize a new categorical public policy exemption for the names of so-called 'lower level' employees disciplined for so-called minor violations," she wrote. "That request is inconsistent with the Supreme Court's direction that courts cannot create any categorical public policy exceptions to disclosure and that any alleged 'exceptional' circumstances must be decided on their own facts."

After the case went to court, Schimel was defeated in his bid for re-election by Democrat Josh Kaul, but the DOJ pressed on with its case. Ultimately, it was to no avail as Dane County circuit judge Valerie Bailey-Rihn dismissed the DOJ's various arguments one by one. The judge said the case did present interesting lines of reasoning, but she said the state had to demonstrate an exceptional reason for refusing access to each individual record that was being denied, and it did not so.

One of the more interesting arguments, Bailey-Rihn wrote, was the fact that internet records, like diamonds, are forever, but she said the Legislature and the courts had not yet grappled with that issue.

"The court appreciates the concerns regarding the openness and longevity of internet search results, but as of yet, there is not a statutory or common law justification for denying full access to records on that basis," she wrote.

Less interesting, and perhaps more troubling, the judge asserted, was that many of the DOJ's arguments had already been argued in state courts and rejected.

"Additionally, many of defendants' listed reasons for redacting information have already been addressed by higher courts," she wrote. "The purpose of the open records law is to allow for transparent and accountable government and public employees."

She rejected the notion that there was no public interest in the names because the misconduct involved work rule violations rather than criminal activity.

"The Wisconsin Court of Appeals in *Kroeplin* stated that the public records law advocates for disclosure of records 'where the conduct involves violations of the law or significant work rules,'" her decision stated. "This implicitly contradicts the DOJ's argument that the records may be withheld because the misconduct was not criminal by including work rules in the court's analysis."

In addition, Bailey-Rihn said the court explicitly addressed the issue in *Kroeplin*, quoting that case: "*Kroeplin* appears to include a third argument. He acknowledges that the public has a strong interest in accessing records relating to employee discipline where the employee is charged with a crime or with a serious work rule violation. However, he asserts, because he was not charged with a crime or because, at least in his view, the DNR did not accuse him of serious misconduct, the public's interest in the disclosure of his documents is slight. We reject this argument."

Bailey-Rihn said three court decisions had considered and rejected the explanation that the reputational interests of public employees are an important factor and that employees whose names are released may be embarrassed, or, in more severe cases, struggle to get hired based on the release of their names. She specifically dismissed the argument that exposed employees may have trouble finding future employment.

"A public interest in continued employment, especially for employees who may have serious work misconduct, would certainly give way to the public interest in transparency," she wrote.

And she rejected the idea that all the misconduct was minor and deserving of nonrelease, saying the agency itself had called some of the incidents serious at the time of discipline.

"Finally, the records at issue are characterized both as 'garden variety' and severe," she wrote. "Defendants assert both that the misconduct is minimal and therefore the public does not need the information while simultaneously stating that release of names could cause challenges in future employment. Having reviewed the facts, it seems that the records likely land somewhere in between the two opposing characterizations."

While it is not entirely clear where each individual record falls on the scale, Bailey-Rihn wrote, the court found that neither justification was adequate to rebut the presumption of openness.

"Defendants have not shown how personal reputation concerns relate to the larger public interest," she wrote.

The judge said the argument that the employees were lower level was not persuasive and that courts in the past have held that generalized concerns that apply to all "public employees" fail the "exceptional reason" requirement. She also noted that courts have held that all public officials are subject to heightened scrutiny.

"Further, as previously stated, the Wisconsin Supreme Court requires that there be particular concerns for withholding information, not issues that could be generalized to all public employees," she wrote. "Based on these tenets, a generalized argument limiting access to lower level employees is not an exceptional circumstance that would favor nondisclosure."

The court was also aware that if this distinction were to be used, it could easily qualify as a blanket exception, Bailey-Rihn stated.

"A records custodian could deny access to any employee not in a supervisory role," she wrote. "Due to concerns over blanket exceptions and the case law favoring full and open access, the court finds the distinction between the authority levels unpersuasive."

Bailey-Rihn likewise rejected the state's argument that releasing the names would deter supervisors from fully and adequately investigating misconduct.

"However, the Court of Appeals in *Kroeplin* rejected the argument that investigators of employee misconduct 'would be less than candid if they feared that their appraisals might be available for public inspection,'" she wrote. "The court rejected the argument stating that there was no indication that disclosing the records would have the purported effects."

Here, Bailey-Rihn observed, there did not seem to be a practical difference between DOJ's argument and the rejected argument in *Kroeplin*.

"As in *Kroeplin*, DOJ fails to point to any evidence indicating that disclosing misconduct records would inhibit supervisors from investigating claims or imposing discipline," she wrote. "There is a statutory presumption of openness; without evidence of an actual chilling effect on investigations, the court is not going to deny full access."

As Barker pointed out at the time, a ruling in favor of the DOJ would have been disastrous for open records if the decision ultimately stood. It was defeated, but it still stands out as an important case to study because of two ramifications.

First, it demonstrates that records officials continually re-litigate reasons for denying access to records that have long been considered settled law: "Releasing the records will have a chilling effect on disciplining employees." "Releasing the records will destroy morale." "Releasing the records will have a chilling effect on recruiting and retaining good employees because of the possibility that their misbehavior will be exposed."

All of those are straw arguments dismissed repeatedly in courts, as Bailey-Rihn observed, and yet government continues to bring them in new cases, and taxpayers continue to pay for them. That's because, in the end, settled law is only settled until it isn't. The ability to overturn precedent is not a bad one, but it also opens the door to mischief.

That's where the Legislature needs to step in and clarify the law to address the baseless arguments that are made over and over again.

The second significant aspect of this case is that it glimpses an argument the state likely will be making again and again—that the right to privacy is especially challenged by the eternal existence of records on the internet. Bailey-Rihn characterized this as a new argument, but it really isn't—it is the same argument that leads opponents of openness to argue for shutting down online court records, that they are too easily accessible and that they linger on.

But it is a curious claim that public records can somehow be too accessible, and that a record, once released, should somehow have a shelf life, and that it doesn't justifies denial. It is important to know whether an employee with some serious misconduct on his or her record in the first five years of employment had a spotless record for the next 25 years, or if a pattern of misconduct persisted all the way through.

This isn't possible when records "do not live forever" as they do online. The DOJ essentially argued that if a record could just dissolve *Mission Impossible* style after a few years it would be OK to release but not OK if it is going to be around 20 years later. Who wants to be dogged forever by youthful indiscretions and "occasional tardiness," the DOJ wanted to know.

But the DOJ missed the point. The crucial question is not about youthful mistakes but the public's right to know about serious misconduct that is considered egregious or unethical or even unsafe. Somehow, in its consideration of a record's longevity, the DOJ forgot to balance the public interest in the nondisclosure of years-old minor infractions leading to discipline against the public's interest in the disclosure of years-old major infractions leading to discipline.

Because major infractions must be disclosed regardless of time, and because only the public can judge what constitutes a major infraction, there should no valid argument against releasing a disciplinary record on the grounds that "it will live forever."

—

All of the foregoing concern the privacy rights of public employees, but a growing concern has centered on the privacy rights of citizens, particularly when it comes to constituent correspondence between a citizen and a lawmaker that might involve personal situations.

The easy answer is that the public records law already allows for the redaction of identifying information in records releases, and, in any case, the idea of a private communication with a public official is an oxymoron.

That's the easy and technically correct answer, but it's not sufficient.

For one thing, as de la Mora pointed out in 1983, the public records law does not even address privacy concerns directly, and the state's right to privacy statute offers no relief for any information available to the public as a matter of public record. That doesn't mean personally identifiable or sensitive information not meeting specific exemptions under the open records law will automatically be released—there must be a balancing test.

But there's no specific protective exemptions based on privacy in the open-records law whatsoever, and, as de la Mora pointed out, the law "fails to give any insight to the judiciary on how the privacy rights of individuals must be weighed in the context of applying the balancing test—a general formula which on its face considers only whether the harm to the public outweighs the presumption of benefit to the public."

Such privacy concerns have come into sharp focus in several cases in recent years, especially involving lawmakers and their desire to keep the names of constituents who correspond with them secret.

In 2010, *The Lakeland Times* sued state Sen. Mark Miller over various issues related to a request for all electronic and written correspondence between Miller and any member of his staff and Tia Nelson, the executive director of the Board of Commissioners of Public Lands, Natural Resources Board member Jonathan Ela, DNR deputy secretary Pat Henderson, and the Gathering Waters Conservancy, as well as all electronic and written correspondence to or from Miller or any member of his staff that pertained to Stewardship access requirements in the 2009 budget bill or to the Stewardship access rule the DNR was then promulgating.

Miller ultimately released the documents but at first redacted all the names and email addresses, saying the information did not have to be released. However, before that issue could be contested in court, the senator quickly reversed his decision and released the information.

But the issue wasn't dead. In her 2016 re-election bid, state Rep. Mary Felzkowski took the same position as Miller did and articulated her reasons for it. Specifically, she said that constituent correspondence sometimes contained highly sensitive and personal information that the public had no right to know or access.

"I think that there are lot of things in this country and in this state that should be looked at as far as the personal rights of people and protecting the personal rights of people," she said. "In open records, you don't need to know whose child has an opioid addiction, that's none of your business. None. It doesn't affect the taxpayers of the state. It doesn't affect how government works. Those are very private conversations and if somebody can't get BadgerCare or their chemo treatments, that's none of your business. And I believe constituents have a right to that privacy."

After the state's Act 10 controversy, state Sen. Jon Erpenbach (D-Middleton) expanded the scope of Felzkowski's thinking, saying constituents' email addresses and names were off limits even when they there were communicating purely political opinions. The MacIver Institute had sued Erpenbach after it had issued an open records request for the emails, including names and email addresses, of people who emailed him at the height of the Act 10 controversy in 2011, when Scott Walker and the Legislature effectively ended public-sector collective bargaining.

Many believed public employees were among the emailers, using government computers on government time to lobby the legislator. Erpenbach released more than 25,000 emails but redacted the names and email addresses of the senders. He won on that count in lower court, but lost in the court of appeals. And, even though he surrendered the names and email addresses, in a 2016 interview with *The Lakeland Times*, the senator continued to say he was right.

"The reason why I didn't want to release the records is that it wasn't detailing legislative activity, it wasn't detailing anything other than the fact that this was a person, and here's their personally identifiable information, here's the content of what they had to say," he said. "And what we have always done in our office prior to this lawsuit was that you can have the content or you can have the personally identifiable information, but you can't have both because, as an elected official, an individual or a constituent approaching me on some issue has to have some sort of right to privacy on that particular issue, and it doesn't matter whether it is Act 10 or a neighbor doing something they shouldn't be doing."

Erpenbach said he understood the need for open government and embraced it, but he also believed releasing the personally identifiable information of a citizen who petitioned his or her government would have a chilling effect—there's that phrase again—on civic participation.

"If an individual contacts me with their thoughts on Act 10 or Donald Trump, whether I agree or I disagree, I have to be able to protect what they believe in and what they are saying because at what point are we going to cross the line where it's like, 'I'm not contacting my legislator on this because I don't want my name all over the place,'" he said. "And, honest to God, that's the only reason why. I've been really consistent on (open records)."

Erpenbach pointed out that those emailing him on government time using government computers during the 2011 Act 10 controversy were legally allowed to do so.

"To me it doesn't matter, if they are within the law, whether they are using a state computer or not, if they are within the law, why don't they have a right to privacy?" he asked.

And there can be real-life consequences, the senator said.

"Let's say the individual who contacts me is all of a sudden the subject of a talk radio show," he said. "Her address, what she makes, what her house looks like—it's all out there, and she's getting ripped on talk radio because she petitioned her government. If you want to know who I am meeting with, fine. But if I have a citizen petitioning me, and this is where we have to figure out a way to delineate—if we can delineate at all—in my mind there's a huge difference between a lobbyist sending me an email and you sending me an email."

The lobbyist is representing a group of people, Erpenbach said, while individuals are telling him how they feel about something.

"I'm very sincere on this," he said. "How do we protect an individual's right to petition their government without recourse and keep our records open? And given how divisive things are right now, and we can't even see each other we are so far apart, if an individual has a legitimate concern about a piece of legislation coming through, and they are contacting me to tell me how they feel about it, and their neighbor doesn't like them, or doesn't like what they think, and it's 'Oh my God, there's that leftie-liberal or rightie-conservative whacko nut job,' where is the protection for the individual?"

For the most part, the senator's claims are frivolous. Erpenbach especially tried to protect politically friendly constituents on a hot-button issue, saying they could face reprisals if their identities were known and that such exposure would have a chilling effect on citizen communications with lawmakers.

The appeals court thought that was frivolous, too, and dismissed the argument out of hand.

"Erpenbach places much emphasis on the 'nuclear environment' which existed in and around the state capitol building while collective bargaining changes were being considered and even after their enactment, and, from this, argues that senders of the emails generally could face threats, harassment or reprisals in one form or another," the court stated. "While Erpenbach has identified threats and harassment levied against public officials and police officers at the Capitol building itself around the time Act 10 was under consideration, he has identified no instances of actual threats, harassment or reprisals against concerned citizens away from the Capitol building who merely communicated their position regarding the public policy changes via correspondence."

Erpenbach had asserted that many of the communications he received expressed concern about reprisal, the court stated, but he failed to identify any emails in the record supporting that assertion, and the court's own review of the emails did not reveal any such concerns by the senders.

"In short, Erpenbach has demonstrated no reasonable probability that citizens merely corresponding with lawmakers regarding their position on Act 10 would be subjected to negative repercussions for sharing their views regarding the legislation," the decision stated.

The MacIver Institute had also argued that it was critical for the public to know who was communicating to lawmakers on matters of public policy, not to mention where those communications came from, and the court agreed. Indeed, after analyzing the emails, MacIver found that 1,020 of the 1,522 emails sent by Wisconsin state government employees were sent during normal business hours.

"Public awareness of 'who' is attempting to influence public policy is essential for effective oversight of our government," the decision stated. "For example, if a person or group of persons who has played a significant role in an elected official's election—by way of campaign contributions or other support —contacts a lawmaker in favor of or opposed to proposed legislation, knowledge of that information is in the public interest; perhaps even more so if the person or group also stands to benefit from or is at risk of being harmed by the legislation."

The "where" aspect was important, too, the court found.

"It is also of public interest to know from 'where' the sender is attempting to influence public policy," the decision stated. "Whether a communication is sent to a public official from a source that appears associated with a particular unit of government (such as Milwaukee County or Waukesha School District), a private entity (such as Northwestern Mutual Life or Marquette University), or a nonprofit organization (such as American Red Cross or Clean Wisconsin, Inc.), or from individuals who may be associated with a specific interest or particular area of the state, from 'where' a communication is sent further assists the public in understanding who is attempting to influence public policy and why," the court determined. "Thus, the redacted information identifying 'who' sent emails attempting to influence public policy and from 'where' the emails were sent is not 'purely personal,' and the public has a strong interest in disclosure of such information."

In the end, the court stated, application of the public records law does not turn on whom the public record is from or who owned the computer from which the public record was transmitted.

"Application of the public records law is the same whether the record is from George Soros, David Koch, or John Q. Public," the judges ruled. "The ownership of the computer upon which the communication was transmitted is not relevant under the law. The public has a right under the law to know who is attempting to influence its public officials. John Q. Public falls in the same league as George Soros/David Koch, regardless of any of their desires to remain anonymous. If legislators do not like the law they created they can repeal it—but until then they must abide by it."

As MacIver's arguments and the court's agreement make clear, abiding by the law is much preferable to repealing it, and, in fact, it would be wise to codify that court's language to make sure there's no lack of clarity in the future.

There's another important aspect about the full release of constituent correspondence—though none hardly as important as knowing whom lawmakers are talking with on matters of public policy—and that is to determine the veracity of the communications, i.e., whether lawmakers are telling the truth about the contacts they are having.

He's now retired, but over in Wisconsin Rapids there was a lawmaker, Rep. Marlin Schneider, who for many years attempted to derail and dismantle online circuit court records as an invasion of privacy. Such records were unfairly used to discriminate against job seekers and apartment hunters, he argued, and he said his constituents often expressed their desire to have that open window into their lives closed, you know, in the interest of justice.

So year after year Schneider introduced bills to do just that. And in late 2009 he did so again, circulating a memo on December 23 of that year seeking co-sponsors. As the *Wisconsin State Journal* reported, Schneider said in the memo —and again at a public hearing—that he had received hundreds of letters from "innocent people who said their lives had been hurt by information appearing on the state's website for court records, popularly known as CCAP."

But, oops, that prompted the Associated Press to file an open records request seeking copies of all the correspondence Schneider said he had received. Schneider complied, but it wasn't pretty. As *The State Journal* reported, since 2006, only 59 people had sent emails or letters to Schneider, and only 22 of those complained that CCAP (now known as Wisconsin Circuit Court Access, or WCCA) records hurt them, even though their charges had been dismissed.

The others who complained were merely offering general comments on the issue, or had actually been convicted, the AP reported. So the names and email addresses of individuals politicking with their lawmakers as citizen lobbyists are not protected, and they shouldn't be. That should be codified.

But we're not out of the woods yet when it comes to privacy concerns. Though she is an outright enemy of transparency, some of the concerns Felzkowski expressed about divulging private conversations about someone's BadgerCare or chemotherapy treatments are well taken. In such letters and emails, the private business of the family intersects with public policy. And while most of us would object to these identities or the actual health or financial scenarios of people being disclosed, there appears to be no statutory protection for redacting them. HIPPA laws would not protect those conversations with a lawmaker, and the open records law, when it comes to health, provides certain exemptions for health information but those pertain only to official health care records prepared by or under the supervision of a health care provider.

Informally telling a family story to a lawmaker to try and get some help might or might not cut it under those exemptions, depending upon whom the custodian or judge is.

While I don't know the proper fix for that kind of situation, some adjustment is needed, with the kind of guardrails mentioned above to prevent lawmakers from abusing the process. Indeed, to be fair, in his interview with *The Times*, Erpenbach endorsed a new look at the entire canon of the Wisconsin public records law, and suggested addressing just that issue.

"Maybe the state could delineate between policy issues and medical or other privacy issues in the open records law," he said, and he further said it was probably time for a comprehensive rewrite of portions of the statute, as long as the news media was on board and signed off on that effort.

"Maybe we should have a rewrite, with editors involved, of what really should be protected and what shouldn't be when it comes to an individual," he said.

I would agree. As a doctrinal matter the constitutional right to privacy already protects the information Felzkowski is worried about. In the U.S., and no less in Wisconsin, the right to privacy applies only when one has a reasonable expectation of privacy, and that reasonableness must derive not from the person seeking to protect the material but from the nation and states themselves, through the crafting of public policy to explicitly define what a sensible and rational expectation of privacy is. The doctrinal foundation is there, but the political application is lacking.

To be sure, who wouldn't think that it's reasonable to protect a family's most private medical histories and similar situations, even when they are discussed with a lawmaker in a way that implicates public policy? Most of us would. But not everybody. And it could be argued that a person engaged in such correspondence with a public official has given an implied waiver of that right. That should not be left to chance.

Many years ago, a custodian had released records to *The Times* that were not redacted out of a fear of trespassing the law. The records did pertain to public matters, but, as letters to a lawmaker might, they contained extraordinarily private and sensitive information. The custodian implored us not to publish that information and indeed we had no intention of doing so. It was information that really was none of our or the public's business. But the narrow construction of records exemptions, the omission of any right to privacy in the open records law, the state's privacy statute's declaration that a claim of privacy is not valid when a matter of legitimate public interest is concerned—all these arguably made that information releasable, and it was in fact released.

It should not have been.

So, as de la Mora suggested so long ago, the open records law needs to address the right to privacy explicitly. At the very least, it should extend HIPPA protections to the open records law, as well as personal finances and other family matters. It should also declare that such discussions between citizens and public officials do not represent any express or implied consent to a waiver of the right to privacy but must be subject to a balancing test.

That should protect the right to privacy, but by itself would leave the door open for the czars of secrecy to exploit any new language. Thus, as counter safeguards, the law should specifically emphasize that any such information deemed to be exempt should be redacted while the rest of the correspondence remains open. And, at that point, to prevent judicial activism and "reinterpretation" of legislative intent, the law should declare explicitly that no right of privacy exists for any record category for which there is no enacted statutory exemption.

Chapter 4

Open Government v. Open Government

Many people will likely remember (or still indulge in) *Mad Magazine's* Spy vs. Spy, two almost identical Cold War creatures, except that one was dressed in all white and the other in all black, who spent most of their time trying to outwit the other, usually with absurd consequences.

Today, in the real world of transparency politics, there is a real Spy vs. Spy drama playing out in what might be called, if it were a cartoon strip, Open Government vs. Open Government. These political creatures are not quite as identical as the spies were, but the consequences of their face-off could be equally absurd. In fact, they could kill the entire movement for government transparency.

On the one side is what is often called the Freedom of Information movement, which is concerned with processes, such as open meetings, and disclosures through public records of the actions of government officials. It is most powerful on the state and local level, and the public records and public meetings laws that enshrine it are what newspapers such as *The Lakeland Times* and the *Northwoods River News* use to ensure and demand accountability.

Put another way, the freedom of information movement—with its requirements for open meetings and the release of public records—lets the public see just how officials are making decisions on a daily basis.

On the other side of the coin is what is often called the open government data movement. Its core idea is that the reams of data the government collects

—from census statistics to government contracts to agency spending to publicly funded scientific studies and agency consumer reports—should be open to the public to peruse and use as the public sees fit.

This growing movement has led to the creation of a multitude of federal and state web portals to such data. For example, Data.gov, the federal government's open data site, says it aims to make government more accountable by increasing citizen participation and informed decision making. Federal law requires federal agencies to publish their information on the website as open data, using standardized, machine-readable formats, with the metadata included in the Data.gov catalog, the site points out.

At first blush, there would seem to be no conflict between these two wings of the transparency movement. And, not surprisingly, activists in one arena are generally supportive politically of those in the other arena, as they should be. After all, one is hardly likely to support public decision making and then oppose publishing the statistical consequences of those decisions.

In recent years, though, tensions have arisen between the two sides, and observers of the overall transparency movement have begun to wonder whether the freedom of information side and the open data side are complementary or competing forces, and, if the latter is the case, what that means politically for an overall transparency movement that has thrived largely by being non-ideological beyond a commitment to openness.

Let's take a look at these questions, as well as how open government vs. open government is playing out right here in Wisconsin.

—

The distinctions and then tensions between freedom of information efforts and open government data initiatives have been around for a while, but one of the first major papers to quantify their significance was published in the *UCLA Law Review* in 2012 by Harlan Yu, a doctoral candidate in computer science and an affiliate of the Center for Information Technology Policy at Princeton University, and David G. Robinson, a visiting fellow of the Information Society Project at Yale Law School.

As Yu and Robinson observed, the early days of the open government movement focused on transparent processes, not transparent data.

"The phrase ['open government'] was first used in the 1950s in the debates leading up to passage of the Freedom of Information Act," Yu and Robinson wrote. "But over the last few years, that traditional meaning has blurred, and has shifted toward open technology."

But, the authors wrote, while open technologies involve sharing data over the internet, all kinds of governments can use them for all kinds of reasons.

"Recent public policies have stretched the label 'open government' to reach any public sector use of these technologies," they wrote. "Thus, the term 'open government data' might refer to data that makes the government as a whole more open (that is, more publicly accountable), or instead might refer to politically neutral public sector disclosures that are easy to reuse, even if they have nothing to do with public accountability."

The bottom line is, the authors wrote, governments that open up reams of data online are not necessarily "open."

"Today, a regime can call itself 'open' if it builds the right kind of website—even if it does not become more accountable or transparent," they wrote. "This shift in vocabulary makes it harder for policymakers and activists to articulate clear priorities and make cogent demands."

And all that made for a new ambiguity in open government, the authors observed.

"Technology can make public information more adaptable, empowering third parties to contribute in exciting new ways across many aspects of civic life," they wrote. "But technological enhancements alone will not resolve debates about the best priorities for civic life, and enhancements to government services are no substitute for public accountability."

Since 2012, concerns within the open government movement have only grown, with many who prioritize the transparency of decision-making processes concerned that the ascendance of open data as the face of the open government movement allows governments to proclaim themselves as open when they are in fact quite closed. That is to say, governments can conceal secretive decision-making processes by simply dumping mountains of data on the internet—data that many times only experts aligned with specific ideologies can decipher or spin.

Michael Canares, an open-data advocate who believes the interests of both camps can be reconciled, has written on the Web Foundation's Open Data Labs website that he heard such concerns raised at an international governance conference in 2014.

"At the time, Freedom of Information (FOI) advocates told us that the open data movement was highjacking the freedom of information agenda by giving governments a new outlet for transparency, relegating FOI requests to the bottom of the priority list," Canares wrote. "They raised concerns that governments might just focus on releasing large amounts of data the average person could not understand or use instead of responding to citizens' questions."

And that's exactly the concerns raised in 2018 in *The Conversation* by Suzanne J. Piotrowski, an associate professor of public affairs and administration at Rutgers; by Alex Ingrams, an assistant professor at Tilburg University; and by Daniel Berliner, an assistant professor of political science at the London School of Economics and Political Science.

"Over the last 50 years, Freedom of Information—or FOI—laws have been one of the most useful methods for citizens to learn what government is doing," the authors wrote. "These state and federal laws give people the power to request, and get, government documents. From everyday citizens to journalists, FOI laws have proven a powerful way to uncover the often-secret workings of government."

And, the authors asserted, while FOI laws have always faced many challenges, including resistance, evasion, and poor implementation and enforcement, the last decade had brought a different kind of challenge in the form of a new approach to transparency: the open government, or data, movement.

"Despite the fact that it shares a fundamental goal with the more established FOI movement—government transparency—the open government movement threatens to harm FOI by cornering the already limited public and private funding and government staffing available for transparency work," they wrote.

First, the authors contended, resources—both money and political attention —are inherently scarce.

"Government officials now have to divide their attention between FOI and other open government initiatives," they wrote. "And funders now have to divide their financial resources between FOI and other open government initiatives."

Second, they contended, the open government reform movement as well as the FOI movement have long depended on nonprofit advocacy groups such as the National Freedom of Information Coalition and the Sunlight Foundation to obtain and disseminate government information.

"This means that the financial stability of those nonprofit groups is crucial," they wrote. "But their efforts, as they grow, may each only get a shrinking portion of the total amount of grant money available."

For example, they pointed to Freedominfo.org, a website for gathering and comparing information on FOI laws around the world that had to suspend its operations in 2017 due to resources drying up. In addition, the authors wrote, the open data movement allows governments to claim credit for politically convenient reforms such as online data portals, while their actual open government agenda may create a false sense of transparency. That's because, they wrote, there's a lot of government data that isn't available through those portals.

Other observers say that many governments declare public records requests redundant, given the amount of information available online, simply telling the citizenry the data is online for them to find, if only they will go looking for Waldo, while avoiding specific answers to specific questions posed in specific records requests.

It's also worth mentioning that the open data movement is so concerned with opening up data portals that it neglects to answer another fundamental question: Why is the government collecting so much data in the first place?

Open data movement advocates disagree, of course. While open data efforts do take sizable resources, they argue, they should also reduce FOIA requests and free up those resources while not damaging the fundamentals of the FOI movement. And, they argue, the information that is generated and collected by the public sector allows the larger body politic to access and use the information—not just individuals making specific requests—which enables many more people to take part in public sector activities and to participate in public decision-making, while giving both public and private stakeholders, including commercial developers, the information needed to develop new added-value services and products.

Three examples of the tensions between the freedom of information movement and the open data movement stand out: The Obama administration nationally, and, in Wisconsin, the administration of Gov. Scott Walker, and the Wisconsin Economic Development Corporation.

On the one hand, President Barack Obama was hailed as a pioneer in the open data movement. In 2013, for example, Obama signed an executive order that made open and machine-readable data the new default for government information, with the president saying that making such data readily available and useful was the core of his promise of a more efficient and transparent government.

Then, too, in 2009, Data.gov went live and was the first platform to deliver federal data to citizens, academics, and anyone else seeking insights from government information, Jason Shueh wrote in *Government Technology*.

According to the federal website, Data.gov has grown to more than 200,000 datasets from hundreds of data sources including federal agencies, states, counties, and cities and has set the example for other open government data catalogs, with hundreds of other countries, states, and cities around the world launching their own open government data sites since 2009.

"One of the things we're doing to fuel more private sector innovation and discovery is to make vast amounts of America's data open and easy to access for the first time in history," Obama said in 2013. " ... And we're making it easier for people to find the data and use it, so that entrepreneurs can build products and services we haven't even imagined yet."

On the other hand, Obama was vilified during his White House years for his aggressive resistance to freedom of information requests and laws. In 2011, the Associated Press reported, the Obama administration "took action on fewer requests for federal records from citizens, journalists, companies and others over the previous 12 months even as significantly more people asked for information."

The AP analysis showed an increase of 41,000 FOIA requests over the previous year, to 544,360 requests at the 35 largest agencies. However, the AP reported, the administration responded to nearly 12,400 fewer requests.

"The administration refused to release any sought-after materials in more than 1-in-3 information requests, including cases when it couldn't find records, a person refused to pay for copies or the request was determined to be improper under the law," the AP stated.

And nearly half the agencies the AP examined took longer—weeks more, in some cases—to give out records that year than during the previous year.

By 2015, the Obama administration had set a new record for failing to fulfill FOIA requests, while under Obama the number of FOIA lawsuits in federal courts reached record highs. Overall, in 2015 and 2016, people who asked for records received redacted files or nothing all 77 percent of the time. The administration was also criticized for cracking down on leakers and whistleblowers and for using the Espionage Act a record eight times to prosecute government officials suspected of leaking classified information.

Also, as far back as 2010, the state department inspector general observed that state department employees had independently raised concerns that former secretary of state Hillary Clinton's private email usage was interfering with federal record-keeping laws.

A side note: While I am using the Obama administration in this example because he was heralded as a champion of the open data movement and thus as a champion of transparency when nothing could have been further from the truth, let's not pretend Donald Trump was any better, or, for that matter, any worse on FOIA issues or on whistleblowers, though the media portrayed him as much worse than Obama. Let's compare the two administrations.

From the Associated Press for 2016: "Overall, in the final year of Obama's administration, people who asked for records last year under the law received censored files or nothing in 77 percent of requests, about the same as the previous year."

From the Associated Press for 2017: "People who asked for records under the Freedom of Information Act received censored files or nothing in 78 percent of 823,222 requests, a record over the past decade."

———

While Obama was a Democrat, the Republican administration of Scott Walker compiled a similar track record in Wisconsin.

Walker, too, was progressive when it came to open data. In 2011, for example, as part of his state budget, the site OpenBook Wisconsin was legislated, allowing citizens to track the amount of money the state spends.

"There have been more than 25 million entries showing payments made for purchasing goods or services, travel and vendor payments for state agencies, the legislature, the courts and the University of Wisconsin System dating back to 2008," the website states.

As of 2017, the data included fringe payment data, employee salary, purchase orders, and contracts that state agencies have with vendors.

"OpenBook Wisconsin brings a historic level of openness and transparency to state government, and this website gives taxpayers an unprecedented level of access to the state's finances," Walker said in announcing the site.

But, as this book has discussed, in a historic but unsuccessful effort, the Walker administration collaborated with Republican lawmakers to include in the state budget measures that would have effectively killed the state's open records law. And, during his re-election campaign in 2014, Walker would not make a judgment about whether the Legislature should abide by the open records law or be subject to the open meetings law, while citing the biggest open government problem to be the inability of the public to review the state's finances online—in other words, open data.

The state's economic development corporation (WEDC), created in 2011 under Walker, is another example of the sharp tensions brewing between open government and open data. Again, the trend is to open up the data but shut down access to the decision-making processes.

In 2019, for example, a report by the Wisconsin Public Interest Research Group and Frontier Group gave the WEDC the nation's second-highest ranking in the nation for economic development-related transparency and online access to information. In 2012, the same annual report had blasted the WEDC for its lack of transparency. According to the 2019 report, a review of economic development subsidy reporting in all 50 states found that a majority of states still failed to meet minimum standards of online transparency, but Wisconsin was fast improving.

"Three states—Wisconsin, Connecticut and Mississippi—are 'advancing' states in economic development subsidy transparency," the report stated. "All three states include itemized grant payments to companies in their online spending portals, a transparency measure both Mississippi and Connecticut require by state statute. Both Wisconsin and Connecticut incorporate their primary economic development agency's grant payments directly into the state's general expenditure checkbook and are two of only three states to publish an annual report detailing statewide economic development grant spending."

OK, but the agency has been criticized for the secrecy in which it has operated. In 2015 and 2016, when Walker was still governor, two Democratic members sought records about 28 economic development awards for more than $126 million after the agency said it could not locate staff underwriting documentation. The records requests went unfulfilled for nearly a year.

Perhaps most egregious, the WEDC's final contract with special interest titan Foxconn was voted on and approved in closed session. That vote came despite a plea for transparency by Democratic lawmakers on the state's Joint Finance Committee.

"Gov. Walker and Legislative Republicans are committing state taxpayers to $3 billion in corporate subsidies while taking money away from classrooms, roads, and health care for decades," said then Senate Democratic leader Jennifer Shilling (D-La Crosse). "The lack of transparency throughout this process shows there is a higher risk to taxpayers and communities than Gov. Walker and Republican lawmakers are willing to admit. Given Foxconn's concerning track record, we need more openness and transparency from Gov. Walker's administration before committing families to years of economic costs and liabilities."

—

So in the world of open data versus freedom of information, the trend is to open up the data but shut down access to the decision-making processes, and to drain resources away from the mechanisms and tools FOIA advocates need to pry information from records custodians.

It's true on the national level, and it's true in Wisconsin.

In 2016, the national Freedom of Information Act celebrated its 50th birthday, but the birthday was hardly cause for celebration. An assessment of that law at 50 showed just how weak the open government movement was, and how fragile open government protections are. It was a national assessment but the same is the case in the various states. During that 50th birthday year, federal lawmakers threw the Sunshine law a party of sorts, more specifically, a hearing to see how the law was doing. The question was, had the FOIA fulfilled its promise in the days since President Lyndon Johnson signed it into law in 1966?

Sen. Chuck Grassley (R-Iowa), the chairman of the Senate Judiciary Committee, which held the hearing, said it had accomplished much.

"Today's hearing is a celebration," Grassley said. "It's an opportunity to reflect upon the good that's come from FOIA. And it's a chance to reiterate why FOIA should matter to all Americans. Without FOIA, countless stories of government waste, fraud, and abuse would have simply remained in the dark."

Before FOIA, Grassley said, people had to justify to the government their need for documents or information. But the law changed all that, he said.

"After FOIA, the government has to justify its refusal to release such information to the public," he said. "Before FOIA, government could largely rest assured that mismanagement would remain hidden behind the curtains. After FOIA, it's the right of the people to know what their government is up to. Put simply, FOIA was created to ensure transparency."

Still, despite all the benefits of the law, Grassley said much work remained to be done.

"Over the years, the government has continued to find ways to undermine citizens' right to know under FOIA," he said. "Where the default setting should be transparency, we still find a culture of obstruction and reflexive secrecy. This has been the case under both Democrat and Republican administrations."

At the hearing, Rick Blum, the director of the Sunshine in Government Initiative (SGI), a coalition of nine media associations, offered up a number of prescriptions for strengthening the FOIA nationally.

SGI members include the American Society of News Editors, The Associated Press, Association of Alternative Newsmedia, National Newspaper Association, Newspaper Association of America, Online News Association, Radio Television Digital News Association, Reporters Committee for Freedom of the Press and the Society of Professional Journalists.

First, Blum said, agencies still look for ways to delay the release of information, and Congress should hold them accountable when they don't meet statutory guidelines. Any agency, Blum said, can cite "unusual circumstances" to justify extending the FOIA's 20-day deadline for responding to requests, if the agency tells the requester it needs to search "voluminous amounts of records," or must locate records in multiple offices, or must get advice from another agency.

"As long as an agency shows progress to reduce backlogs or can show an unexpected uptick in requests, long wait times are tolerated," Blum said. "Probably the single biggest factor deterring journalists from using FOIA is the long waits."

Second, Blum said, FOIA suffers from insufficient investment in technology —a direct result of competition from the burgeoning open data movement and the rush to buy expensive data portals for every level of government and for every agency. A portal for Freedom of Information requests, similar to those for posting other government data, would level the playing field, and Blum proposed requiring the Office of Management and Budget (OMB) to build a single public interface for all agencies to accept FOIA requests and to allow OMB to add additional features.

And, Blum said, it should not be simply a series of links to agency request forms, or a single form that is sent to any agency of one's choosing.

"A true portal is a request-to-response processing and tracking tool so that agencies and requesters alike can manage their requests and responses through a seamless system," he said.

Third, Blum said, Congress should defend FOIA from efforts to savage the law by knifing it with an endless stream of statutory exemptions.

"These statutory exemptions, recognized under (the statute), are proposed many times each year," he said. "Over the years, this committee's bipartisan work, along with counterparts in the U.S. House, has helped stop or narrow over-broad proposals to put information beyond the public's reach. I respectfully suggest we need better gatekeeping—and earlier reviews—to ensure any new proposed statutory exemption to disclosure under FOIA meets strict, clear criteria to ensure new secrecy is justified, necessary, narrowly tailored to the need, clearly defined and time-limited."

Finally, he said, Congress should strengthen leadership on FOIA at all levels and should reconsider the way the government captures, organizes, and stores electronic information so disclosure is built in at the front end, not the back end.

Dr. David Cuillier, the director of, and associate professor at, the University of Arizona School of Journalism, was not so sanguine overall. The law is broken, the professor said.

"FOIA has been co-opted as a tool of secrecy, not transparency," Cuillier said. "I hear from journalists and citizens nearly daily about their problems in maneuvering through an intimidating system fraught with delays, confusion, and excessive fees that often results in no records or pages delivered in unusable formats blacked out entirely or in part. As a result, information that can shed light on unsafe drinking water, inappropriate expenditures, and inefficient government operations remains hidden from the public."

Cuillier said it was no exaggeration to say a tipping point—a crisis situation—had been reached when it comes to freedom of information in the country.

"We are frogs in the kettle of slowly heating water, and if we don't jump out now we will find ourselves in a sticky and murky stew," he said.

The professor said the research was clear.

"Requesters are having a harder time than ever in getting the information they need," he said. "While agencies are becoming more efficient in processing 700,000 requests a year, denials and the use of exemptions to hide information are rising. An Associated Press analysis this year of FOIA request data showed that the Obama administration has set a record in the rate requesters are denied information or told that it doesn't exist—77 percent of the time."

In 2012, Cuillier added, agencies' use of exemptions to deny requests increased 22 percent over the previous year.

"Comparing the last three years of the George Bush administration to the first three years of the Obama administration, the percentage of denials among most agencies has increased," he said. "The culture of secrecy grows beyond FOIA as journalists struggle to receive basic information about schools because of the Family Educational Rights and Privacy Act, and through excessive message management through public information officers. Journalists have become so frustrated that last year the Society of Professional Journalists and more than 50 other journalism organizations sent a letter to the White House urging a stop to the excessive secrecy."

A delegation met with White House staff to discuss the problem, the professor testified, but had yet to see any action. Cuillier said transparency in the U.S. government doesn't even look good when compared to other nations.

"Ratings of FOIA laws in the 105 nations that have them indicate that U.S. FOIA ranks 46th in its strength, behind such countries as Uganda, Kyrgyzstan, and Russia," he said. "Even Mexico's FOIA ranks better than ours, at ninth place."

Other countries have incorporated significant elements into their laws, Cuillier said.

"For example, a dozen nations, such as Liberia, have declared the right to know as a constitutional right, and some international courts have even deemed it a basic human right," he said. "In some nations, such as South Korea, FOIA applies to the judicial and legislative branches. South Africa, Brazil, and Estonia require that government contractors doing the government's business adhere to FOIA."

How could these nations pass us by? Cuillier asked.

"It makes sense, really, since the majority of other FOIA laws have been passed in just the past 15 years," he said. "Technically, Congress enacted FOIA as an amendment to the Administrative Procedures Act of 1946, which was created to deal with the growing federal bureaucracy. Amendments through the years tinkered with FOIA, but as we know, significant leaps do not occur often in our political system."

The professor said the FOIA might be better thought of as a 1966 Ford Mustang, a revered classic.

"A 2016 Hyundai, however, has better mileage, safety features, sound, reliability, and air conditioning," he said. "If we look past sentimentality and focus on efficiency, then perhaps it is time to garage the Mustang, trade up, or at least give it a complete overhaul."

Among other things, Cuillier called for FOIA training for all employees, reining in statutory exemptions, and adding new enforcement mechanisms.

"Expecting a grandma from Topeka to hire an attorney to sue an agency is unreasonable," he said. "The deck is stacked against the citizen, and journalism organizations are less likely to sue for public records than they were in the past. Some states provide penalties for agencies or officials who fail to follow public record laws, such as suspension or removal, or sometimes even criminal repercussions. Those provisions are rarely enforced, but send a strong message."

—

So the FOIA has been weakened over time, and in part—but only in part—because of the open data movement.

But let's be clear. The open data movement itself is not trying to eviscerate the freedom of information movement. Far from it. But two things are going on. The first is that those devoted to darkness exploit the open data movement for their own secret aims—ah, we'll throw reams of data on the internet (but not all of it, mind you) and proclaim ourselves to be champions of openness, even as we are quite confident that most citizens can make neither heads nor tails of it.

Those same exploiters will also drain away as many resources as they can from freedom-of-information tools, using resources disproportionately to build massive data portals, making it easier to obstruct the prompt and complete delivery of records and to thwart technology that would provide complete access to government, records, archives, and streaming media and meetings. And they can argue all the while that open records and open meetings laws are less important than they used to be, precisely because of all the data portals the government has made available.

That's not to say, as I previously mentioned, that the open data movement has not played an unwitting role in this subterfuge. It has.

In a critical 2013 post at the Partnership for Open Government, Pedro Prieto-Martin, at the time a researcher at the Institute of Development Studies, put his finger on what we might call a conceptual flaw in the mainstream thinking of the open data movement that, arguably, has allowed advocates of secrecy to pit open data activists against FOIA proponents.

Let's take a look.

Prieto-Martin began by pointing out that the term "open government" had been used for decades to refer to efforts to reduce "bureaucratic opacity" and create avenues for public scrutiny.

"These efforts materialized mainly in the enactment of legislation on access to information, privacy, data protection and administrative procedures, and by creating ombudsman offices and supreme audit institutions," Prieto-Martin wrote.

Then, in the 2000s, Prieto-Martin continued, a new vision emerged and gained traction. That vision embraced open government as those efforts to "improve government capacity and modernize public administration based on three principles: transparency, participation, and collaboration." In other words, open government wasn't so much about providing private citizens with the information they sought. Though that wasn't excluded as a goal, it was more about offering up mass catalogues of data that the citizenry could use, the by-product of which, at least theoretically, would be more civic participation and collaboration.

Interestingly, Prieto-Martin wrote, the person who popularized those principles in 2009 was none other than Barack Obama, when on his first day as president he issued a "Memorandum of Transparency and Open Government," in which he committed to creating an unprecedented level of government openness.

"We will work together to ensure the public trust and establish a system of transparency, public participation, and collaboration," he wrote. " ... Government should be transparent. ... Government should be participatory. ... Government should be collaborative."

Prieto-Martin went on to laud Obama's leadership by example and his enthusiasm for openness. I, of course, have already expounded on his failures and downright obstinance went it came to freedom of information and day-to-day openness, while at the same time providing more and more raw data, and we can agree to disagree on that point. But Prieto-Martin did put his finger on a critical conceptual failure in Obama's three principles, failure that led to an actual undermining of open government, whether or not it was intentional.

"However, Obama's memorandum had also negative consequences: It contributed to extend a superficial and inaccurate understanding of OG [open government], as something consisting of three successive pillars—transparency, participation and collaboration—with a growing complexity and importance," Prieto-Martin wrote. "The first limitation of this OG's conceptualization is that it presents as different two concepts which, in fact, cannot be conceived separately: participation is collaboration, collaboration is participation, or they are nothing. Attempts to draw a clear boundary between the two are fairly arbitrary and artificial."

Even the promoters of Obama's three principles could not clearly articulate the differences between the two, or the reasons why participation should precede collaboration, Prieto-Martin continued.

"It is also remarkable the lack of agreement on what tools or activities constitute each of them, eg, the use of social networks strengthens the participatory or the collaborative dimension of an OG strategy? The answer depends entirely on the resource consulted," he wrote.

In practice, Prieto-Martin asserted, that had had important negative and unintended consequences.

"Most of the studies and research on OG developed so far have assumed this conceptual triad to a greater or lesser degree," he wrote. "The same is true regarding benchmarking models, implementation models, and even the very OG initiatives and strategies. Typically, those resources only provide detailed guidance for the subject of Open Data—which is often equated with the level of 'transparency'—while the other two levels remain in a limbo of conceptual vagueness."

And that is the crack in understanding through which the Spy vs. Spy, open government v. open government conflict escapes into the open. Prieto-Martin's is a critically important point:

"This is where the second issue originates: By conceiving OG as something that starts with transparency and gradually matures into the stages of participation and collaboration, governments can stand as champions of OG even when they are just promoting Open Data initiatives, which do not represent a substantive change in the way governments act or interact with the citizens," he wrote.

Escalating to the higher levels of open government would require a renewal of the mindset, habits, and organizational models of public administrations and political bodies, and both are institutions that traditionally dislike novelties and risks, Pietro-Martin argued.

"Thus, much of the actions taken so far have focused on the level of transparency," he wrote. "… However, transparency and open data do not add value by themselves, as they have an instrumental function: They provide the foundation on which to establish the accountability of public institutions and the collaboration with all kinds of stakeholders. If transparency is not accompanied by participation and accountability activities, its usefulness is limited."

And thus we have reached that stage in Wisconsin and nationally. Government data portals are everywhere, and everywhere governments stand as champions of transparency, while all the while the means by which citizens may participate are increasingly frustrated and dismantled.

Prieto-Martin prefers a different set of pillars, and on the whole they are indeed more workable: participation, accountability, and transparency. True participation is not the ability to sit in front of a computer and try to stay coherent while digesting raw data; true participation is the ability to access and oversee the daily activities of government, and to seek, most often in collaboration with others, to influence the deliberations.

But let's take Prieto-Martin's formulation one step further. What if the foundational principles of open government were not just participation, accountability, and transparency? What if we added another element, namely, what if those foundational principles were participation, accountability, transparency, and inclusion?

Ah, inclusion. It's a nice term that long ago was co-opted by partisans but which should be returned to the public domain where everyone can claim ownership. So what is inclusion, and how does it differ from participation?

Well, participation is the act of taking part in something. It requires effort on the part of the people. It also requires that government provide a means of access so that people, when they make that effort, can indeed find their way in. So open government laws require that records requests be answered and filled with few exceptions, and that meetings be open, to look at the general framework. The posting of meetings and agendas is required, too.

But notice that the focus in all this is on what the government must do to provide access rather than what it should do. After the government fulfills its basic requirements, then the people can do what they must to take part.

Imagine it this way. Imagine all of government as one single capitol building. In our current way of thinking, the law would require that, when the Legislature convenes, one or two doors must be open to let the people in. If someone arrives at the back, they might have to walk around to the front.

That might satisfy the 'participation' principle, but in its formulation it is a rather exclusionary, not inclusionary, approach to open government. The fact that any government official would even consider locking some doors indicates an attempt to frustrate access. It is exclusionary thinking.

Some might object that, in this age of mass violence, the number of entrances to government buildings must be reduced, but that's a different matter not relevant to the simile's real point. But here is a real-world application. In this book I have talked of attempts by some lawmakers to abolish the state's online court records for various reasons. One of the traditional fallback positions is that they really wouldn't be dismantling any transparency or access to those actual records because they would still be available for public inspection at the courthouse.

Really? It's obvious that making someone drive or take public transportation to a courthouse rather than walking to the computer in the next room is an attempt to reduce the participation level. If this were the case, the government might still be providing an access to participation, but its approach would be exclusionary rather than inclusionary, in the same way that simply providing open data portals and declaring transparency as a mission accomplished is exclusionary rather than inclusionary.

So inclusion must be a foundational principle of open government, and it should be reflected in state statutes. Interestingly, Wisconsin's statutory language already makes this a part of its governmental policy: "Further, providing persons with such information is declared to be an essential function of a representative government and an integral part of the routine duties of officers and employees whose responsibility it is to provide such information."

That's pretty inclusionary but because the declaration is so often ignored it must be strengthened by adding an "inclusionary" requirement that would mandate that governments, in providing that information and in fulfilling its essential function, shall make every effort to provide the most expansive and inclusionary means to access.

However it is written, government must be required not simply to provide minimum access but to provide as much access as it possibly can, in as many venues and formats as it possibly can, with the right of citizens to appeal instances where the government has fallen short. In sum, such a standard would automatically rule out limiting court records to public inspection at a courthouse. A public record is a public record and an inclusionary approach to providing access to those records requires their online availability.

To use another more recent example, during the Covid-19 pandemic, many governments at all levels have begun providing access to their meetings via phone teleconference or Zoom or other platforms. The question is, why haven't they been doing so all along? What would prevent them from continuing these means of access? Holding an in-person meeting should always be the standard, but just holding such a meeting and compelling the public to attend when existing technology would allow much greater participation is an example of an exclusionary approach to government, and is a signature of the Dark State.

Open government, to be truly open, is about being proactive rather than passive. It is about including people—not merely about breaking down barriers to participation but actually pursuing ever wider participation.

Chapter 5

Attorney-Client Privilege

Of course, ever wider participation is not what most bureaucrats and politicians want, and over the years many intricate methods for making sure they achieve ever narrower participation—let's call them performance techniques—have been developed, and one they developed into an art form is the use of attorney-client privilege to shield documents from public view that the public has every right to see.

In the old days, they were just brazen about it. You're don't hear it much anymore, but up until the early 2000s many local government officials would just openly direct that sensitive documents be marked as attorney-client privilege to keep them out of the hands of reporters and other troublemaking citizens.

"Just run that by the attorney and have him stamp that as privileged," a good old boy or good old girl would bellow, and that was that. Everybody could laugh among themselves and go on about their business.

The growth of the open government movement changed things somewhat. Courts first ruled that documents were not necessarily protected by attorney-client privilege just because an attorney had marked them that way. The content was crucial, and other court decisions made clear that, for documents to actually be protected by the privilege, the attorney for the government has to be offering legal advice that the client has solicited.

Unsolicited policy opinions from a government attorney would not be sufficient.

Even so, while the brazen and routine stamping of policy documents as privileged because they happened to pass before an attorney's eyes for a fleeting second has gone by the wayside, this performance technique is still a widely, if more subtly, used method of circumventing the open records laws.

For one thing, the aforementioned court cases notwithstanding, most judges are lawyers, not to mention human, and so many if not most have a knee-jerk tendency to act like attorneys when such cases present themselves, and side with the government attorneys. For this very reason, even open records lawyers are loathe to take such cases.

Attorney-client privilege just might be the third rail of open government politics. So let's take a look at the way the privilege has been recently applied, and why it is so dangerous. For that we need to travel to—well, wonder of wonders—Oneida County.

—

In the summer of 2020, Oneida County responded to a months-old records request from *The Lakeland Times* for several supervisors' emails, as well as for those of the county board chairman, Dave Hintz, by handing over a series of completely redacted emails between county officials and the county's attorneys, asserting a blanket privilege for them all.

The only problem was (and is), no such automatic privilege exists in the state, and county officials either knew it or they should have known it. Case law is pretty clear that the privilege attaches only to explicit and confidential legal advice sought by the client, and to correspondence from lawyers that would expose that legal advice.

In the newspaper's requests, *Times* publisher Gregg Walker asked for all emails sent by two board supervisors and by Hintz, and for all emails received by them, for the previous three months, that related to their jobs as supervisors and to Hintz's role as chairman of the Oneida County board of supervisors.

The two supervisors fulfilled their requests on July 9. Hintz had acknowledged his request July 21 but did not send any records until August 15, about two-and-a-half months after the records request.

In the Hintz records, virtually all the communications between the county's attorneys and county officials were redacted. In addition, a series of nine email strings dated between May 16 and May 20 were completely devoid of content, with many recipients' names blocked out. The back cover of this book (if you have the paperback) is an example of the many pages the newspaper received.

As anyone can see, the responses showed a brazen disdain for the state's open records laws. It also demonstrates how much government officials hold average citizens in contempt, for instead of responding with a document in which every word was blacked out, the county could just have denied the document and refused to release it at all, asserting the privilege. But Mr. Hintz and the county's corporation counsel, Brian Desmond, apparently wanted to rub our faces in it.

"The response by Mr. Hintz takes obstruction of transparency to a new level," Walker said of the response. "It is established in case law that there is no automatic privilege for all correspondence between attorney and client, only for specific legal advice sought by the client."

Not only that, but the county did not merely redact content but the names of some of the recipients of the emails in question, making it impossible to know the entire recipient list. That's important because, if some non-qualifying clients or third parties received the email, then that would likely forfeit any privilege.

In sum, county officials said the redacted communications were subject entirely to attorney-client privilege merely because they said they did, without any evidence of privilege and without any way to determine the validity of the claim. In his response letter, Hintz cited several court cases that he said showed that all communications between attorneys and clients were privileged and exempt from release.

"In discussing the predecessor statute to [the current attorney-client privilege statute], the court in [*Dudek v. Circuit Ct. for Milwaukee County*] recognized that 'the law is well settled that once the professional relationship is established, all communications, oral and written, between attorney and client are privileged from production ...,'" Hintz wrote. "Based upon the common law exception to the public records law for attorney client communications, any records reflecting communication between agents and officials of the county and the county's counsel are exempt from disclosure under the public records law."

Actually, what is really well settled is just the opposite. In his letter, Hintz cherry picked a quote from the Supreme Court's *Dudek* decision. Indeed, even the judges in the *Dudek* case repudiated it. In fact, the Dudek court made the explicit point that not all correspondence is automatically protected.

"In applying the privilege to the particular facts of our case, we can say *generally* [emphasis added] that the privilege prevents attorney Dudek from producing any correspondence between himself and his client or his client's agents, *which correspondence is relevant to the lawsuit* [emphasis added]...," the Dudek decision states.

The Dudek court also emphasized that such legal advice must be sought by the client and does not include extraneous general discussions and materials.

"It appears, generally, that all matters other than those just specified including reports of experts prepared for use by Mr. Dudek before or at trial are not protected by the attorney-client privilege," the decision stated.

What's more, the *Dudek* court made it clear that not all communications are privileged, just those giving relevant legal advice to the client, in the paragraphs immediately preceding the sentence cited by Hintz.

"Wisconsin, like most jurisdictions, has recognized only a narrow ambit to the communications included within the attorney-client privilege," the *Dudek* decision stated. "This narrowness in scope of the privilege has resulted in a number of cases which make clear the type of communications which are not protected by the privilege. In its landmark case on work product, *Hickman v. Taylor, supra*, at page 508, the United States supreme court summarizes often troublesome items which it considers not protected by the attorney-client privilege."

Those examples, the Dudek court stated, included "memoranda, statements and mental impressions," and "writings which reflect an attorney's mental impressions, conclusions, opinions or legal theories." That would include policy discussions in which attorneys take part, rather than offering specific and sought after legal advice.

The *Dudek* court also observed that "[o]ur court has also had the opportunity to hold a number of communications not protected by the privilege of [the attorney-client privilege statute]."

—

The *Dudek* decision was handed down in 1967, after which the attorney-client statute was amended and a new general rule of privilege enacted. However, that statutory amendment still requires an attorney to be giving specific legal advice to the client: "A client has a privilege to refuse to disclose and to prevent any other person from *disclosing confidential communications made for the purpose of facilitating the rendition of professional legal services to the client* [emphasis added]..., " the statute states.

Since then, multiple court decisions have clarified the intent of that statute.

First, it is to be narrowly construed, ruling out any blanket exception, as expressed in multiple court decisions, as in the state Supreme Court's decision in *Lane v. Sharp Packaging Systems*: "Furthermore, because the lawyer-client privilege is 'an obstacle to the investigation of the truth' it should be 'strictly confined within the narrowest possible limits consistent with the logic of the principle.'"

In 1994, in *Journal/Sentinel v. Shorewood*, the state court of appeals ruled against a school district that had sought to protect a memorandum of understanding related to the settlement of a breach-of-contract and defamation lawsuit brought by the district's superintendent. The district's law firm largely drafted the memorandum and possessed custody of it, the court observed.

The court also determined that it was a public record and further determined that the document was the product of the law firm's provision of legal services, that it was produced during the course of the law firm's representation of the district, and was, in effect, the culmination of that representation.

But far from declaring that the document was thus protected by attorney-client privilege, the court rejected the district's argument that releasing the memo would be a breach of the privilege.

"This argument is without merit," the decision stated. "The privilege applies only to confidential communications from the client to the lawyer; it does not protect communications from the lawyer to the client unless disclosure of the lawyer-to-client communications would directly or indirectly reveal the substance of the client's confidential communications to the lawyer."

In *State v. Boyd* in 2011, the court of appeals reinforced that interpretation: "First, the privilege only encompasses confidential communications from the client to the lawyer, and those communications from the lawyer to the client if their disclosure 'would directly or indirectly reveal the substance of the client's confidential communications to the lawyer.'"

In 1996, in *Wisconsin Newspress v. Sheboygan Falls School District*—a case that Hintz cited as an example of the courts' support for a blanket exception for the privilege—the Supreme Court again rejected a blanket exemption for all correspondence between attorneys and clients. It did find that a letter was covered by the privilege not because of a blanket exception but because the letter was properly privileged under the "narrow ambit" of communications the state recognizes.

"Although the newspapers only seek the disclosure of a portion of the letter, the release of such portion of the attorney letter would reveal information protected by the attorney-client privilege," the decision stated. "The newspapers argue that the attorney-client privilege generally does not apply to communications from the lawyer to the client, citing *Shorewood*. However, an exception is where disclosure of the communication would indirectly reveal the substance of the district's confidential communications to its lawyer. We conclude that such an indirect revelation would occur *in this case* [emphasis added]."

That the court took the time to review the communication to see if the privilege could be exercised proves that no blanket privilege existed for the communication, for in that case the court would not have had to review the letter at all.

Hintz's other reasons for denying access to all attorney-client communications were similarly flawed. In his response, Hintz cited an evidentiary privilege and an exemption in the open meetings law that he says were sufficient to deny access to certain records. To wit, Hintz argued, the public policy supporting the privilege is so strong that the Wisconsin Department of Justice calls it a sufficient basis for denial without resorting to the balancing test.

So Hintz's major claims about attorney-client correspondence were all blanket claims—the common law claim, and an evidentiary privilege claim that it is always in the public's interest to deny attorney-client communications. But the latter claim was every bit as much a blanket claim as the common law claim, albeit a policy one, that the courts have rejected.

Finally, Hintz wrote, even if the balancing test was applied, the open meetings exemption allowing closed sessions for consulting with officials about litigation supports denial for some correspondence because the public records law says the exemption is indicative of public policy. In other words, if discussion of the content would justify a closed session, that would justify redactions and denial of the content in written communications.

But, in his response, Hintz never denied any records or justified complete redactions for any specific correspondence, or offered any hint of the subject matter of any such communications, saying only that the open meetings law exemption applied to "certain communications reflected in the responsive records."

Sorry, but merely citing the exemption as the reason for the denial of the records, without any further justification, fails. The DOJ compliance manual states that a closed session "must contain enough information for the public to discern whether the subject matter is authorized for closed session." According to the compliance manual, the attorney general has advised that notice of closed sessions must contain the specific nature of the business, as well as the exemption(s), and that "[m]erely identifying and quoting from a statutory exemption does not reasonably identify any particular subject that might be taken up thereunder and thus is not adequate notice of a closed session."

As such, a denial or redaction of a record based on that open meetings exemption must likewise not merely identify the exemption, as Hintz and other supervisors did, but give the specific nature of the business in the letter. Hintz and other officials failed to give any subject matter or even identify the communications they redacted under the exemption. Indeed, nowhere in their responses did Hintz or other officials ever offer any evidence that the redactions were justified under the attorney-client privilege claim, and they certainly did not do so by merely citing the open meetings exemption.

What's more Hintz's claim of privilege failed under other court-declared tests. For instance, he does not provide any explanation or evidence that the communications represented any relevant legal advice to the clients and were not merely the attorneys' 'mental impressions, conclusions, opinions or legal theories,' or, for that matter, merely entailed broad policy discussions. Hintz simply said the records were privileged because he said they were.

By contrast, in a 2015 case, *Wisconsin Professional Police Association v. Marquette County*, the court of appeals ruled that authorities must demonstrate that withheld records actually merit the privilege.

"As an authority seeking to redact information from records that are otherwise accessible under the public records law, the county has the burden to show that the redactions are justified," the court determined. "The question, then, is whether the county has met its burden to show that the material in the requested redactions in this case is, as the county asserts, privileged attorney-client communication or protected attorney work product."

What's more, the county redacted the name of many email recipients of the alleged privileged communications, making it impossible to determine if people who would not be authorized under the privilege received any of the emails.

If that were the case, the privilege would collapse.

According to the *Boyd* court, a communication is 'confidential' under the rule only if it is "not intended to be disclosed to 3rd persons other than those to whom disclosure is in furtherance of the rendition of professional legal services to the client or those reasonably necessary for the transmission of the communication."

While certain third parties might be included in a communication without sacrificing the privilege—one argument that can be made—that argument misses the point. The point is, the names should have been released because they did not disclose the content of any privileged communication, merely the names of those receiving the communication, as the *Wisconsin Professional Police Association v. Marquette County* ruled about billing invoices.

"Moreover, our review of the unredacted versions of the invoices reveals no reason to suppose that the redacted portions, on their face, reveal the substance of privileged communications," the court found. "Indeed, many of the redacted portions do not appear to even arguably reflect the content of communications, but rather, appear simply to refer to the fact that there was a contact between parties or a contact between the county with its attorneys. The county fails to explain here, as it failed to do in the circuit court, how any of the proposed redactions contain information that directly or indirectly reveals the substance of confidential communication."

Ditto in Oneida County. Likewise, as Oneida County has done, the court found that, like the circuit court before it, all it "had in front of [it] was little more than the bald assertion that these were attorney/client documents."

"Therefore, like the circuit court, we conclude that '[a]bsent more information, the strong presumption of public access was not overcome' on summary judgment with respect to the redactions made on the basis of the attorney-client privilege," the *Marquette County* court concluded.

The newspaper believed the same applied in Oneida County. Disclosure of the recipients would disclose no substance of allegedly privileged communications, but it would have allowed the newspaper to see if the recipients were indeed covered by the privilege, which would fail if they weren't.

In the end, Hintz's reasoning—more precisely, the corporation counsel's reasoning—was severely flawed, and the newspaper believed Hintz and the county violated the open records law by applying a blanket exception that doesn't exist to many records and by failing to provide any proof that the communications' content represented confidential legal advice requested by clients. In addition, the redacted recipient names revealed no privileged content but would verify that persons receiving the communications were covered by privilege.

—

There's even more to this story that is relevant to the entire state, and it deserves a deeper dive into the flawed logic of the county's arguments. Fortunately for us, the county made those arguments readily available during an open meeting.

That meeting itself was an absurdity that serves to underscore just how bad things are in Wisconsin when it comes to open government. For starters, after we had published the county's response in the newspaper—as well as a photo of one of the entirely redacted documents, the one on the back cover of this book—Hintz wanted to take the county board into closed session to explain the county's actions.

That's right, the county board chairman wanted to discuss in secret why the county was being secretive.

And it's even worse than that. Hintz had proposed the closed session under an exemption in the open meetings law allowing such sessions for supervisors to confer "with legal counsel concerning strategy to be adopted by the governmental body with respect to litigation in which it is or is likely to become involved."

Never mind that *The Lakeland Times* had not filed a lawsuit in the matter, nor had it threatened one. That's right, Hintz was calling a closed session to discuss a non-existent lawsuit, and this was too much for even most supervisors to swallow. Supervisor Jack Sorensen immediately objected, for example, saying there was "no need" for the closed session, and supervisor Scott Holewinski followed, arguing that the county should not move into closed session every time a potential lawsuit "that might happen" emerged.

Supervisor Bill Liebert underscored the point.

"If we don't have a lawsuit, there's no reason to just go into closed session at all," Liebert said.

Liebert also said the listed agenda exemption was misleading and could cause some members of the public to believe a lawsuit had been filed.

By an 11-10 vote, the county board nixed the closed session, handing Hintz a significant defeat, and, in remarks after the county board meeting, supervisor Billy Fried said he was shocked at the way the records requests had been handled.

"I'm dumbfounded at how long it takes to get an official reply to an open records request," he said. "Just a reply. Are you going to do it? Are you not going to do it? Are you releasing some and more coming later? I'm just dumbfounded."

In a general discussion of the county's open records policies and ordinances before the vote was taken, three signifiant and controversial points emerged— points that likely exist in other county and local ordinances.

The first is that the county code requires that each custodian—and supervisors are the custodians of the records they possess—submit records requests to the corporation counsel for review before releasing them, if any question exists about their releasability.

Here is how the ordinance reads: "If a record contains information that may be made public and also information that may not be made public or a question as to public access arises, each authority shall consult with the corporation counsel before releasing any information under this section."

In addition, under the "separation of information" section of the county ordinance, the corporation counsel shares power with the records custodian about what information must be released and what information must be withheld. If in the judgment of the custodian and the corporation counsel, there is no feasible way to separate the exempt material from the nonexempt material without unreasonably jeopardizing nondisclosure of the exempt material, the entire record shall be withheld from disclosure, the ordinance states.

At the county board meeting, Hintz translated the language from his perspective.

"The way I interpret it is, if you get a complicated request and that includes many, many emails, some of which are releasable and some of which are not, you are to consult with corporation counsel before releasing them," he said. "Every law is complicated, so that is what I would do if given a significant information request—determine what records are requested and get guidance from the corporation counsel on how to proceed. That is our general policy."

Corporation counsel Brian Desmond added his take.

"The ordinance does say that the corporation counsel shall be consulted when you have questions or concerns about emails," he said.

But Desmond also said he was not consulted on every request, citing as an example the sheriff's department's receipt of hundreds if not thousands of requests every year for accident reports. The department did not consult him on every report, Desmond said.

"Those that they don't have questions on, they don't contact me," he said. "The same would go for county board supervisors. It's when you have questions, concerns, things of that nature, that's when my office should be contacted."

But that general policy requiring consultation on every questionable call—rather than the custodian conducting the balancing test himself or herself—conflicts with state statutes, which give each records custodian complete power, as well as responsibility, over the disposition of a records request.

For instance, under "separation of information" in the state statutes, the law states that if a record contains information that is subject to disclosure .... and information that is not subject to disclosure, "the authority having custody of the record shall provide the information that is subject to disclosure and delete the information that is not subject to disclosure from the record before release."

There is no requirement to seek legal review and abide by that review in the language. What's more, the statutes give custodians the complete legal power to make those calls and carry out the review functions by themselves: "The legal custodian shall be vested by the authority with full legal power to render decisions and carry out the duties of the authority under this subchapter."

That language—"vested by the authority with full legal power to render decisions"—would seem to preclude local governments from adding more restrictive review language, unless they designate more than one custodian, which Oneida County did not. Indeed, such review power as that given to the Oneida County corporation counsel could endow noncustodial authorities with the power to obstruct the release of records they may not want released, which would subvert the entire intent of the law.

To be sure, the ordinance requirement raised questions and concerns on the county board floor.

"We have had a handful of public records request in the last three years, but at no time in the two-and-a-half years here do I remember any records request coming in where I needed to converse with corporation counsel," Liebert said. "I've always looked at it that my response would go to our clerk and then it gets dispersed from there, but I do not remember anybody talking to me that I was required to send something to our corporate counsel."

Supervisor Steven Schreier said he considered the separation of releasable information from non-releasable information to be the responsibility of the custodian.

"What needs to be reviewed by corporation counsel—if you have questions about whether there needs to be a redaction, removal or some such, that is our responsibility as the custodians of the records," Schreier said.

But Schreier also wondered what the policy actually was—turn over a request immediately to the corporation counsel for review, or review the records and turn over questionable items to the corporation counsel. Desmond said there was no set policy, and that records requests were handled in countless ways, though he suggested consultation was recommended for questionable records because of such things as evolving case law and liability concerns.

"I don't think there is any definite procedure or practice that we have followed, or are required to follow, here in Oneida County," he said. "We're here to help."

In the discussion, Liebert also referenced what he called a history of contentiousness between the local newspapers and the county over open government issues, and he said that gave him some concern.

"I'm a huge advocate for open records," he said. "As far as I am concerned, virtually everything that goes on in this county should be public."

The second significant point concerns a record custodian's right to waive attorney-client privilege. Desmond put it bluntly, telling supervisors that individual custodians don't have the power to waive attorney-client privilege and release records otherwise protected by the privilege.

"There's one caveat to that [the individual custodian making the decision to release or not release records]," Desmond said. "That is attorney-client privilege, which can only be waived by the entire county board. The privilege is held by the client, which is Oneida County, which is represented by the county board."

While some governments make that claim, it is highly arguable.

Practically speaking, such a position would either require supervisors to vote on a privilege claim concerning records they haven't even seen, or would obligate all supervisors to carry out reviews of every records request supervisors receive, a non-delineated and burdensome role for elected officials. Beyond practicality, as reported, the statutes vest each custodian "with full legal power to render decisions and carry out the duties of the authority." That statute contains no "caveat" that the custodian's full legal power does not include the power to waive attorney-client privilege.

Moreover, the question of who is the "client" when it comes to government bodies is a question well traveled in case law on both the federal and state levels. The bottom line is, though, no federal court has actually determined the question of whether government attorneys can represent individual government officials, or whether the client is the organization, though certain decisions have tip-toed around the edges.

In *Re: a Witness Before the Special Grand Jury 2000-2*, the U.S. Court of Appeals determined that the client was the agency itself, which would fit into Desmond's framework. The court further declared that, as a result, the attorney-client privilege did attach between the attorney and the agency but did not extend to individual employees and officeholders,

So, if the client is always the organization, Desmond's analysis would hold, but many have argued that if government lawyers cannot represent individual custodians, then there is no privilege at all for records in the possession of the individual custodian, as opposed to those held by the county itself.

For example, the records of the county's administration committee, held by the county clerk, would obviously be protected by the privilege because they are held by the county and belong to a county entity, while the records held by individual supervisors belong to the individual supervisor, who would not be represented by the attorney because the individual supervisor is not the client.

What's more, the court noted the higher duty to the true client: the public: "Just as a corporate attorney has no right or obligation to keep otherwise confidential information from shareholders, so a government attorney should have no privilege to shield relevant information from the public citizens to whom she owes ultimate allegiance, ..."

To be sure, that case concerned a criminal matter, and in that instance a grand jury represented the public, but the privilege has likewise been constricted in noncriminal cases. For example, in 1998, in *Reed v. Baxter,* the court found that conversations between a city attorney and members of the city council were not only not privileged, but, in the particular case, the interests of the individual council members were adverse to the interests of the city council as a whole.

The case involved a reverse discrimination claim, and a meeting between a city attorney and two council members who were fact finding about the promotion of an individual. The court determined that "[t]he interests of the councilmen and the interests of the city executives were not the same. The councilmen were not clients at a meeting with their lawyer. Rather, they were elected officials investigating the reasons for executive behavior."

Thus, no privilege to the conversation attached, the U.S. appeals court determined.

That case does not unquestionably settle the question of who is the "client" in any given situation, but it does determine that the interests of individual supervisors are not always the same as those of the government body as a whole, and that, in such cases, the government lawyer cannot represent both the organization as a whole and the individual supervisors who are part of that body.

So it raises the question: If the client in this case is the county and not the individual supervisors—who may perceive the responsibility to provide relevant information to constituents differently from the organization—would no privilege at all attach? On the other hand, if the individual supervisors are the clients, then they would be free, as the clients, to waive the privilege if they felt it was in the public interest to do so.

A question by a supervisor led to the third area of contention. The supervisor asked: Can a request be made for all emails over a period of time without a specific subject area identified? Desmond said a subject matter was required.

"The law states that it has to have a time period and a subject matter," he replied. "Again, each request has to be looked at as a fact-specific kind of endeavor."

In fact, the law does not state any such thing. The law states: [A] request for a record without a reasonable limitation as to subject matter or length of time represented by the record does not constitute a sufficient request."

Desmond rewrote the statute to substitute "and" for "or," changing the requirement for a sufficient request from either having a defined time period or a defined subject matter—one or the other—to a requirement that every request must have both. In his records response to *The Times*, Hintz made the same argument as Desmond.

On the state level, Gov. Tony Evers has made the same argument in denying a request for his emails from FOX6 in Milwaukee. The governor was sued over the matter and lost in circuit court (see next chapter), but in the meantime other governments have begun to follow the governor's lead.

———

My pappy used to tell me that the truth was always somewhere in the middle. OK, not really, but generally I think that's where the truth usually is.

So when reading this chapter and other episodes in this book, one might be tempted to believe that Oneida County officials are the biggest open government gangstas in the state, but that's not exactly the case. To be sure, reported shenanigans are not nearly as nefarious elsewhere, but there is a caveat that is important for readers to know.

That is to say, the most important word in the previous sentence is "reported." Sadly, most communities simply don't have watchdog newspapers like *The Lakeland Times* and the *Northwoods River News* that dig into records and hold officials accountable.

That's not to toot our own horns, it's just the way it is. Yes, we put a high premium on open government, and we feel some other newspapers don't rank it as highly as they should, but it's also true that many newspapers do value it as we do but simply don't have the resources we have had. We've been blessed.

So, on the one hand, the crowd in Oneida County is pretty bad and probably would rank higher on the odious meter than your average obstructionist, but that's not to say other local governments are angels. They are likely doing much of the same stuff in their counties, and getting away with it because they lack public oversight.

The appalling lack of watchdog newspapers or any other media to hold officials accountable underscores the importance of citizens not only getting involved but demanding transparency and being vigilant about it. No doubt the transgressions listed in this book only scratch the surface of what is happening across the state, and taxpayers should be outraged, not merely by the denial of information without any reason but by the deeply offensive mockery of the law and of the people such behavior represents.

To use an analogy, the courts have determined that there is no wiggle room for officials when presented with a records request. They must deny the request or fulfill it. Period. The same should go for elected officials everywhere now. There should be no wiggle room. Government officials must declare themselves to be on the side of openness or secrecy.

For, in the end, when it comes to attorney-client privilege, there should only be one real client: the public. Artificial legal entities—incorporated governments and bureaucracies that assume the voice of the people and assert rights "for the people" that actually trump individual rights—more often create barriers to access than they increase participation.

Indeed, that is exactly what they are designed to do. It's time to tear down those artificial constructs, and attorney-client privilege should be one of the first of those constructs to crumble.

Chapter 6

Elected officials: The Governor

YIKES!

Just when we thought we couldn't get a governor any more opposed to transparency than Gov. Scott Walker, along came Tony Evers and made us pine for the good old sunshiny days of Evers's predecessor.

As it turns out—and I know a lot of Scott Walker fans have been wondering if I would ever get to the current governor—Evers is one of the most devoted practitioners of the Dark State ever, not just an enemy of freedom of information and open processes but of open data as well. He doesn't like any of it, and he gets a whole chapter. So smile, Scott Walker.

Right off the bat, when he took office, Evers denied a request by the Associated Press for a handwritten note left to him by the former governor. Evers later relented and released the note, but it was an important early signal.

Later in his first year, Evers's office denied multiple records requests for the governor's emails by television station FOX6 news reporter Amanda St. Hilaire, on the grounds that they lacked a specific subject matter, even though each request had a specific and reasonable timeframe. He later released one day of emails but continued to insist he did so because he wanted to, not because he had to.

In this ploy, the governor's office was literally trying to rewrite the law to say that both a subject matter and a timeframe are needed when the law plainly says a reasonable request must contain one or the other, not both, as was reported in the last chapter.

FOX6 sued the Evers administration over the request, and prevailed in the circuit court. In fact, in Evers's first year in office, there have been three lawsuits filed against the administration over open government. If it's not a record, it must be pretty close.

Besides FOX6, the conservative MacIver Institute sued Evers because it says he refused to give it the same access to email advisories and events that he gives to other news outlets. MacIver says that's a violation of the First and Fourteenth Amendments of the U.S. Constitution, and I agree.

In the other lawsuit, Rep. John Nygren sued the administration for denying a request for records related to farmer mental health initiatives. Nygren wanted records that would help him understand how the Evers administration came up with a specific amount of funding requested for those initiatives, but the governor's office said the requests were overly broad.

This is a dangerous trend because there are cases in which the courts have ruled that requests were either overly broad or too burdensome, given the number of records involved. So those pursuing this strategy have a chance to really close down open government in significant ways. So far, Tony Evers is nothing less than Gov. Darkness.

Let's take a look at these lawsuits one at a time.

—

First, there is the case of Amanda St. Hilaire, who has established herself as one of the most talented and aggressive open government reporters in the state.

It all started in September 2019 with a pretty routine request for the governor's emails. St. Hilaire requested about a month's worth of emails to and from Evers and to and from his chief of staff, Maggie Gau. As FOX6 reported, on September 27, assistant legal counsel Erin Deeley denied the request.

Specifically, the station requested Evers's emails that were sent and received from June 14 through June 30 and from September 2 through September 18, and it requested Gau's emails from June 4 through June 30 and from September 2 through September 18.

The reason for the denial? Deeley said the requests were insufficiently specific because they lacked a subject matter.

"The public records law provides that a requester may deny a record request that lacks 'reasonable limitation as to subject matter or length of time,'" Deeley wrote, citing the open records statute.

Deeley emphasized that she had followed up by phone to request a subject matter.

"You declined to give a subject matter," Deeley wrote to St. Hilaire. "Instead, you offered to make multiple requests for smaller periods that would culminate to cover the same period described above. As I explained on the phone, this does not alleviate the problem or make your request sufficiently specific."

Though Deeley said it wasn't determinative in the decision to deny the requests, she said the requests generated an estimated 10,975 items when she reviewed the identified users' email records.

"As I explained on the phone, we cannot provide you approximately 10,975 items without individualized review," she wrote. "This review would require an employee to devote weeks of time working on your request alone, ignoring their other job responsibilities and all the other requests our office receives. And while you could not be charged for the time it would take to conduct that review, Wisconsin taxpayers should not be asked to pay the salary of a state employee to work exclusively on an insufficiently specific request for weeks, to the detriment of all other requests, requesters, and job responsibilities."

Deeley also defended Evers's open government track record.

"During the first six months of Gov. Evers's administration, our office responded to 149 public record requests with an average response time of 22.78 calendar days," she wrote. "In 2018, Gov. Walker's average reporting time, per their own tracking records, was 26.5 business days, meaning they did not include weekends or holidays in their calculation."

Walker's office completed 170 requests in all of 2018, Deeley observed, while Evers's office had already logged 226 requests since inauguration. Deeley also said that the amount of requests the governor's office receives means the law needs to be strictly followed.

"However, given the volume of requests our office receives, in order to be fair and responsive to all requesters and fair to the Wisconsin taxpayers paying for the staff needed to fill record requests, it is important we apply the law as written and uniformly to all requesters," she wrote.

After that denial, the station reduced the request to one week's emails, but that merely brought another denial, and for the same reason: the lack of a subject matter. So the station tried again for a third time, this time requesting one day's emails, and again the request was denied.

"For the same reasons articulated in my September 27, 2019, denial, and reiterated in my October 3, 2019, denial, this request is denied because it lacks a subject matter," Deeley wrote.

An open records request may be denied if it does not include a reasonably specific subject matter and a reasonably specific time frame, Deeley argued, and she cited the attorney general's open records compliance guide to back up her assertion.

"Per Wisconsin Department of Justice guidance, '[a] request must be reasonably specific as to the subject matter and length of time involved,'" she wrote, quoting the manual. "While you have provided a time frame, you have not provided a subject matter, only a medium/format."

What's more, Deeley continued, the station had already offered to make individual, multiple single-day requests that would culminate to cover the same larger period referenced in the original request.

"This does not make your request sufficiently specific under [the law]," she wrote. "The law requires a requester to provide a subject matter."

Deeley also clarified that she had not denied the earlier requests simply because they had the potential to produce many documents.

"A request, if properly made with the requisite specificity, may very well generate a large number of records," she wrote. "The prior request referenced above required review of over 3,000 pages of responsive records prior to release."

But with the volume of requests the governor's office receives and the amount of records maintained—the office had received another 49 requests for records since the station made the initial request a month earlier, Deeley wrote—the governor's attorney said it was imperative that the law be applied as written, and applied uniformly to media and citizens alike.

"Wisconsin taxpayers should not be asked to pay the salary of a state employee to work exclusively on an insufficiently specific request for weeks, to the detriment of all other requests, requesters, and job responsibilities, when that requester need only provide a subject matter, as the law requires," Deeley concluded.

But open records lawyers such as April Barker, who has handled and won multiple open records cases both for *The Times* and others, and open records advocates such as Bill Lueders, the president of the Freedom of information Council (FOIC), said Deeley's reading of the law was mistaken.

"It's part of a concerted effort, unfortunately, to come up with ways to limit public access," Barker told FOX6.

In an email to state media and others, Lueders said that, while Evers's office was arguing that email requests for an entire month or even a single day were not reasonably specific, legislators routinely respond to similar requests by providing records.

As for Deeley's interpretation of the law that a reasonable open records request must include both a specified subject matter and a timeframe, and her quote from the attorney general's compliance manual to make her case, that's just not what the law says, as St. Hilaire pointed out in one of her requests to Deeley.

"The next sentence in the statute says a request is insufficient if it does not have 'a reasonable limitation as to subject matter *or* length of time,'" St. Hilaire wrote. "This part of the statute does not require a subject matter; it gives the choice of subject matter or time. In this case, I gave a very specific and short period of time. Although the statute does not require me to provide a subject matter, I would argue the emails themselves are subject matter in the same way expense reports themselves are subject matter."

St. Hilaire has also pointed out that the DOJ compliance guide referenced by the governor's office cited a 1997 case in which a requester asked for three hours of tape on each of a sheriff's department's sixty 911 channels, which constituted 180 hours of audiotape. The requester also requested a transcript to be prepared for each of the tapes and a log identifying the time of each transmission, according to the court's decision. The judges agreed that requiring a records custodian to engage in copying 180 hours of tape and the creation of a log to identify the time and the order in which the transmissions were received represented an unreasonable burden.

A close reading of the case, however, shows that the judges never concluded that there must be both a specific subject matter and a reasonable timeframe, only that the overall request was unreasonably burdensome. In fact, the judges observed that the sheriff's office had asked for one or the other but was turned down.

"A letter requesting Schopper narrow his request suggested that he identify specific times of the transmissions he was seeking or that he identify a specific incident to which the transmissions would relate," the judges wrote.

In other words, the judges upheld the request's denial not because a subject matter was not included but because the requester refused to provide a specific incident or reduce the burdensome timeframe. The judges' quote of the sheriff's response suggests that either a specific timeframe or a specific subject matter would have worked, not a subject matter and timeframe, as the compliance manual wrote.

"Here, Schopper's request was far in excess of that which was necessary for his announced purpose," the judges wrote. "Because he could reasonably have limited his request but failed to do so, and because the request placed an unreasonable burden upon the custodian in preparation of the documents necessary to fulfill the request, we conclude that the court did not err by finding the request to be so over broad as to be inadequate under the open records law."

It should be pointed out at this point that Evers is not the first governor to use this gambit, including citing the Schopper case. In 2015, amid all the hoopla over Gov. Scott Walker's and the GOP's bid to send the entire canon of open government law to the trash bin of history, Walker did the same thing to *The Lakeland Times*.

It could be argued that the FOX6 case is analogous, that if the four-weeks timeframe was overly burdensome—and that's 'if'—narrowing the request to a week or a day should surely have fixed the shortcomings. What's more, as St. Hilaire also points out, the language of the law does not state that it must be reasonably limited by "subject matter *and* [emphasis added] length of time involved, as the compliance guide puts it incorrectly" but by "subject matter *or* length of time."

Simply put, the governor is trying to rewrite the open records law, and, in the circuit court decision in November 2020, Dane County circuit judge Stephen Ehlke agreed.

In the decision, Ehlke said the dispute turned on the proper interpretation of a portion of the open records law: "A request ... is deemed sufficient if it reasonably describes the requested record or the information requested. However, a request for a record without a reasonable limitation as to subject matter or length of time represented by the records does not constitute a sufficient request."

In pondering that question, Ehlke observed that, when interpreting any statutory language, the starting point is the language of the statute.

"If the meaning of the statute is plain, we ordinarily stop the inquiry," he wrote, quoting case law and pointing out that statutory language is given its common, ordinary, and accepted meaning.

The specific dispute in this case, Ehlke wrote, was the second sentence in the sufficiency test: "However, a request for a record without a reasonable limitation as to subject matter or length of time represented by the records does not constitute a sufficient request."

The judge proceeded to break down the grammar of the sentence in question.

"The second sentence of the statute begins '[a] request ... without a reasonable limitation as to subject matter or length of time...'" he wrote. "The phrase 'a reasonable limitation' is singular and denotes that a requester must provide *a* single reasonable limitation. Had the Legislature intended to require more than one reasonable limitation, the statute would read, 'without reasonable *limitations* as to ...'"

What's more, Ehlke continued, the use of 'or' is disjunctive, meaning that two or more separate things need not be combined or considered together.

"As a result, I read the statute to say: A request for a record without a reasonable limitation as to subject matter *or* a reasonable limitation as to length of time does not constitute a reasonable request," he wrote. "That is, one reasonable limitation is required under the statute, and it can be either as to subject matter or to length of time."

The governor made his own grammatical arguments, but Ehlke found them wanting.

"The governor argues that the use of 'or' in this sentence means 'and' because the statute is written in the negative," he wrote. "The governor argues that the use of a single negative flips the disjunctive meaning of 'or' to the conjunctive meaning of 'and.'"

Apart from the statute's explicit use of 'or' rather than 'and,' Ehlke said he found the argument unpersuasive for two reasons.

"First this interpretation ignores that the statute is worded in the singular ('*a reasonable limitation as to* ...')," he wrote. "I read this statute, attempting to give effect to every word, to mean the Legislature intended that a records request include 'a reasonable limitation as to' one of two options. Hence, the use of a singular 'reasonable limitation' and the word 'or.'"

Second, Ehlke argued, as the TV station pointed out, the governor's interpretation ignored that the sentence was written with a double negative, not a single negative (a records request *without* a reasonable limitation ... *does not* constitute a sufficient request).

"Using two negative expressions gives a sentence or clause a positive meaning," he wrote. "In other words, a statute written in the positive or written using a double negative has the same meaning. The positive form of the statute would be: 'A request with a reasonable limitation as to subject matter or length of time .... is sufficient.' In this form, the statute would be clearer and would plainly state that a reasonable limitation as to one of two options is sufficient. Writing the statute using a double negative, however, leads to the same result."

Ehlke also said the TV station's interpretation of the statute comported with the Legislature's declared presumption in favor of complete public access, and its policy that access may only in an exceptional case be denied.

Finally, Ehlke observed that in its briefing, FOX6 also contended that its requests actually included a reasonable limitation as to subject matter, that is, the subject matter was Gau's and Evers's emails themselves, and thus the requests were sufficient even under the governor's interpretation.

But, given his conclusion about the language of the statutes, Ehlke said he did not need to decide that question.

———

In another 2019 case, the MacIver Institute, a free-market non-profit news organization, sued Evers for excluding its journalists from press briefings and for refusing to provide them with press material that was shared with other news outlets.

The suit claiming First and Fourteenth Amendment violations was filed in federal court. MacIver lost a decision in federal district court, but the case is under appeal. According to MacIver, the Evers administration refused to include MacIver News Service reporters on invitations to press events, which made it harder for the reporters to stay up-to-speed on the governor's activities. The Evers administration also blocked MacIver journalists from participating in a budget press briefing that was open to other journalists, the lawsuit alleged.

"Gov. Evers should not block MacIver journalists from public press briefings and limit their access to government activities," Brett Healy, president of the MacIver Institute, said. "Our reporters have the same constitutional rights as every other journalist in Wisconsin, and we have a duty to keep the public informed about what's happening in state government."

Healy said the MacIver News Service had approached the administration numerous times in attempts to rectify the situation amicably, but its efforts were ignored. For example, the institute says the MacIver News Service hand-delivered to administration officials a letter from attorneys for the journalists, demanding that MacIver reporters receive the same access to public press events and information as journalists from other news outlets. Even after the letter, however, the Evers administration persisted in its course of conduct, continuing to exclude MacIver journalists from media advisories and press briefings, the institute said.

"We now have no option but to sue," Healy said. "A free and vibrant press is critical to democracy, and to ensuring the people of Wisconsin are informed and engaged on what's happening in their state. We hope to quickly resolve this issue, not just so that our journalists can go about their important work but to ensure no future governor engages in the same unconstitutional practices."

The MacIver Institute is represented by the Liberty Justice Center, a public interest law firm based in Chicago. Daniel Suhr, an associate senior attorney at the center, said the First Amendment guarantees freedom of the press.

"Courts nationwide have held [that] this means government officials can't pick and choose which reporters cover their public events," Suhr said. "Gov. Evers has spent the past six months excluding the MacIver journalists from his press conferences and briefings. That's wrong. Our country relies on vigilant watchdogs from the news media, and government officials can't duck hard questions by barring anyone who might ask those questions in a briefing."

While MacIver had been barred from press invitations, the list of invitees did include multiple left-leaning contacts, MacIver alleged, including *The Progressive Magazine*, Devil's Advocate Radio, *The Capital Times* newspaper, the Democratic Party of Wisconsin, Democratic legislative offices, and left-wing advocacy groups such as One Wisconsin Now.

In an email to members and supporters of the Wisconsin Freedom of Information Council, as well as to some media, FOIC president Bill Lueders expressed concern over the allegations in the lawsuit.

"The lawsuit alleges that Evers has refused to include the MacIver Institute on its media email send list and has barred its reporters from attending press briefings," Lueders wrote. "These allegations are deeply troubling and merit the attention of all members of the press and all defenders of open government."

Not being a lawyer, Lueders said he didn't know whether the alleged conduct was a violation of law, but he said it certainly was not in keeping with the state's tradition of open government.

"If Tony Evers has what it takes to lead state government, he ought to be able to withstand the inclusion and presence of reporters from a conservative news outlet," he wrote.

Gregg Walker, the current president of the Wisconsin Newspaper Association in addition to being the publisher of *The Lakeland Times* and *Northwoods River News*, said the allegation underscored a disturbing trend.

"Open government and free speech issues should not be partisan issues, not left or right, but based absolutely on a defense of the freedom of speech and press and due process," Walker said. "We have been warning about the politicization of open government issues for some time, and these allegations certainly underscore that troubling trend."

The whole idea of the First Amendment is to allow dissent and disagreement with those in power, Walker said.

"Deny due process and free speech to anyone, regardless of their political viewpoint, and that's the same as denying it to everyone," he said.

More specifically, the lawsuit alleged that the Evers administration violated both MacIver's First and Fourteenth Amendment rights.

"The First Amendment guarantees the freedoms of speech and of the press, and those rights are incorporated against the states by the due process clause of the Fourteenth Amendment," the lawsuit stated. "The Fourteenth Amendment also guarantees citizens equal protection of the laws, including equal treatment by their government."

As such, the lawsuit contended, the freedoms of speech and of the press and equal protection include a right of equal access among journalists to generally available information and events.

"A public official may not target particular news media outlets or journalists for exclusion from access made generally available to other media," the lawsuit asserted, citing previous case law in *Anderson v. Cryovac, Inc.* "To do so violates several constitutional doctrines, particularly the right to news-gathering and the prohibition against viewpoint discrimination."

And that's just what the Evers administration had done, the lawsuit claimed: "Gov. Evers and his staff have targeted plaintiffs for exclusion from generally available media advisories and press events."

The MacIver News Service is indisputably a credible and legitimate news organization, the lawsuit asserted.

"Writers for the News Service post to its website and social media, and occasionally its stories are run by other news outlets," the lawsuit states. "Its reporters often contribute directly to other outlets as well. The MacIver Institute has gone to court before to defend the rights of journalists and the public to access important information, and has won an 'Opee' from the Wisconsin Freedom of Information Council for its commitment to openness and transparency in state government."

In addition, MacIver news director Bill Osmulski previously won several awards working as a television news reporter in the Milwaukee and Eau Claire markets and produced a regular public-affairs program for WVCY-TV 30. What's more, the lawsuit continued, the MacIver News Service was credentialed by the Wisconsin Legislature to cover its activities as part of the Capitol press corps, and MacIver journalists regularly interviewed state legislators and other public officials in and around the capitol.

The lawsuit also described how MacIver's exclusion unfolded.

"When Gov. Evers took office, Osmulski and his former MacIver News Service colleague Matt Kittle asked the governor's office to add them to the media list," the lawsuit stated. "They received no response and never received a media advisory of an upcoming event by the governor in the subsequent six months, although numerous media advisories have been sent out to an email list of approximately 1,000 local, state, and national reporters and news outlets."

Access to media advisories is critical because it provides reporters with information about the governor's public events, which also are the context in which he is sometimes available to answer questions as part of a media availability before or after an event, the lawsuit contended.

"Media advisories also alert reporters to press conferences with formal opportunities to ask questions of the governor," the complaint stated. "As a result of this exclusion, it has been practically impossible for the MacIver journalists to attend the vast majority of the governor's public events and press conferences."

On Feb. 28, 2019, the governor's office held a press briefing for members of the Capitol press corps to explain the governor's forthcoming budget on an embargoed, on-background basis, the lawsuit alleges.

"The office invited 26 members of the Capitol press corps but did not invite reporters from the MacIver News Service," the complaint stated. "The invitation email described it as 'a budget briefing for media' with 'staff from the state budget office and the governor's office' that would 'include an overview of key budget initiatives on background, as well as a brief opportunity for questions.' The email also promised a printed copy of the Budget in Brief, which was not made available to the general public until the governor's budget address later that night."

Alerted to the briefing by a colleague in the press corps, the lawsuit continues, Kittle and Osmulski emailed the governor's staff to RSVP.

"They then went up to the conference room at the designated hour and were denied access," the complaint stated. "Watching their colleagues in the press corps file by, they were told that they were not on the RSVP list and that the senior staff member in the governor's office who could permit their access was not available to talk to them. Numerous messages and requests via email and voicemail asking the governor's communications staff for a conversation to discuss went unreturned."

Briefings such as that are important for journalists to thoroughly and accurately report the news in a timely manner, especially in a competitive news business, the lawsuit alleged.

"By targeting the MacIver News Service for intentional and selective exclusion from this briefing, the governor's office made it substantially harder for these journalists to report the news in a timely, thorough manner," the complaint stated.

In sum, the lawsuit asserted, by targeting the MacIver News Service and Osmulski for exclusion from generally available press information and events, Evers violated their First Amendment right to freedom of the press, their First Amendment right to free speech, and their Fourteenth Amendment right to equal protection of the laws.

MacIver asked the court to declare that excluding the MacIver News Service and Osmulski from the information concerning the time and location of the governor's public events and press conferences was unconstitutional and that excluding them from generally available press events like the February 28, 2019, budget briefing was likewise unconstitutional.

The lawsuit asked the court to enjoin Evers from excluding MacIver News Service and Osmulski from generally available press events and lists announcing such events. Whatever the outcome, the behavior of the Evers administration is intolerable, and, if the courts won't deal with it, the Legislature should through legislation forbidding discrimination against media outlets.

—

In yet another 2019 case, Evers settled an open records lawsuit filed against him by then state Rep. John Nygren, releasing 10,000 records and paying $40,000 in legal fees.

In a statement, the governor did not admit to breaking the law but said he had no time to waste in court during the Covid-19 crisis, which was at a fever pitch at the time of the settlement in 2020. But Nygren retorted that breaking the law is exactly what the governor was admitting he did.

In November 2019, Nygren, then the Assembly chairman of the Legislature's Joint Finance Committee (JFC), sued Evers in Dane County circuit court over what Nygren called the governor's practice of concealing public records related to mental health for farmers.

In July, after the Department of Agriculture, Trade, and Consumer Protection (DATCP) had requested the release of funds from the JFC for counseling vouchers for farmers, Nygren said he and Sen. Alberta Darling (R-River Hills) informed the agency that it needed to work with the Speaker's Task Force on Suicide Prevention. Instead, Nygren claimed, the DATCP, acting at the direction of the governor's office, attacked the JFC, claiming insufficient funds existed at DATCP for farmer mental health. At the time, agriculture secretary-designee Brad Pfaff accused the GOP of abandoning farmers; the Republican-controlled Senate later refused to confirm Pfaff's nomination, effectively firing him.

Nygren also said the agency continued to withhold information from the task force chairwoman, Rep. Joan Ballweg, though it provided similar information to media outlets, and he pointed to what he said was a discrepancy in available funds for counseling vouchers for farmers. OpenBook, which tracks government expenditures, reported a higher available balance than what DATCP claimed publicly, the senator said.

Nygren issued a records request to the DATCP and to the governor's office related to farmer mental health and several other topics over a one-month period. The agency fulfilled the request, but the governor's office denied it.

Nygren's lawsuit sought to have the court require that Evers and his staff turn over public records related to the original records request. In May 2020 the state Department of Justice reached a settlement on behalf of Evers, in which it released more than 10,000 documents. The state also agreed to pay $40,000 in attorneys fees.

Nygren said the settlement was long overdue and could have been avoided.

"It took over six months, but Gov. Evers finally realizes he broke the law and has now agreed to fulfill the original request for records," he said. "DATCP fulfilled the exact same request with no complaints, in a timely fashion, and without legal action."

Had Evers done the same or at least worked with Nygren to address any concerns the governor had, Nygren said there would have been no lawsuit, saving taxpayer resources.

"Instead, he denied the request outright," Nygren said. "Once sued, the governor could have owned up to his obligations, admitted fault, and avoided further cost. But he dragged out the legal fight."

Nygren said it was obvious that Evers wanted to blame Covid-19 for his lack of transparency.

"Months before Wisconsin was dealing with Covid-19, Gov. Evers was sued not once, but twice for hiding records from the public," the lawmaker said. "No amount of finger-pointing can distract from Gov. Evers's abysmal record of hiding documents from the public."

If Evers was concerned that the original request was overly broad, Nygren said, his staff could have contacted Nygren to seek a resolution.

"In fact, Gov. Evers's staff has done this for other records requests I have sent to his office," the senator said. "Instead, Gov. Evers denied the request without any contact or follow-up. My only option was to seek court action to force Gov. Evers to comply with the law. And because of that lawsuit, he is finally going to comply with the law."

To be sure, Evers's responses to the settlement show how disconnected the governor's office is when it comes to transparency. For instance, Evers accused Nygren of the same thing Nygren accused the governor of—not reaching out and negotiating. The governor's office said Nygren initiated a costly legal battle rather than work collaboratively to resolve what the governor considered an overly broad request. Evers's office also pointed out that the Legislature has exempted itself from the open records laws that apply to the governor and hundreds of other government entities and officials around the state. To be precise, the Legislature has exempted itself from the open records retention law, which in the real world is much the same thing.

But a couple of points. While the Legislature's self-exemption from the records law isn't entirely irrelevant—it's hard to take lawmakers' open records requests seriously when they refuse as a body to abide by the public records retention law—it's no excuse for the governor's office, which isn't exempt, to break the law.

As for the broadness of the request, the governor's office said it was overly broad because it would apply to everyone in the office and that Nygren asked for every document that contained one or more common terms, such as "mental health" or the names of several lawmakers. The governor's denial to Nygren—

that his request was overly broad—was an echo of the FOX6 request denial, which the governor's office deemed insufficiently specific because it lacked a subject matter.

This case, when taken in context with the FOX6 case, shows that the governor's game is all about obstruction, not about the burdensome nature of requests. In the FOX6 case, the governor's office said it only wanted a subject matter along with the time frame, and then it would be willing to comply, no matter how large the request; but when Nygren gave him both, there was yet another reason to deny the records—this time the subject matter itself was too broad.

Well, it's hard to see how a request for a specific subject matter and for records containing the specific names of lawmakers for a one-month period could be overly broad, and it's time to make this point: Officials who want to conceal records will create excuse after excuse to do so, and they often try to bully requesters to narrow their requests in a way that would allow them to not release many important documents.

Indeed, sometimes requesters can't specifically know what they are looking for until they see it. They know the broad category of records, or they know the date range, but it's unrealistic to expect a requester to ask for the smoking gun when it has been cleverly concealed. In these instances, the open records request is like a search warrant to look for evidence in a larger file.

Requesters must be able to sort through the files of public records if transparency is to mean anything at all. In an open records case against Lakeland Union High School in 2018, in a request similar in nature to that made to the governor by FOX6, this newspaper asked for all current faculty and staff disciplinary records for the previous five years.

Just as the governor's office later argued, LUHS likewise contended that our request was not specific enough, and, what's more, claimed that asking for the disciplinary records of all 78 LUHS staff members amounted to nothing more than a "fishing expedition" that would encourage ever more blanket requests and turn the purpose of the open records law "on its face."

Vilas County judge Neal A. Nielsen—one of the greatest judges of all time when it comes to transparency—pondered the argument and rejected it, ordering the records to be released and giving the newspaper one of the greatest open government quotes of all time:

"The school district says *The Lakeland Times* is on a fishing expedition," Nielsen said. "It might be, but (in Wisconsin) there's no closed season, no bag limits, and no license required for that kind of fishing."

Amen to that. Let's make sure the fishing stays good in Wisconsin, from the governor's office on down.

———

No matter how the remaining lawsuits are settled, the first two years of the Evers administration have been chilling in its hostility to openness in all forms, open data as well as open processes. Evers and his colleagues have opened up a new and large Black Hole in an already Dark State.

But it isn't just lawlessness. Sometimes the conduct is more subtle, a careful dismantling of the mechanisms of openness that were in place when he arrived. That's perhaps even more appalling because it represents not just a reaction to unexpected events, or at least the unmasking of an attitude that, while uncooperative, did not indicate forethought and malice. Bad enough, perhaps, but not indicative of evil.

But the almost immediate undermining of the established underpinnings of transparency by newly elected Evers suggests premeditation. In October 2019, for instance, the Wisconsin Institute for Law & Liberty (WILL) called out the governor for a lack of transparency a month after Evers pledged to "better present accurate information about public records to the public."

"Evers's promise came in response to a WILL report, released in September, that revealed the administration deliberately shuttered an open government website and has failed to re-issue Walker-era executive orders that instituted best practices for government transparency," WILL stated.

CJ Szafir, then WILL executive vice president, said the Evers administration pledged to do things better than the Walker administration when it came to government transparency.

"A month later, there is no plan, there is no visible progress, and the public remains in the dark," Szafir said. "We're calling on Gov. Evers to keep his promise to open up state government and follow Walker's best practices."

In the review of the open government practices of Evers, Lt. Gov. Mandela Barnes, and various state agencies, WILL found what it called a disturbing departure from two best practices in the Walker administration.

I would hardly call Walker's record a proud legacy, but, as noted previously, the Walker administration did strike two blows for openness in those late-tenure executive orders, issued in 2016 and 2017.

As WILL stated in its study, which was written by Libby Sobic and Szafir, Walker issued executive orders that directed executive offices and state agencies to respond to records requests in 10 business days, keep and maintain an organized tracking system, and develop a dashboard website for the public to monitor how the administration was complying with records requests and best practices.

WILL set out to examine whether and to what extent the Evers administration was following those directives, and, in doing so, submitted identical open records requests to 11 offices and state agencies. By the end of August, WILL said it received responses on nine of the 11 requests and reviewed over 4,000 records.

The results were abysmal.

WILL found that Walker's open-government website was no longer active and the public could no longer determine how the Evers administration was practicing government transparency. What was dark before was dark again in the Dark State.

WILL also concluded that the system to track records requests in Evers's office was disorganized and dysfunctional.

"There are scores of missing data making it impossible to know whether the governor's office is complying with open government best practices," the authors wrote. "One out of three of all open records requests are either unfulfilled or not recorded properly."

Barnes was no open records wizard, either, the WILL study found. His office received only 13 requests but took an average of 22 days to respond. In all, WILL found, five state agencies—DATCP, DNR, DHS, DOA, and DOR— responded to WILL's requests for tracking documents, and all five agencies continued to respond, on average, within 10 business days.

That wasn't true for such agencies as the Department of Transportation (DOT) and the Department of Children & Families (DCF). They had not complied with the requests 49 days after they were sent. Agencies such as the Department of Public Instruction and the Department of Justice's Office of Open Government were mixed, WILL stated.

"DPI's response time has slipped from, on average, within 12.5 business days, to responding for the last six months within 15 business days," WILL stated. "DOJ's Office of Open Government, founded by [former attorney general Brad] Schimel, continues to provide an unprecedented amount of transparency, including publishing a monthly metric of the department's open records request responses."

After the study, WILL called on Evers to quickly reissue the Walker executive orders that defined the best practices for open government and revitalize the open government dashboard website.

"If the Evers administration does not act, the state Legislature should consider oversight hearings to determine why the Evers administration is taking Wisconsin backwards on transparency," the group urged. "The state Legislature should require all government offices and agencies to comply with open records laws and create clear and up-to-date tracking systems."

WILL also called upon the Legislature to ensure full transparency by instituting low records request fee policies to ensure that all citizens have access to the inner workings of government.

Of course, Evers did not re-issue those executive orders, and the administration did not revive the transparency website. And the Legislature did not convene any hearings on the governor's backsliding on open government.

When it comes to executive orders, the governor has recognized the need to convene task forces on various issues he considers critical and in need of stakeholder dialogue and urgent solutions, ranging from student debt, climate change, retirement security, reducing prescription drug prices, and caregiving, but there's been no executive order to restore Walker's best practices, no executive order to convene a task force on open government, and no executive order even mentioning open government.

The Legislature's inaction was no surprise (see next chapter), but Evers's hostility to transparency was unexpected, at least the depth of it. Szafir put it mildly when he said Evers was clearly not prioritizing government transparency.

"This is dangerous because open government is not just an ideal but a critical tool for the public in a democracy to hold their elected officials and public employees accountable," he said. "Evers threatens to turn Wisconsin's proud legacy of transparency in state government into a bureaucratic black box."

A Black Box or a Dark State, call it what you will. A black rose is a black rose by any other name.

Chapter 7

Elected officials: The Legislature

When it comes to transparency, one does not have to look far to figure out why these are dark days in a dark state. Just look at the conduct and beliefs of our state Legislature and it's obvious.

While the governor may represent the head of the snake, the Legislature—the elected body that makes our laws—is surely the beating heart of the Dark State, pumping the blood of blockage and obstruction through the veins of all state and local government. Just how could this have possibly happened, and what does it mean for open government?

To be sure, the Legislature has for years now consistently opposed transparency and not just passively. It exempts itself from records retention laws, which effectively exempts that body from the open records law; its members thwart open records requests any way they can, and with bravado; and it generally has refused to release investigative records about its members and staff.

All this aside, lawmakers and governor are all committed to transparency. Just ask them. In real life, though, the Legislature is a particularly odious body, perhaps the worst in the nation, though I admit that might be stretching it. It's a top fiver for sure.

For starters, the Legislature exempts itself from the open meetings law and from the records retention law, which mandates that state agencies and local government entities keep records for a set amount of time, as set by the Public

Records Board. That board supervises the state's public records, management, and preservation programs. For most records, the required retention is seven years. But while the Legislature has mandated this program for others, it has refused to mandate it for itself, so lawmakers don't have to keep public records for any amount of time.

It's a pretty crafty way of end running the law. Technically, while some state Legislatures exempt themselves from open records laws outright, our Legislature achieves the same goal but in a way that allows them to say they are bound by the law, and proudly so. And, technically, they are bound. If you ask a legislator for a public record and that lawmaker has that record, he or she must release it. But if he or she just happened to destroy it the day before, it's the requester's tough luck. So legislators can use and then extinguish documents they don't want anybody to see. It effectively exempts them from the law.

That they can still proclaim themselves champions of transparency—we aren't like those lawmakers in other states who don't have to abide by open records laws!—shows just how devious lawmakers are in wanting to camouflage their hostility to due process.

A little story about this illustrates the point about why ending the retention exemption for the Legislature was and still is so important.

The Lakeland Times was the first news media to focus attention on the retention issue way back in 2010, when the newspaper requested records from the DNR and from then Northwoods state Sen. Jim Holperin. (D-Conover).

That's when we discovered the Holperin Hole, as we fondly called it, a veritable rabbit hole for legislative openness that still outrageously exists in 2021.

In June of 2010, seeking information about a Northwoods shoreland zoning issue, *The Times* asked the senator and the state Department of Natural Resources for any email communications between Holperin and then DNR water division administrator Todd Ambs. The DNR complied with the request, which included several such exchanges. However, Holperin's record release included none of those exchanges.

That prompted *Lakeland Times* publisher Gregg Walker to ask Holperin why he had not supplied the emails in question. In response, Holperin said he provided all the records in his possession at the time of the request.

"That fulfills my duty under the open records law," Holperin wrote.

The senator then cited a 1961 statute exempting the records and correspondence of lawmakers from the permanent use collection of the state's public records board and said he had also begun to routinely delete many of his office emails.

"You have raised questions regarding the retention of Senate records," Holperin wrote to Walker. "On advice of the Senate Chief Clerk and pursuant to Senate Policy and (statute) 16.61(2)(b)1, my current office policy is to not retain emails that are judged not to be substantive exchanges."

Holperin said there were certain exceptions to that policy, including emails subject to a pending open records request.

"Regular deletions pursuant to this office policy prevent unnecessary demands on legislative computer system capacity," Holperin wrote. "This policy has dramatically reduced the number of electronic exchanges compared to what we have previously had on hand."

At the time, Holperin's stance apparently represented a new approach by the lawmaker, given his response that the policy had reduced the number of emails his office stored. Earlier in 2010, in fact, the senator had supplied the newspaper with a substantial number of emails from another open records request.

After Holperin's response, *The Times* asked attorney general J.B. Van Hollen for a legal opinion, but his office replied that it had no statutory jurisdiction to offer one. Assistant attorney general Lewis Beilin nonetheless said lawmakers should promote the cause of transparency, even when laws do not obligate them to perform certain functions.

The retention of records was an essential element of open government, Beilin wrote.

"For obvious reasons, the public's right to 'the greatest possible information regarding the affairs of government' depends to some extent on the retention of records memorializing those affairs in the first place," he wrote.

With that bit of sanity, *The Times* called upon lawmakers to rectify the situation. Gubernatorial candidate Scott Walker also called for ending the exemption, though that support evaporated after he was elected.

"Why should they be exempt?" candidate Walker asked. "It's just like the Congress. They make laws that apply to everybody else but exempt themselves and that just seems to be fundamentally wrong."

Now here's the part of the story that would be hilarious, if it was not so sad.

After the brouhaha, Holperin, in an interview at *The Times*, pledged to introduce legislation to end the exemption, though he predicted it would go nowhere in the Republican-controlled Senate.

Yes, though he was himself responsible for exposing the retention loophole by using it aggressively, he was now Ready Freddy to fill up the Holperin Hole so no one else could throw records into the abyss. We always gave him credit for that, even if we were skeptical about his true motives.

The senator turned out to be right about Republican support, to no one's surprise, but he also got the cold shoulder from most Democrats. After circulating the bill for co-sponsorship, Holperin got only two of his colleagues in the state Senate to sign on as co-authors, while only four representatives in the Assembly joined up. Neither of the Northwoods two local representatives at the time, Rep. Dan Meyer (R-Eagle River) or Rep. Tom Tiffany (R-Hazelhurst), signed onto the legislation, and overall only one Republican enlisted.

Ultimately—and here's the most important point about all of this—Holperin offered backhanded testimony that not only showed his own disingenuousness on the issue but unintentionally underscored why ending the exemption is so important. In his testimony, Holperin said he introduced the legislation at the request of *The Lakeland Times*, which he said had pursued the matter for several years as a crusade and "maybe an obsession." Holperin also told the panel he didn't think the bill was of statewide interest or significance. Nonetheless, he said, he supported the measure.

"I think there's no reason the Legislature needs to exempt itself from the current records retention law," he said. "It's been my experience after 15 years of service in both houses of the Legislature that all legislators in nearly all circumstances do retain the records which are created by their offices and by their day-to-day activities."

Not only was compliance virtually universal, he said, but the Legislature should comply with the same requirements of open government by which other agencies must abide.

"I hope all committee members will support this to demonstrate that the Legislature is not above our records retention law, that it should not be exempted therefrom, and every public agency, every local unit of government, every legislator, and every legislative body should be covered by not only the open meetings law, not only the open records law, but by the records retention law in the state of Wisconsin."

For a time, Holperin acknowledged, his office had a policy of deleting insubstantial emails, such as those notifying people of an earring lost in the bathroom or an announcement of hockey tickets or Girl Scout cookies for sale.

"As legislators we get, typically speaking, a dozen of these really irrelevant email messages every day," he said, and, he added, he had decided to delete them to prevent staff from having to comb through them when open records requests did come in, and out of a concern for the amount of storage space such messages consumed. The senator said he had since rescinded that policy, and he said it made sense for the Legislature to live by the same rules that governed other government agencies.

"But again, if the electronic capacity exists to keep it, and if all agencies have to keep it, as I guess they have to do pursuant to the records retention law —there's nothing that can be deleted, really, practically speaking—I think we should, too," he said.

In pushing the measure, *The Lakeland Times* has often cited the potential for abuse of the exemption, the senator's presumption of universal compliance notwithstanding, and in fact has disputed Holperin's definition of insubstantial email messages.

So let's examine the veracity of Holperin's testimony.

First, he said, it was a newspaper "obsession" that carried little significance, but it was the right thing to do because the Legislature had imposed the mandate on everybody else in government. In other words, the exemption wasn't important except that it represented a double standard.

In that case, why didn't he just introduce legislation to end the retention requirement for everyone? After all, he testified, record retention was a matter of little public policy significance. And why was it not significant? Because after 15 years in the Legislature, Holperin testified, he knew that "all legislators in nearly all circumstances" did retain records.

Besides the fact that he could not possibly know that, his own conduct betrayed that testimony, for, as he acknowledged in the same testimony, his own office had a policy of deleting those "insubstantial emails." He said he had rescinded that policy, but it's important to observe that he rescinded it only after stories appeared in *The Lakeland Times* about the Holperin Hole.

But wait. Holperin was only deleting insignificant emails that lacked substance, right? You know, those hockey game announcements and Girl Scout cookies for sale.

But that wasn't true, either, because, as part of that policy of routine deletion, Holperin's office had deleted the email string that started the whole thing—the exchange he had with the DNR's Todd Ambs. As he was required to do, Ambs had turned it over, but Holperin's office had made it go poof as an insubstantial email.

But was it? Well, let's take a look. Though it is about an old issue, it is critical to understand why lawmakers must be required to keep such correspondence. The exchange was about the potential effects of new shoreland zoning regulations on what was then a proposed library expansion in Minocqua.

In the emails, Ambs tried to reassure Holperin that the proposed library expansion could proceed despite a new rule that limited impervious surface amounts within 300 feet of an ordinary high water mark in unincorporated areas. The library and town community center sat within that perimeter and could not meet the terms of the revised NR115, but Ambs told Holperin the library could proceed under the old rule.

"If the rules were already in place and everyone knew what to expect (i.e. the folks working on the library expansion knew the parameters of NR115 before they put their plans together) then I would say that the new NR115 would not allow them to expand without getting a specific variance for the project," Ambs wrote.

Having said that, he continued, he was "quite comfortable" that the project could continue under the old rule. But, he cautioned, property owners within the 300-foot zone who did not have plans underway should not expect to be able to substantially expand their impervious surfaces later.

"Once the new rule and applicable new county ordinances are in place, owners of property in Water Quality Management Areas should plan accordingly to protect water quality," he wrote.

Notably, Ambs did not want his conclusions circulated publicly. Holperin said, essentially, no problem.

"Thanks for this," Holperin replied. "I understand the library can go ahead under the old rule . . . and probably will . . . and that's the message that will go out for public consumption."

But the communications didn't stop there. Holperin said he was still disturbed by Ambs's views on what property owners might or might not be able to do later. Specifically, he said, the library project would be denied under the new rule simply because it was in Minocqua, an unincorporated town, and that wasn't right.

"If the library expansion were occurring in Madison or Milwaukee or Rhinelander or Eagle River or Crandon [all incorporated cities]. . . it gets the go-ahead," Holperin wrote. "Well, of course, this is just not fair and simply cannot be justified. Either all downtowns by water should have these new building projects restricted . . . or none of them should."

That said, Holperin asked Ambs to discuss exempting "little downtowns," and, he said, he had another idea.

"Or, better yet, will you join me in applying the rule everywhere, including incorporated areas," he asked. "Why should Madison be exempt, exactly?"

To be sure, shoreland zoning rules in general and the exemption of incorporated cities and villages specifically were hot-button issues at the time, especially in northern Wisconsin, and clearly this was a serious public policy discussion between a lawmaker and a major state official, not only discussing the potential ramifications of a new state rule but potential legislative plans of action by Holperin.

So how many people think this isn't substantive? How many think that's no more important than the announcement of a cookie sale? How could Holperin think it wasn't substantive enough to retain as a record?

Indeed, if that is not a substantive public record, nothing is. Yet, Holperin deleted it because he could. And that's the point. In the mindset of legislators, as Holperin himself proved, lawmakers can deem everything to be insubstantial. Perhaps that is why Holperin determined that there was universal compliance with retention.

It's a simple proposition: Through its exemption from the state's records retention laws, legislators have been and still are slaying transparency by the death of a thousand deletions. As Holperin's exchange demonstrates, the retention exemption allows lawmakers to erase policy negotiations they might be having with state agencies and special interests without the public or the media ever finding out.

And there's only one possible reason that, in 2021, lawmakers still refuse to end that exemption. It's because records are still vanishing down the Holperin Hole.

In 2016, after the GOP's spectacular debacle in trying to repeal the entire statute in 2015, then Senate majority leader Scott Fitzgerald (R-Juneau) told *The Lakeland Times* he would be open to repealing the exemption. Fitzgerald said things would be different in the next legislative session—that GOP lawmakers would support more open government—and he said that may well take more resources to ensure compliance with the open records law.

Specifically, Fitzgerald told *The Times* that he and his committee chairpeople would be more than willing to support a hearing to examine bringing the Legislature under the retention law.

"I don't think anybody would be opposed to maintaining [records] for a certain period of time because we have to anyway," Fitzgerald said. "You get these constituent contacts and oftentimes, the case in a file, it's a long-term look or a project that you're working on for the constituent. So I've never been concerned that that isn't something that would be palatable, so I certainly wouldn't rule it out. I have kind of an internal process that I've always used to make sure that constituent contacts are maintained."

By all indications, all that was sweet talk. No hearing was ever held, and the Senate leadership failed to address the issue. For instance, that same year, running for re-election, JFC member Sen. Tom Tiffany refused to say whether he would support such legislation.

"My records are open" was all Tiffany said on the matter, the same refrain heard from other lawmakers.

In the last legislative session (2019-20), as he has in the past, state Sen. Chris Larson (D-Milwaukee) circulated a bill to end the Legislature's exemption of itself from the retention law, but predictably, once again, the bill went nowhere. Tiffany, who is now in Congress but who was still a senator for most of that session, said much the same thing as he did in 2016 when Larson introduced the bill, telling *The Times* he would not co-sponsor the legislation and would reserve judgment on supporting the bill until after it moved through the committee process.

"As we have discussed in the past, I think it is a legislator's responsibility to be open and transparent with the public," he said. "Me and my office conduct ourselves in that manner on a daily basis. We comply with open records requests and I go the extra mile to keep constituents informed about my positions on issues."

Larson correctly argued that more was needed. In a column, he said he viewed the exemption as an invitation to trouble.

"They say what's good for the goose is good for the gander, but when it comes to public records, the state Legislature doesn't seem to believe in this principle," he wrote. "…This quirk in the law has been used by some legislators to protect constituents' personal information, and by others to hide their communications with corporate interest groups like the American Legislative Exchange Council, or ALEC. And I know that some of my colleagues in the Senate make it a point to delete their calendars daily."

For a state with a rich history of transparency and with technological advancement, Larson said such a double standard should no longer stand.

"I believe, as I recently told a Milwaukee TV station, that the ability of lawmakers to destroy records is an invitation to corruption," he wrote. "… Our public tax dollars pay for all of the functions the lawmakers perform. The public has a right to see records that show who is exerting influence over these allocations."

———

When they are asked to explain why they don't support bringing the Legislature under the retention law, lawmakers have a pat answer, a la Tiffany: All I know is that I retain all my substantive records, and you're welcome to come and inspect them anytime.

That's problematic. As we saw with Holperin, what is significant and what is not is in the eyes of the beholder. And, even if that particular lawmaker is keeping all of her or his records, that doesn't mean the lawmaker next door is. The retention law is designed not for honest officials but for the dishonest official, just like locks are designed to keep criminals, not honest people, out of a house.

The likely truth is, most lawmakers probably do keep all their substantive records. But that doesn't mean they are ecstatic when they receive an open records request. Quite the opposite. The history of the Legislature over the last decade is a history of lawmakers looking into every nook and cranny of the law to find other ways to keep as much information as secret as possible. We have already reviewed the Erpenbach email case as one example of that, but let's take a look at some other ways lawmakers seek secrecy (some, because frankly, an exhaustive accounting would require volumes).

In 2013, Sen. Leah Vukmir (R-Wauwatosa) carried legislative privilege even further than most, and tried to add a lesson to the playbook in a most creative way. Not only do lawmakers not have to retain records, Vukmir effectively argued, but they are immune from being sued for a violation when they are caught with records and don't turn them over.

In response to an open records lawsuit filed against her that year by the Center for Media and Democracy (CMD), which was seeking records that the group maintained would shed light on Vukmir's relationship with the conservative American Legislative Exchange Council, Vukmir claimed she had legislative immunity.

Simply put, Vukmir asserted in a motion, the state constitution prevented a legislator from being served with a civil summons while the Legislature was in session, and an open records lawsuit is a civil process. Per Senate resolution, the motion contended, the Legislature was in session until January 2015.

Then attorney general J.B. Van Hollen filed the reply motion for Vukmir.

"The rationale behind this provision of the constitution is to prevent members of the Legislature from being distracted by civil lawsuits and minor criminal violations," the motion stated. "A civil lawsuit can interfere with a member's full participation representing her constituents, and when a legislator cannot appear because of a civil lawsuit 'then the people whom the legislator represents lose their voice in debate and vote.'"

Critics said such a position, if successful, would have eviscerated the open records law, and they accused Van Hollen of kowtowing to partisan politics. It was indeed a strange motion to make: I can't be sued for violating the public interest when I'm on the clock supposedly working in the public interest, even if the lawsuit would validate whether I'm really working in the public interest while I'm drawing a public paycheck.

But here's the real kicker. As noted above, Vukmir contended the Legislature was in session until January 2015—until the next Legislature was sworn in—and the point is that the Legislature is virtually always in session. Here's how Richard A. Champagne, chief of Wisconsin's Legislative Reference Bureau, and Madeline Kasper, an LRB legislative analyst, put it in a 2019 report on special sessions:

"Nineteenth century legislatures met in regular session for only a few months and then adjourned sine die, that is, 'without a day' set for reconvening, which effectively abolished the Legislature," they wrote. "... Since the 1961 session, the established legislative practice has been to meet for periods throughout the biennium and then to adjourn sine die, if at all, only on the day the succeeding legislature is sworn in. In recent decades, the Legislature has not adjourned sine die at all."

As such, the analysts wrote, at its first meeting in January of the odd-numbered year, the Legislature organizes itself to conduct business during the biennium through adoption of a joint resolution establishing the session calendar, and the legislative schedule is divided into regular session floor periods interspersed with periods for committee work. In addition, the governor can call a special session at any time, and the Legislature may convene an extraordinary session in addition to regularly scheduled floor periods.

But the bottom line is, the "calendar" stretches from January of an odd-numbered year to January of the next odd-numbered year, and, as Jessica Karls-Ruplinger, the deputy director of the Wisconsin Legislative Council, and Mike Queensland, its senior staff attorney, summed it up in 2019: "Each biennial session of the Wisconsin Legislature begins and ends on the first Monday in January of the odd-numbered year, unless the first Monday falls on January 1 or 2. ... In effect, the Legislature may be in session at any time during the biennial period from inauguration day to inauguration day."

Again, as the LRB observed, in recent decades, the Legislature has not adjourned at all. Because the Legislature is always "in session," Vukmir's immunity argument would essentially shield her and her colleagues from ever being sued civilly, including for open records violations, during the entire time they were in office.

Talk about stretching an exemption. Talk about hutzpah.

The senator's detractors were quick to point out her departure from normal procedure, whereby lawmakers either accede to requests or fight them in court. Those at the Wisconsin Freedom of Information Council said they were 'shocked and saddened' by Vukmir's unprecedented legal argument.

"Our state's openness laws are fundamental to its ability to function as a democracy," the FOIC said in a statement. "Members of the Legislature, which passed these laws, ought to respect that. We call upon Sen. Vukmir to reconsider her position in light of the damage it could cause to the state."

The FOIC described Vukmir's position as a ruse and said the attorney general had in the past initiated legal action against members of the Legislature.

"In fact, lawmakers have been sued for violating the Open Records Law on a number of occasions," the FOIC stated. "They sometimes lost, sometimes settled, and sometimes won. But in no prior instance did they claim to be above the law. Wisconsin's traditions of open government, including the ability to litigate cases of alleged noncompliance, have served the state well. That is not a tradition with which we should dispense."

One such instance cited by the FOIC was a case in which *The Lakeland Times* sued state Sen. Mark Miller (D-Monona) for not providing records in response to a request. The case was settled with Miller agreeing to pay fees and costs, the FOIC observed.

For his part, state Sen. Jon Erpenbach (D-Middleton), who was still embroiled in his email lawsuit at the time of Vukmir's controversy, said he was shocked to hear of Van Hollen's opinion because it did not square with what the attorney general told him when Erpenbach sought advice from the Department of Justice about his own case.

"I find it amazing that, in the defense of a conservative organization, attorney general Van Hollen now claims that a legislator should not be required to comply with an open records request for emails," Erpenbach said. "This is the opposite of his stance two years ago, when a conservative organization sued me in an attempt to gain an unprecedented level of personally identifying information from emails sent to me by constituents. At that time, I sought the advice of attorney general Van Hollen, who is a constitutional officer sworn to represent the Legislature without prejudice. He refused to provide any counsel other than to tell me to acquiesce to the conservative organization's request."

Erpenbach said Van Hollen's about-face was a blatantly partisan political maneuver.

After the *Milwaukee Journal Sentinel* added to the salvo with an editorial of its own, Van Hollen defended his position. The attorney general said the editorial unfairly accused him of turning his back on a commitment to open government. Open government, Van Hollen wrote, is an essential tool to citizen-informed democracy, and he said he remained committed to using his position to facilitate compliance with the law. But he said he also took an oath to uphold the state constitution, including the section protecting sitting lawmakers from civil actions.

"The framers of the constitution inserted this provision—common among state constitutions—to give temporary protection to lawmakers from civil suits while they are doing the people's work," Van Hollen wrote. "Whether the framers' decision to provide this unique protection to legislators was a proper balancing of interests is a debatable question. What is not debatable is my responsibility to defend its application when it is invoked."

An attorney general cannot simply pick and choose parts of the constitution to disregard because they may act to frustrate a different policy goal, Van Hollen continued.

"... Sen. Vukmir chose to invoke her privilege from civil process—as she is constitutionally entitled to do," Van Hollen wrote. "Some legislators make that choice, some do not. But neither Sen. Vukmir nor I believe legislators are above the public records law."

Indeed, Van Hollen added, Vukmir believed she had fully adhered to the public records law by releasing all records subject to the request.

"This is unlike the position taken by the other legislator mentioned in your story (Erpenbach), who asserted that he had no obligation under the public records law to disclose the name of any person who contacted his office about a controversial piece of legislation," the attorney general wrote.

The issue then, Van Hollen continued, was not if the public records law applied to legislators.

"It does," he concluded. "Legislators, like other public officials, are under a legal duty to respond to public records requests as soon as practicable and without delay. The only question is when they may be sued for an alleged violation. If they choose to invoke their temporary privilege, that is a question the constitution answers."

For her part, Vukmir said it was all one big misapprehension.

"Despite media accounts stating otherwise, I have met my obligations regarding the requests for records sought by CMD," Vukmir said. "I do not believe legislators are above the public records law. My position is that I have fully complied with the public records law and have produced all records subject to this open records request, as I have done with the five previous requests from CMD since the beginning of April."

Vukmir said she had always believed in transparent government and would continue to comply with all future requests for records, including two recent requests by CMD.

"This has proven to be an unfortunate and largely misunderstood matter ...," she said.

But CMD disagreed that the senator had satisfied its request. Pointing out her position as ALEC's national treasurer, and her appearance at the group's Oklahoma City meeting—not to mention her sponsorship of model ALEC legislation—the group said it was hard to believe she did not have a single record relating to that legislation, her position as a leader of ALEC, or the Oklahoma meeting, except for text messages and a few emails showing her attendance.

"When Sen. Vukmir says she has provided all records 'subject to this open records request,' her claim must be viewed in light of the fact that ALEC has been stamping its bills and communications to legislators with a disclaimer asserting the documents are 'not subject to' any state's public records law," CMD said in a statement. "We have no confidence she is complying with Wisconsin's public records laws versus abiding by ALEC's claim that materials it provides to lawmakers are not subject to any public records law."

What's more, the group said it was not known whether Vukmir withheld any materials distributed to her via an Internet dropbox, which it said ALEC has used in the past. The bottom line was, CMD stated, the two sides factually disputed whether the senator had observed the law, and court was the appropriate venue to sort it all out.

"It is Sen. Vukmir's claim that she has complied with our public records requests, and it is CMD's position that she has not," the group stated. "The proper place to resolve this is in court. If she has fully complied with our request, why is she taking the extraordinary and unprecedented step of asserting legislative immunity to block the case from proceeding? What is she hiding that she won't allow this matter to be resolved on the merits?"

Vukmir was not the only lawmaker to have been on the receiving end of CMD open records requests about ALEC. The organization sued five other lawmakers that year; those five released the records.

Ultimately, Vukmir, too, settled the case but the issue of immunity continues to hover in the sky. As it turned out, an independent investigator discovered more emails in a private email account that should have been released. Vukmir attributed it all to a glitch in which multiple searches of her email accounts had produced inconsistent results.

"I regret the technical issues we had fulfilling this request, but I have now fulfilled the request and turned over all records," she said then in a statement. "Additionally, I have worked to identify the problems we encountered through this process and have taken action to ensure that this will not be an issue in the future."

As part of the settlement, Van Hollen's office agreed to withdraw the immunity argument, though that leaves the issue unsettled and so potentially available for lawmakers to use in the future.

For her part, according to the settlement, Vukmir agreed to pay $12,500 in lawyer's fees and $2,500 in punitive damages, but—wait for it—she didn't pay the settlement, taxpayers did.

At least when it came to transparency issues that didn't involve her own records, Vukmir believed in accountability. In 2007, she cosponsored the "Earmark Transparency Act," a bill that would have obligated public debate on all earmark spending, as well as public disclosure of the identity of lawmakers seeking earmarks. The legislation did not pass.

—

When they are not busy trying to extend legislative exemptions and immunities from the law, lawmakers make use of other tools in their toolbox to obstruct records requests.

One way has been to ignore requesters' wishes to have records sent in digital format, you know, the format most records are created and housed in these days. Instead, until recently, some lawmakers liked to have the records printed out, drawing out the time involved in fulfilling requests, increasing costs to requesters, and concealing digital information.

In 2018, to cite one illustrative example, the Wisconsin Institute for Law & Liberty, which has done yeoman's work on transparency issues these past few years, sued state Rep. Jonathan Brostoff (D-Milwaukee) for doing just that—refusing to turn over electronic records, opting to print them instead and to charge what WILL said were unnecessary fees.

The case started the year before when WILL research fellow Collin Roth made an open records request to Brostoff for emails related to occupational licensing reform, an issue WILL had been integrally involved with over the past several years. Roth specifically asked Brostoff to provide the emails in an electronic format.

However, Brostoff printed thousands of pages of documents and sent Roth an invoice for more than $3,000. That prompted WILL's attorneys to point out that the law requires custodians to provide electronic records when requested and also does not allow charging for paper copies of electronic files. Brostoff refused to budge, and so WILL went to court. In its court filing, WILL said the law explicitly defines records to include electronic files, and pointed out that a printout of the text of an email doesn't reproduce everything in the actual electronic file. Just as a transcript captures only one facet of a video recording, WILL asserted, a printout was no substitute for an original email file.

Tom Kamenick, who was then deputy counsel and open government specialist at WILL and who has since formed the Wisconsin Transparency Project, argued that such tactics were all about making it more difficult for the public to access records.

"I see this all too frequently," Kamenick said. "Instead of doing things the easy way, custodians intentionally make the process difficult and expensive, discouraging people from even making records requests. We shouldn't put up with that."

WILL also pointed out that a similar case existed, which produced a ruling that January by a Dane County circuit court judge that state Rep. Scott Krug (R-Nekoosa) needed to provide electronic files when requested. WILL said Brostoff was informed of that case but still refused to comply.

WILL president and general counsel Rick Esenberg said the case was not about ideological differences. Brostoff is a liberal Democrat and Krug is a Republican.

"Unfortunately, both Republicans and Democrats occasionally fail to meet their obligations under our open records and open meetings laws," Esenberg said. "We've worked with advocates across the political spectrum to fix that. This is just the latest fight."

In addition to a requirement under the law, providing records electronically is the smart thing to do, WILL contended.

"Why would a public servant waste taxpayer resources printing out copies of electronic files?" the group said in a statement. "That method is slower, more expensive, and less convenient for everybody than just copying the files onto a CD or flash drive (or even just emailing the files directly to the requester if the request is small)."

Roth said WILL had been on the frontlines of an effort to reform Wisconsin's occupational licensing laws and that openness on the matter was crucial.

"We believe citizens have a right to earn a living and that burdensome and unreasonable regulations often stand in the way of meaningful work," he said. "As with any public policy debate, government transparency is critical."

According to the complaint, on July 10, 2017, Roth wrote Brostoff requesting all emails sent to or from his or his legislative staff's email accounts, whether government or personal, that included a list of key words related to the occupational licensing issue.

"If these records are stored electronically, please provide them in that electronic format," Roth wrote.

Brostoff responded the next day, saying the request would be fulfilled but the documents would be reproduced as paper copies and a fee would be required for the cost of the paper copies. On December 6, Rebecca Frank in

Brostoff's office emailed Roth, stating that they had completed the request. She provided a cost estimate for producing the records, the complaint stated.

The cost was either $3,239.76 or $1,808.84, depending on the way the key words were searched for. On January 3, 2018, the complaint continued, Kamenick, acting as Roth's legal counsel, wrote Brostoff, reminding him that the records request asked specifically for the electronic records in their original format and that, because the request specifically asked for electronic records, they had to be provided that way.

"Providing electronic records in paper format does not comply with the Open Records Law," the letter stated.

Frank responded the same day, saying the Assembly chief clerk had confirmed that the law permits the documents to be provided in paper format, and that, per Assembly policy, they must be provided that way, the complaint stated. On February 2, Kamenick sent Brostoff a final letter requesting that he fulfill his obligations under the open records law and produce electronic records in the requested electronic format.

"In that letter, plaintiff's counsel informed defendant that the Dane County Circuit Court recently ruled against defendant's colleague, Wisconsin state Rep. Scott Krug, 'and determined that Assembly representatives are required to provide records in electronic format when requested,'" the complaint stated.

Kamenick also attached an attorney general's opinion letter from 2011 saying that electronic records should be transferred to some "electronic medium" to be provided to the requester and concluding that charging "per page" for such records was inappropriate.

Brostoff remained defiant in the face of the law.

"As directed by the chief clerk, I am again informing you that the open records request you submitted has been printed and is ready for you to pick up," he wrote in an email on February 5, 2018.

According to the complaint, the email contained the same cost estimates provided previously and was unresponsive to counsel's February 2 letter. WILL's underlying legal position was that, under the law, a records custodian must provide files in their native format, if requested, and Kamenick had argued that position in his January 3 letter to Brostoff.

"Providing electronic records in paper format does not comply with the open records law," he wrote. "The open records law does not permit a custodian to create a new and substantively different record in response to a request."

Kamenick also pointed out that, under the law, a record was defined as "any material on which written, drawn, printed, spoken, visual or electromagnetic information is recorded or preserved, regardless of physical form or characteristics, which has been created or is being kept by an authority." Under this definition, Kamenick wrote, an electronic file on a government computer is a "record."

"It is material on which electromagnetic information is recorded and preserved, being kept by an authority," he wrote. "Regardless of the type of file, it is a record."

That created two distinct rights, Kamenick contended.

"A record requester has the right to inspect a particular file—for example, an email file—by appearing at the government office," he wrote. "A record requester also has the right to receive a copy of that same email file. Not a paper document with some of the same information, but an identical copy of that file with all the same information in it."

If a 'copy' differs in some significant way for purposes of responding to an open records request, then it is not truly an identical copy but instead a different record, Kamenick asserted.

"A paper printout of an email file does not contain the same information as the original file; it differs in a significant manner from the original," he wrote. "A printed document lacks substantial amounts of information, sometimes referred to as 'metadata,' from the original file ..."

Metadata includes such things as the author or creator of the file; the date the file was created; hidden header information, including blind carbon copy (bcc) recipients; and the server and folder location where the file was located, Kamenick wrote.

"Metadata is part of the 'electromagnetic information' maintained by an authority, and therefore meets the statutory definition of a record," he wrote. "Converting an email file into a paper document will erase all of that information. In no sense can a paper document be considered an identical copy of an email file. It is analogous to providing a transcript of an audio or video recording when the recording itself is requested, which is not permitted."

Roth had the right to obtain a copy of the email records he requested in the same native file format in which those emails are kept on government computers, Kamenick concluded. Before even answering WILL's arguments, Brostoff flipped and handed over the records, agreeing to pay nearly $2,000 in attorney's fees and costs.

Though it was settled, this case is important because of the arguments WILL raised and because of the troubling patterns it represents.

First off, Brostoff and Krug and, by extension, their fellow lawmakers employed what has become a new tactic in the arsenal of Dark State obstruction and that could carry far beyond the Legislature. That is, one of the new ways lawmakers attempt to exploit the original law's lack of specificity, beyond merely proffering absurd interpretations of such provisions as the length of time it takes to respond to requests, is to toy with the definitions in the law itself.

Just what is a government meeting? Just what is a public record? Just what is a government body subject to the law? The broad statutory language in all these definitions has been contested as lawmakers and others try to hard-channel those definitions away from the original intent of lawmakers and toward their own narrower constructions.

Specifically, the Assembly had adopted a policy that only paper copies of records would be provided. In Krug's case, the defense had tried to take refuge in statutory language, arguing that it gave requesters a right to control the format of a record: "If a requester appears personally to request a copy of a record that permits copying, the authority having custody of the record may, at its option, permit the requester to copy the record or provide the requester with a copy substantially as readable as the original."

Of course, in that case, the requester had not appeared personally, so it was irrelevant. And, in any case, a document is not a copy of record if it does not contain all the information of the original record. Lawmakers tried to interpret "substantially as readable as the original" as "almost the same as," allowing them to omit information, when readability clearly refers to the printed clarity of the information provided, not to the information itself, in other words, it must be "substantially as legible as the original."

In both the Brostoff case and the Krug case, the Legislature's position would be that a paper record was a legitimate copy of a digital record, even though it contained much less information, or metadata, than the digital record. That was a definitional sleight of hand—an attempt to rewrite the very definition of a public record, or at least to create a definition for the copy of a record—that, if it had stood, would have modified the meaning of the statute.

Finally, the Brostoff case represented a troubling pattern of contesting in court issues that the courts have already settled. In *The Times's* case with the DOJ that I wrote about earlier, the very issue had been decided years before in *Kroeplin*. In the Brostoff case, Krug had just lost on the same issue the year before.

More and more, opponents of transparency keep challenging the same precedents that favor openness, throwing cases against the judicial wall in hopes some will stick. It's not that overturning precedent is necessarily wrong, but relentless challenges against settled law can bring uncertainty to that law, which is exactly the goal of Dark State strategists. To wit, even when they don't succeed in overturning precedent, they make it more cost prohibitive to challenge records denials by making litigation likely, and that discourages legal challenges to official decisions in the first place.

In addition, in an era in which courts have taken somewhat of a turn against transparency, there is the increasing likelihood that a challenge to precedent will succeed, and the government will be upheld, so hey, why not go for it?

The answer is not that courts can or should be restrained. But, given the new reality, the Legislature must be keen on overturning bad decisions with new law, when such law is constitutionally appropriate and, indeed, called for. The Legislature has taken such action multiple times in the past several years—to correct an awful Supreme Court decision on conditional use permits, for instance—and it must be prepared to do so in open government matters.

These days, that will take electing a new Legislature.

—

Another issue bandied about in the Legislature these past few years has been a proposed merger of the Legislative Reference Bureau (LRB) with the Legislative Council and—the real point of the merger—to close off legislative drafting files.

As the Center for Media and Democracy (CMD) explains, legislative council attorneys act as general counsel to the Legislature and provide procedural and substantive policy advice to legislative leadership, individual legislators, and committees, while LRB attorneys draft all bills, resolutions, and amendments for introduction in the Legislature, as well as legislation for the governor, executive branch agencies, the courts, and other legislative service agencies.

But the agencies have different confidentiality requirements under Wisconsin statutes, CMD points out, expressing further concern that the merger would lead to greater secrecy, especially in the bill-drafting process if lawmakers suddenly asserted attorney-client privilege between drafting attorneys and lawmakers. Changes in access to the drafting files could impede the public's ability to see who has influence in writing various pieces of legislation, the group states.

"Drafting files become open records after a bill has been introduced and in a few other instances," CMD stated in a 2019 release. "There citizens can see how a bill becomes a law and who had input into it, including lobbyists and special interest groups."

In February 2019, Mary Bottari of the CMD sounded an alert about ongoing efforts to close down the drafting files. She noted that in 2015 an effort had been made to do so, reportedly with the support of the LRB itself. That attempt failed, Bottari wrote in a February 28, 2019, email to a wide array of media, but, even so, the LRB had gone on to make significant changes to its drafting manual that she found troubling.

It was all the more serious at the time because Republicans in the Legislature were pushing the merger of the LRB and the Legislative Council, a move that could subject the drafting files to attorney-client privilege. Maintaining access to those files was important, Bottari wrote in her email, because the files have traditionally included the drafters' notes.

"Drafters' notes are used for many purposes to ask questions, seek clarification, provide explanation, give a legal opinion, or to otherwise communicate important information to the legislator for whom the draft was being prepared," she wrote. "These notes were always placed in the file. Limiting this information defeats the very purpose of the drafting file."

When Richard Champagne became LRB chief in 2015, things changed, Bottari observed, saying Champagne's philosophy was to avoid emails and written notes and to encourage communication with legislators and legislative staff by telephone to avoid a written record.

The drafting file manual revised after Champagne became chief reflected that philosophy, Bottari asserted. Essentially, Bottari explained, the revised manual reduced 55 pages of general policies and procedures, and general rules for drafting and revising, to three pages, tossing "out the door decades of best practices on how to keep a robust drafting file and even deal with the media."

"Missing from the introductory pages are important reminders, such as, 'LRB policy (1) General: The LRB policy is to serve all legislators alike regardless of party affiliation, political views, seniority or other factors,' and the LRB 'must maintain a nonpartisan attitude in dealing with legislators and the public.'"

In the earlier drafts and for decades, the 'client' of the LRB was the Legislature as a whole, Bottari wrote, not individual legislators. In addition, there was no assertion of attorney-client privilege. And that's not all that was missing from the earlier version, Bottari continued.

"The earlier version stresses that 'the importance of maintaining confidentiality cannot be over emphasized,'" she wrote. "And both agencies have clear confidentiality requirements in law. Drafting files for instance are confidential until a bill is introduced or the bill is discussed by governmental bodies in a public manner."

But, Bottari stated, Champagne had gone a step further to assert in the manual that LRB attorneys must maintain an attorney-client relationship with each member of the Legislature and other persons with drafting privileges, with respect to the provision of drafting and other legal services.

"The emphasis on attorney-client privilege indicates that the LRB believes that state politicians should have greater rights to declare exemptions to the open records [law] than are provided to the LRB in the statutes," she wrote. "Would an LRB attorney actually claim attorney-client privilege in a judicial proceeding? In contrast, the Legislative Council does not claim attorney-client privilege and U.S. courts have been moving in the opposite direction."

Indeed, Bottari continued, multiple federal courts had rejected the government lawyers' assertion of attorney-client privilege in relation to their politician bosses, even if the boss is the president.

There was even more pruning.

"The earlier version of the drafting manual instructed that there are nine pieces of information required for opening a drafting file," she wrote. "Item number five instructed drafters to note if 'the person who requested the draft is different from the person for whom the request is to be drafted. If the person who requested the draft is a lobbyist, note the organization that the lobbyist represents.'"

The earlier version, Bottari wrote, also discussed explicitly the "open records exception to confidentiality requirement" that "an un-introduced draft may become an open record available for inspection under 19.35 (1) if the draft is discussed in an open meeting by a government body."

"The earlier version instructs under 'drafting files' that drafters 'place any written drafting instructions received from or on behalf of the requester and a description of any oral drafting instructions provided by or on behalf of the requester,'" she wrote. "The earlier version instructs under 'constitutionality' that 'if there is reason to question seriously the constitutionality of a measure call this to the requesters attention preferably by writing a memorandum and putting a copy in the file or by writing a drafters note.'"

All those important issues, which facilitate transparency and best practices, appeared to be missing from Champagne's version of the drafting manual, Bottari wrote. In short, the drafting manual was no longer a training book on open government, it was another pathway toward the Dark State.

Despite the sweeping changes in the manual, current lawmakers have not given up on just scrapping any access whatsoever to the drafting files. What's important, these lawmakers argue, is the final version of a bill, not all of the various manifestations leading to it, especially the early versions, which often contain what one lawmaker called "very irresponsible or ridiculous" provisions.

But such information is not only beneficial to the public but critical. Those early notes and drafts tell the public who exactly was first proposing the legislation, what provisions—some of them admittedly irresponsible—these interests might be seeking, and which legislators were willing to do their bidding. That's pretty important information.

Allowing the public to track only the activity pertaining to a final version is akin to allowing the police only to investigate the immediate crime scene of a murder and to arrest only the person who pulled the trigger, without ever digging into whether someone might have hired the killer and arranged the homicide. The real fingerprints of the crime are covered up.

Likewise, without being able to vet the entire chronology and origin of legislation, the real fingerprints of secrecy are sealed.

Lawmaking needs to be a completely transparent process. Closing down the drafting files allows special interests unfettered access without being exposed to the public, and it allows lawmakers to hide who they are actually making their policy bed with.

—

While shutting down drafting files is bad enough, sealing off the files of internal investigations into alleged lawmaker misconduct takes secrecy to a whole new level. Yet that is exactly what the Legislature has traditionally done, even after the Supreme Court, in the *Kroeplin* decision, declared the files of closed disciplinary investigations of public employees to be open.

For lawmakers, what's good for thee is not good for me—again.

The history of the Legislature's attempts to shield lawmakers from public exposure when it comes to alleged misconduct is a long one. According to the *Milwaukee Journal Sentinel*, as late as 2017 both Assembly speaker Robin Vos (R-Rochester) and Assembly minority leader Gordon Hintz (D-Oshkosh) said they wanted such records kept secret.

In early 2020, four news organizations and a former *Lakeland Times* reporter brought an open records lawsuit against the state Assembly and its chief clerk for records they requested related to a sexual harassment investigation of Rep. Staush Gruszynski (D-Green Bay).

The plaintiffs were the Associated Press, *Wisconsin State Journal*, *The Capital Times*, the *Milwaukee Journal Sentinel* and Jonathan Anderson, the former *Times* reporter who is now a University of Minnesota doctoral candidate who researches public and press access to government-held information.

In the case, a legislative staffer filed a complaint, and a subsequent investigation substantiated the allegation. Gruszynski admitted making inappropriate comments to a female legislative staffer in October 2019, but, despite his admission, the complaint and the detailed investigatory findings were not released, leading to the open records requests and the lawsuit.

In his December 20, 2019, request, according to Anderson's lawsuit, Anderson sought all records related to allegations that Gruszynski sexually harassed the female staffer, including complaints containing the allegations; records created and/or obtained in the course of investigations related to the allegations; and all reports, findings, and/or conclusions related to the allegations.

The day before, on December 19, Scott Bauer of the Associated Press and Riley Vetterkind of the *State Journal* asked for the complaint, Briana Reilly of *The Capital Times* asked for the complaint and investigation, and Molly Beck of the *Journal Sentinel* requested any records pertaining to the complaint.

According to the lawsuit, all the requests were denied. The response, which the complaint asserted was written by Amanda Jorgenson, the human resources manager within the Legislative Human Resources Office (LHRO), said the Legislature had applied the public records balancing test and determined that the public interest in nondisclosure outweighed that of disclosure.

"The only information provided in the response was a paragraph indicating that a complaint was filed, an investigation determined that the allegations were substantiated, and remedial actions that were required as a result," the lawsuit's complaint stated. "No records were provided. Plaintiffs have received no other response to their requests."

In the response, the LHRO said the Legislature determined that the public interest in protecting the privacy and dignity of past and future victims/complainants/witnesses and instilling employee confidence that the Legislature would handle sensitive internal complaints confidentially to ensure that future victims/witnesses felt safe reporting concerns and cooperating with internal investigations outweighed any public interest in disclosure of the requested records, even in redacted form.

"Specifically, staff have requested that the materials related to the request above not be released and expressed concerns that release of the materials related to the requests above, even in redacted form, would compromise the privacy and dignity of the complainant/witnesses based upon the fact that the complainant/witnesses could still be easily identified," the response stated.

"Staff had also voiced concerns that releasing such records, even in redacted form, would have a chilling effect on future victims coming forward to report concerns and future witnesses cooperating with internal investigations."

All of which would compromise the Legislature's ability to be informed of and to timely respond to and resolve such concerns and complaints, the response stated.

In an attempt to balance all those public policy concerns and the public interest in disclosure of such information, the response said the Legislature did acknowledge that a legislative employee filed a formal complaint with the LHRO against Gruszynski.

"The LHRO investigated the employee's complaint and determined that the employee's allegations were substantiated," the response stated. As a result of the substantiated findings, the response said remedial actions as determined by Gruszynski's leadership would be applied, and he would attend anti-harassment training with the LHRO.

The plaintiffs contended that those explanations and reasonings were not sufficient. According to the complaint, under the state public records law, it is the declared public policy of the state that every citizen is entitled to the greatest possible information regarding the affairs of government and the official acts of government officers and employees.

"[State statute] thus provides that the open records law 'shall be construed in every instance with a presumption of complete public access, consistent with the conduct of governmental business,' and further, that '[t]he denial of public access generally is contrary to the public interest, and only in an exceptional case may access be denied,'" the complaint states. "The open records law provides that a requester has the right to inspect any record, subject only to extremely narrow and well-defined exceptions, and to receive a copy of a record."

Clearly, the complaint asserted, the records requested by the plaintiffs were 'records' subject to disclosure under the open records law, and the response contained no valid basis for denial.

"Defendants have accordingly violated the open records law," the lawsuit stated. "Defendants' actions have caused and will continue to cause injury to the plaintiffs by depriving them and the public of their rights under the open records law."

The plaintiffs sought to have the court declare that defendants violated the open records law, and to issue a mandamus order directing them to produce for the plaintiffs a copy of the requested records without delay.

Meanwhile, soon after the incident surfaced, Gruszynski himself acknowledged he had made a mistake after drinking too much in a Madison bar. He apologized to the staffer and acknowledged that his conduct was unprofessional and completely unacceptable. He also said he had taken steps with his family to rebuild what he had broken and that he had sought counseling for himself as well as his family.

However, that didn't stop many Democrats from calling for his resignation, including the Assembly Democratic leadership, led by Hintz.

"This week, the Legislative Human Resources Office (LHRO) completed a formal complaint resolution process into a complaint that Rep. Staush Gruszynski verbally sexually harassed a legislative employee while in an offsite location after work hours," the Democrats said in a statement. "This investigation found the complaint to be substantiated, and in violation of the policies laid out in the Wisconsin State Assembly policy manual."

The Democratic leaders said they were committed to preventing and stopping incidents of harassment whenever they occurred in the Legislature.

"It's our job to create a culture of accountability and to ensure members and legislative employees are held to a high standard of conduct," they wrote. "Rep. Gruszynski failed to meet these standards with his actions. In recognition of the seriousness of this substantiated investigation, we have immediately stripped Rep. Gruszynski of his committee assignments. Rep. Gruszynski will no longer be caucusing with the Assembly Democrats, and should resign."

State Democratic Party of Wisconsin chairman Ben Wikler echoed that sentiment.

"We are grateful for leader Gordon Hintz's swift and thorough response to this troubling report of sexual harassment," Wikler said. "We have zero tolerance for sexual harassment at the Democratic Party of Wisconsin and expect elected leaders to hold themselves to the same standard."

Wikler said it was up to all people to create a culture of mutual respect and trust in the workplace and in communities.

"We are deeply disappointed that one of our own members contributed to this pervasive issue," he said. "In acknowledgment of the gravity of Rep. Gruszynski's actions, we echo leader Hintz's request that he step down."

Gruszynski not only refused to resign but ran for re-election, though he lost in a landslide.

Now there are two important points to make about all this. First, what's interesting about the Democratic Party's response was not its support for the punishment meted out by the Democratic legislative leadership, nor its call for Gruszynski's resignation—the lawmaker did admit to it after all—but its lack of support for those seeking details of the incident and its silence on the Legislature's lack of transparency.

That's not to say Gruszynski deserved that party's or anybody else's support, but he did run for re-election and the voters did judge him but without the full knowledge and details of what transpired. That could have been easily remedied by releasing the records, and by protecting the victim in the case.

And that brings us to the second point, which demolishes the LHRO's most important reason for denying the records in the first place, that release of the incident's details would still allow the victim to be easily identified. (The LHRO had also asserted that releasing the details would have a "chilling effect" on future victims coming forward, but the "chilling effect" argument is made in almost every open records lawsuit, and is always rejected.) But, incredibly, two days after Gruszynski lost his re-election bid in 2020, LHRO officials did release the records, ostensibly because the complainant in the case had spoken to a newspaper reporter and the officials said they had a "new understanding that the victim no longer objects to details of the incident" being released, so long as she remained anonymous.

"The LHRO has determined the legislative policy recognizing the strong public interest in allowing access now outweighs any interest in preserving the confidentiality of the details surrounding the events involving Representative Gruszynski," a letter to *The Cap Times* of Madison said.

So the LHRO denied the records because they asserted that the details would allow the complainant to be easily identified, but suddenly they no longer believed the details would allow the complainant to be identified. Or they no longer cared. In other words, the complainant made the call about releasing the records, not the records custodian. This is not good public policy.

Victims' rights are important, of course, and, if certain details would have in fact enabled the victim to be identified, that is grounds for not releasing that specific information.

But that should be the custodian's call, not the complainant's. The custodian should balance the rights of the complainant—could she be identified or not?—against the public's right to know what lawmakers are doing. Indeed, what about the public interest in allowing the voters of Gruszynski's district to have that information prior to the election, rather than two days after it? What's fair about that? Especially when the story in which the complainant spoke to the newspaper appeared four days before the election and the Legislature only released the records six days later, after the election.

What's more, the state also redacted the names of lawmakers, some of whom were witnesses who were present for a portion of the night in question. But there's no excuse for withholding the names in misconduct cases, including those who are merely witnesses. By the mere fact of being a witness, the lawmakers likely have material information that the public has a right to know, not to mention that taxpayers and residents have the right to know what lawmakers are doing or not doing to make them witnesses in the first place.

So one take away from the Gruszynski case is that custodians need to conduct balancing tests and make their calls, not any of the parties involved in those requests. The second take away is that the Legislature should be statutorily required to release internal investigatory records when those investigations are completed, just like others in state government. The specious reasons offered for denying the records in the first place is proof enough that that should be the case.

Such sexual harassment and assault incidents by government officials are happening not just in Wisconsin but across the nation, and, remarkably in the MeToo era, they are increasing in frequency, making public access to those records essential. A review by the Associated Press in 2020 showed that at least 101 state legislators have been publicly accused of sexual harassment or misconduct since the start of 2017.

In the AP review, at least 39 lawmakers had resigned or were expelled from office since January 2017 following sexual misconduct allegations and an additional 37 faced other forms of repercussions, such as the loss of committee leadership positions. A few were cleared, the AP stated, and investigations were ongoing against others; the list of 101 accused lawmakers included at least one person from three-fourths of the states.

However, while the allegations and actual incidents have grown, so has resistance by legislative leaders of both parties to release investigatory records.

———

Exemptions from the retention laws, legislative immunity, exploiting and redefining statutory terms away from openness, closing off work records to foreclose public access to special-interest players in drafting legislation, sweeping misconduct allegations under the rug—that's just the tip of the iceberg, the more complex machinations of a secrecy-obsessed Legislature.

Lawmakers can be just as aggressive in undermining transparency in the open. To cite just one of many examples, even though Rep. Marlin Schneider retired, other lawmakers have continued to attempt to kill or restrict the state's online circuit court database. That trusted enemy of openness, state Sen. Mary Felzkowski, has mostly championed that effort. Mainly, she has wanted to narrow the information listed on the database, specifically by removing the records of charges when there is an acquittal or the charges are dropped.

"People who are falsely accused or found innocent, that that information can still be public just blows my mind," she has said. "The information would still be out there in paper form, so it's a matter of how ambitious you are to go find it. It's just not readily available to be used to discriminate against people."

A related issue is expungement. In a 2019 piece in *Isthmus*, Wisconsin Freedom of Information Council president Bill Lueders addressed a bill that would have expanded the availability of expungement for people convicted of minor offenses (the bill failed to pass). As Lueders pointed out, it would have ended Wisconsin's rule that expunction can only be granted if it is sought at the time of sentencing and would have allowed expungement to be sought by anyone, not just those under 25, as it is today. What's more, it would have clarified that an expunged case cannot be considered a conviction for employment purposes.

Lueders said he supported changes in the expungement statutes, but he disliked what happened after expungement, namely, that the conviction was sealed and it disappeared from the online circuit court database. In that context,

Lueders went on to address the larger arguments raised by those who, like Felzkowski, would like to deep clean the database—that people with records or who have been arrested will be discriminated against by prospective landlords and employers.

Lueders took issue with that argument.

"No study has ever nailed down how often this happens," he wrote. "Legislators never check out the stories of people who accuse 'CCAP' of ruining their life. No one questions claims that people with criminal records cannot get jobs or housing, no matter how minor the offense or how long ago it happened."

He quoted a report by the Wisconsin Policy Forum that asserted that "[i]n Wisconsin, an estimated 1.4 million individuals have criminal records, which may pose a major impediment to securing a job."

Then Lueders did the math.

"Wisconsin has a workforce of around 3.1 million people and an unemployment rate of 3 percent, or about 94,000 workers," he wrote pre-pandemic. "If there are 1.4 million people with criminal records and only 94,000 workers without jobs, that means at least 1.3 million people with records have jobs."

And not only do lawmakers never question the claims made about "CCAP," or WCCA, ruining their lives, oftentimes, as noted earlier when Schneider was found to have dramatically inflated the number of letters he had received on that very topic, lawmakers are themselves the sources of fabrications about the damage caused by the online database system.

There's also a flip side to this argument, as any print journalist will understand. If we assume the argument is true that employers and landlords are busy scouring online records for criminal records—which I do not—then purging arrest records from WCCA could well lead to even more discrimination against innocent people than keeping them publicly available.

That's because newspaper court reporters are hired to search arrest logs. Even if an arrest isn't dramatic or involves no big names, it's more than likely going to show up in weekly court reports, and that generates a lot of stories. But the dirty little secret is, unless there's a conviction, the fact that there is an acquittal or the charges are otherwise dropped or dismissed is virtually never reported in a newspaper follow-up, except in major cases involving notable names.

If a person's arrest and ultimate lack of conviction doesn't show up in online records because they have been dismantled, then the only information available to those landlords and employers is what they read in the paper, and what they will read in the paper will be the arrest, not the lack of any conviction. The person will almost always be presumed guilty.

Let's cite a second example. Another brazen effort by lawmakers in the past few years has been to reduce the public notice requirements of the meetings government bodies hold. In 2017, Gov. Scott Walker included in his proposed state budget a provision to eliminate requirements that most public notices be published in newspapers. Rather, governments would have been able to simply post proceedings on their own websites.

It was a terrible idea, and, besides that, not a proper one for the budget. While it was technically a fiscal item, eliminating that requirement would have saved the state only about $24,000 a year in a budget that totaled $76 billion.

That budget amendment did not survive, but that didn't stop a host of lawmakers—including, guess who, Felzkowski—from introducing separate legislation to accomplish much the same thing. In the Assembly, 32 of 99 lawmakers signed on to co-sponsor the legislation. The bill failed, but it was shocking that anti-transparency forces had come so close so quickly to a majority in the Assembly.

The bill's supporters had many arguments—red herrings were they all.

State Sen. Duey Stroebel (R-Saukville) said in a hearing that the bill was really benign and that bill opponents had created a lot of confusion about what the legislation would accomplish.

"You may have seen the advertisements in your local paper claiming the public's 'right to know' is going away," Stroebel said. "This narrative is false. This bill does not shield the public from government proceedings. The bill requires all meeting minutes to be published in the local newspaper or, as an alternative, in a public place and on a website maintained by the local government board."

The bill would allow any local government to maintain their current relationship with the local newspapers but simply offered an alternative to costly newspaper publication, Stroebel said.

"I would remind the committee that in many cases newspapers require subscriptions or payment at a newsstand to read any published material— including the minutes newspapers claim is 'your right to know,'" he said.

Stroebel also said all meeting minutes would remain public records.

"Under Wisconsin's public record law, an individual must receive the record if they request it," he said. "Many local government clerks are more than willing to create email lists, mailing lists, or other alternatives for those interested in receiving the proceedings on a regular basis."

Stroebel challenged newspapers' assertions about the cost-effectiveness of the current requirements.

"Local units of government are willing to provide any proceeding document free of charge to any requestor," he said. "Are newspapers willing to offer the same service? Most likely these minutes remain behind a paywall. Newspapers seem to be concerned about the revenue, not providing a service. Under free-market principles, newspapers must provide content their readers want or risk losing readers."

Already, Stroebel said, many types of proceedings were not included in publication requirements.

"For example, the record of committee proceedings from today's hearing will not be published in the state's newspaper of record," he said. "Nonetheless, the proceedings are available on the Legislature's website, the chairman's office, the office of the chief clerk, and the Wheeler Report. Members of the media do not complain the proceedings are hidden."

In a twist, Stroebel said the bill was yet another example of local control.

"Local control is a buzzword we hear in Madison," he said. "That is what this bill is about: local control. Contrary to the opponents, this bill offers more avenues for the public to read and review what is going on in their government."

But opponents quickly knocked down those straw arguments.

For one thing, the Wisconsin Newspaper Association, which represents more than 200 Wisconsin newspapers, pointed out that, in the previous year, a joint Legislative Council study committee concluded that the current publication requirements should remain in place. WNA executive director Beth Bennett told lawmakers that the newspaper industry had a long-standing practice of making all public notices available electronically for free on a website, WisconsinPublicNotices.org.

Because it was not part of government, the WNA argued, and because the information could not be modified, it provided accountability and ensured public access to critical information.

"The goal of WisconsinPublicNotices.org is to enhance government's distribution of public information and assist citizens who want to know more about the actions of their local, county and state representatives," the WNA stated. "This permanent, third-party documentation—unalterable and independent of government itself—ensures the protection of 'your right to know' for each and every citizen."

In the end, Bennett told lawmakers at the hearing on the bill, the legislative council committee did not recommend that legal notices be moved from newspapers in favor of government websites.

"The legislative council's review of why legal notices exist and why they are published in newspapers demonstrated that there is far more to the publication of a legal notice than simply informing the public via a printed notice in the newspaper," she said.

Meanwhile, a representative of the 840,000-member AARP of Wisconsin said repealing the requirements would be a disservice to elderly citizens who depend on newspapers, both print and their websites, for essential sources of information. Older Americans are less likely to proactively seek information online and rely on newspapers and other traditional media to stay informed, AARP's Helen Marks Dicks told the committee.

"We're probably the biggest readers of the minutes," she said. "... We assume if (information) were important, it would come to us."

The WNA also pointed out that the legislation was being pushed by statewide associations that represented units of local government. And while the bill's sponsors called the publication requirements an "unnecessary expense," Robb Grindstaff, general manager of Hometown News Limited Partnership and W.D. Hoard & Sons Publishing in Fort Atkinson, told lawmakers that publication in newspapers was still the most cost-effective way to reach larger numbers of citizens.

"Transparency and accountability of government bodies and public servants —elected and unelected—require this positive, active communication from the government to the people they serve," Grindstaff said. "There exists no more effective and cost-efficient method to reach the largest number of citizens possible than through the pages of the local community newspaper, the news medium used by more people to find out what's going on in their community than any other source, in print or online."

Andrew Johnson, publisher of the Dodge County Pionier in Mayville, called the bill a threat to the public's right to know.

"The idea of open government involves three things, as most of you in this room probably know," Johnson said. "There's open meetings, open records, and public notices. If any one of them falls, our open government doesn't work correctly."

In his testimony, Gregg Walker, the publisher of *The Lakeland Times*, said it was important to remember that when minutes and notices are published in a newspaper's print edition, they also go on a newspaper's website. In addition, Walker said, technology has changed how people gather news information.

"The news market has become more fragmented in the last 10 years than in the previous 50 years," Walker testified. "These days, people still read newspapers and watch TV, but now many go to a website for their news, or use mobile phones. Sixty-three percent of all Facebook users now get daily news from their news feeds, while Twitter has become a preferred platform for receiving breaking news."

As technology has changed, newspapers have changed with it, Walker said, and newspapers were reaching more people than ever.

"Indeed, the most recent numbers from Comscore, a leading company that measures digital audiences and brands, indicate that it would be absurd to cut back government publication requirements for any type of notice, including and especially minutes," Walker asserted. "Not only is the newspaper digital audience massive, it is growing faster than the overall internet audience. And that doesn't count traditional readership. In other words, this bill would take important public information away from newspaper audiences at a time when newspaper audiences are becoming more important in the distribution of news and information, not less important."

In August 2015, Walker observed, according to Comscore, the digital audience engaged with newspaper content reached a new peak, totaling 179.3 million adult unique visitors. That represented a 10-percent increase in adult unique visitors measured by Comscore over the previous year. Over that 12-month period, that 10-percent growth rate of the newspaper digital audience was double that of the internet overall, which grew by 5 percent, Walker pointed out. And the growth in digital newspaper readership was not just among the elderly. More than nine in 10 men (93 percent) and women (92 percent) ages 25-44 who were online in August 2015 engaged with newspaper digital content.

Overall, 83 percent of adult men and women online during that month visited digital newspapers, either on their desktop machines or via mobile devices. Among 18-24 year olds, 81 percent of men and 77 percent of women were part of the newspaper digital audience, while those aged 25-34 and 35-44 reached 93 percent of men and 92 percent of women.

As Jim Conaghan, the vice president of research and industry analysis at News Media Alliance, put it, "These impressive net reach numbers demonstrate the importance consumers place on engaging with newspaper digital content and further reveal the vitality of newspaper media in an era where all businesses are challenged to enhance performance."

Walker said those numbers were well known, or should have been to those researching the proposed legislation.

"The bottom line is, to do away with any publication requirements for such a large and growing audience is not merely foolish, it is sinister," he said. "It makes one wonder what the real motive for this legislation is."

Walker said *The Times's* own numbers reflected the overall trend of growth.

"Last July, when I testified before a legislative task force studying these issues, *The Lakeland Times* in Minocqua had a press run of 9,300 for its print edition," he said. "We had 7,139 Facebook likes, and, for the week of July 18-24, we had 56,012 unique visitors to our website and 79,984 page views. All those people have access to our public notices, and that is at no extra charge to the government entities placing those notices with us."

Contrast that with government websites, Walker challenged the lawmakers.

"In our coverage area, there is no government entity with this ability to reach this number of people the way our newspaper does," he said. "The biggest town in our coverage area is the town of Minocqua, and they don't even have a Facebook page; all they have is a basic webpage."

Meanwhile, Walker continued, technology changes ever faster.

"There is no way towns will keep pace like newspapers," he said. "Five years ago, desktop computers and websites were the rage, now they are on the verge of extinction to mobile. And what is the leading news gathering on mobile? Newspapers."

Walker also challenged Rep. Jeremy Thiesfeldt's assertion said that no one reads newspapers anymore and that readership was down from 41 percent to 23 percent, calling it bogus and laughable.

"First, that number reflects, over the course of a decade, the number of people who said they read a print newspaper the previous day," Walker said. "In our busy lives, it's probably an accurate number."

But just because a person does not pick up a print newspaper every day does not mean they don't do so on a regular basis to check out what is going on in their communities, Walker countered.

"Second, Rep. Thiesfeldt's numbers are just for print," he said. "He completely ignores the exploding number of readers who engage newspapers online as the principal source of their news and government information, numbers that I have just relayed to you."

Finally, Walker took issue with the idea of local control that Stroebel had advanced.

"First, local control over government transparency is a horrible concept," Walker testified. "That would be like having local control over our constitution. The reason these statutes exist, and local communities of government have to follow them, is because it helps keep corruption out. Can you imagine if a government has no obligation to post notices and minutes in a place easily and already accessible to the public?"

Thiesfeldt also said 80 percent of citizens have access to the internet, Walker said, but that doesn't mean they go to government websites.

"Government websites are known as digital ghost towns—and whether they are up-to-date is another big question," he said. "Gov. Walker just came out last week saying that the very government website that was put in place about 10 years ago to make government transparent isn't being used or updated, and it's the law. Maybe you should clean up your own back yard before you spout how great the internet is."

The assault on WCCA and newspaper notices are just two examples of the brazen way lawmakers today attempt to narrow the scope and content of information the government releases to the public. But their shamelessness underscores an important point, and that is, only so much of this aggressive pursuit of secrecy can be averted by codification. As soon as one open government problem is solved through legislation, lawmakers quickly devise loopholes to get around it.

While major transparency issues need to be resolved by statute, the other critical remedy is—and one that is just as important—people need to make transparency a central issue in election campaigns. They need to elect lawmakers who pledge themselves to transparency and hold them accountable once they are in office.

Citizens need to let lawmakers know they won't stand for secrecy. Legislators need to be given a firm choice by voters: Cancel your membership in the Dark State, or cancel your membership in the Legislature.

It's a simply remedy, if voters will embrace it.

Chapter 8

Rewriting the Law: The Judiciary

These days the judiciary is a beehive of anti-transparency thought and activism.

None of which is to say there aren't good court decisions being rendered; there are. It's just that when the case files are reviewed in toto, there is an increasing tendency of state courts to back officials trying to increase secrecy. Worse still, the courts—even ostensibly conservative courts—are engaging ever more in rewriting the open records law rather than in interpreting it.

But there are good decisions, and it would be dishonest not to mention some of them. Long ago, in another case prompted by *The Times*, *Kroeplin v. DNR*, the court ruled that the closed investigatory records of state employees were public. That was a huge step forward in ensuring accountability in the conduct and behavior of officials paid by taxpayers.

More recently, in 2018, *The Lakeland Times* won a significant victory against the state Department of Justice when Dane County circuit judge Valerie Bailey-Rihn ordered the DOJ to release unredacted disciplinary records of 19 employees after the DOJ had refused to release their names.

I have also mentioned the work of the Wisconsin Institute for Law & Liberty (WILL), and that organization has secured a number of open government wins in the courts, including a finding that records must be released in digital format when requested and a settlement in a case in which a lawmaker tried to redact the names in constituent correspondence.

In another WILL case, the state Supreme Court ruled unanimously that the Appleton school district violated the state's open meetings law when a school committee held closed sessions to review ninth-grade reading curriculum.

In that case, John Krueger, an Appleton resident, sued the school district for an open meetings law violation. WILL attorneys asked the Supreme Court to find that the district violated the law when they formed a committee to assist in the development of a curriculum without properly noticing the committee's meetings to the public.

Over a period of six months, a special committee of teachers and district administrators had reviewed works of fiction for possible inclusion in a ninth-grade reading curriculum. None of the meetings was open to the public, WILL asserted, depriving parents, taxpayers, and even other teachers of their right to observe the process. The question was whether the school board could, by rule, delegate authority to create a committee to school administrators—a committee with a defined membership and the power to act collectively—without such a committee being subject to the open meetings law.

In this case specifically, school administrators had created the review committee without being specifically directed to do so by the school board. The circuit court and the appeals court sided with the school district, but the high court came down on the side of Krueger and WILL.

"Where a governmental entity adopts a rule authorizing the formation of committees and conferring on them the power to take collective action, such committees are 'created by . . . rule' under (the law) and the open meetings law applies to them," then justice Michael Gableman wrote in the decision.

WILL president Rick Esenberg said the ruling was significant.

"The critical thing about today's decision is that it affirms Wisconsin's open meetings law is to be construed and applied liberally," Esenberg said. "The school district here strained to find reasons not to follow the law. Today the court made clear the presumption is to be in favor of transparency."

There are other solid court decisions, including those already mentioned, such as finding that government entities cannot charge for redacting records as well as favorable outcomes when government agencies fail to respond to records requests in timely fashion. Unfortunately, the import of those decisions, numerous though they may be, pale in comparison to significant actions and decisions by state courts that significantly undercut current law.

For instance, while would-be thieves of openness in the Legislature were doing their best to take WCCA away by statute, judges were already purging the database of information. One way they do so is by sealing the records of cases that should not be sealed. In 2018, USA TODAY Network announced the results of an investigation it conducted of Wisconsin court records that had been sealed or in which the defendant's name had been redacted. The newspaper company found 208 felony cases that had been sealed or redacted between 2005 and 2014—cases ranging from sexual assault of a child to theft. Of course, as USA TODAY observed, sealing that information not only denied the public access to important information about those charged with serious crimes—a matter of public safety—it protected judges themselves from accountability.

Court decisions, too, are setting precedents for secrecy, and two cases have loomed large.

In one 2016 decision, the state's high court ruled on a 5-2 vote that then attorney general Brad Schimel did not have to release Wisconsin Department of Justice training tapes. The attorney general had argued that the tapes would reveal techniques used by prosecutors and by law enforcement to catch child predators. However, as lower courts pointed out, those techniques were already in the public domain and so the tapes were not revealing anything not already known.

The Democratic Party of Wisconsin brought the case, to see what Schimel had said on the tapes, if anything significant, so the case was brought for political purposes. Still, critics of the decision argued, the public has a right to know just what techniques police and prosecutors consider appropriate and are using. A democratic and civil society certainly demands such transparency, for without transparency anything goes. A society blind to the techniques of law enforcement can see only the specter of a police state before it.

In a second case, the high court decided that then Milwaukee County sheriff David Clarke did not have to turn over records pertaining to immigration hold requests, specifically federal forms asking local jails to hold some prisoners for an additional 48 hours when they were suspected of immigration violations. Critics of the decision argued that those prisoners were in state and not federal custody—thus subject to the state's open records laws—and they argued that the public has a right to know who was being detained, whether they were properly or improperly being detained, and whether they were being ultimately released.

In the end, a conservative court surrendered state prisoners to the rules of federal jurisdiction, odd for a conservative court and one that prompted critics to call into question whether the court had political motives.

That wasn't the only problem with the court case, as the Wisconsin Institute for Law & Liberty pointed out. Specifically, WILL observed, the high court allowed Clarke to make a new argument that a certain regulation blocked his ability to release the names, an argument he did not make in his initial denial of the records request.

"He never argued this regulation prohibited release until the court of appeals," WILL stated. "For decades, a cornerstone of the open records law has been that custodians are limited to relying on the reasons for withholding records they actually put in their initial denial of a request."

Otherwise, custodians can either intentionally sandbag requesters or be negligent and sloppy when considering whether to grant or deny record requests, WILL stated: "It encourages custodians to 'deny now' and work out a justification later."

All these are troubling decisions, but they are not as troubling as the disturbing and aggressive activism of the courts in actually rewriting the state's open government laws to suit their own political whims.

Let's take a look at three of the most important such cases, two of them involving *The Lakeland Times*.

—

In the first case, the Supreme Court allowed officials to withhold the names of those who had voted midway through a three-week union election after the union requested them because, according to the court, union officials might have used those records to pressure those who had not yet voted.

In a 5-2 decision, the high court effectively rewrote the statute because it allowed the motivations, or potential motivations, of requesters to be considered in an open records request, contrary to the plain language of the law, namely, that an open record is open to anyone and for any reason.

Specifically, the justices determined, officials could delay the release of voter lists during union elections because those records could be used to harass eligible voters during those elections. The case pitted Madison Teachers, Inc., against James Scott, the chairman and records custodian of the Wisconsin Employment Relations Commission (WERC).

The teachers' union had submitted multiple requests during a 20-day recertification election between November 4 and November 24, 2015, for a list of those who had voted at that point in the election. WERC denied two requests, but after the election released the names of all who had voted.

To release the names during the election could subject those who had not yet voted to potential coercion and intimidation by the union, WERC reasoned. The union went to court, saying the delay violated the public records law and that the union had not intended to use coercion but to target non-voters in a get-out-the-vote effort. A circuit court sided with the union, but the Supreme Court disagreed. The case bypassed the state court of appeals.

Saying Scott had properly used the balancing test of the open records law, the court majority found that the public interest in delaying disclosure outweighed the public interest in immediate disclosure.

According to chief justice and majority-opinion author Patience Roggensack, the case presented one issue: whether the public interest that elections remain free from voter intimidation and coercion in the certification election was sufficient to outweigh the public interest in favor of openness of public records.

Notably, Roggensack wrote, under the law a labor organization must receive the votes of at least 51 percent of the total number of employees in the bargaining unit, not just those who vote.

"Therefore, a non-vote in the election is for all intents and purposes a 'no' vote," Roggensack wrote. "Certification elections are conducted by secret ballot."

A week before the vote started, the decision continued, the union wrote to Scott, notifying him of its intention to submit requests for records of those who had voted at specific points during the election. The union emphasized that it did not intend to coerce anyone but was fully committed to exercising its First Amendment and statutory rights within the law. On November 10, the union submitted the first of its requests, requesting that the records be delivered "as soon as possible, but not later than 5:00 p.m., November 16," the decision stated.

But on that day, Scott denied the requests on three grounds, Roggensack wrote: "[F]irst, because WERC utilized the [American Arbitration Association], a third-party vendor to collect votes, the commission did not possess the requested documents; second, because the annual certification election is conducted by secret ballot, disclosure of the names of employees who had voted would violate the secrecy of the ballot; and third, because the common law balancing test weighed in favor of 'maintaining the secrecy of the ballot and of avoiding the potential for voter coercion while balloting is ongoing . . . .'"

As evidence for the balancing test argument, the decision stated that Scott was aware of a complaint submitted to WERC by the Racine Unified School District, alleging that voters had been coerced and harassed into voting during its 2014 annual certification election.

The union submitted a second request when the first one was denied, which was also denied. It issued a third request just after balloting ended. That request was fulfilled in timely fashion.

In considering the claims before it, the Supreme Court majority said it did not take the issue of possible voter intimidation lightly.

"All 50 states have employed the secret ballot method of voting to limit voter intimidation during elections," Roggensack wrote. "As explained in [the Supreme Court case] *Burson*, the history of election regulation in the United States shows that voter intimidation and coercion are long-standing evils that election regulations sought to prevent."

Indeed, the decision stated, the *Burson* case is instructive in the Madison teachers' case because it is instructive of the policies that underlie the use of secret ballots. In *Burson*, Roggensack summarized, a political party worker sought to enjoin enforcement of Tennessee statutes that prohibited solicitation of votes and display of campaign materials within 100 feet of entrances to polling places on Election Day.

"The party worker claimed that the statutory regulation violated her right to communicate with voters, in contravention of her First Amendment rights," Roggensack wrote. "Tennessee contended that its statutes were narrowly drawn to serve compelling state interests of preventing voter harassment and intimidation."

In the case, Roggensack stated, the Supreme Court reviewed the history of the secret ballot method of voting in the United States and how it has had an immediate and positive effect in limiting intimidation and coercion. It deemed the Tennessee statute constitutional.

"The Court concluded by explaining that the contest over Tennessee's election regulation involved 'the exercise of free speech rights [in] conflict[] with another fundamental right, the right to cast a ballot in an election free from the taint of intimidation and fraud,'" the chief justice wrote.

On balance, Roggensack wrote, the court said that removing the opportunity for intimidation of voters must prevail. Roggensack also pointed to 2011 Wisconsin Act 10, which specifically prohibited employees from coercing or intimidating other employees in regard to joining, or refraining from joining, a labor organization.

"Under current law, one of the primary goals of certification elections is to give employees an unintimidated voice in deciding who, if anyone, will be their representative," she wrote. "Consistent with that goal, certification elections are conducted by secret ballot to lessen intimidation of voters."

But how to safeguard against intimidation in the electronic age? Things had changed since *Burson*, Roggensack stated.

"Mechanisms to lessen voter intimidation when an election is carried out electronically over 20 days cannot be the same as they were in *Burson* when paper ballots were used at designated polling places," she wrote. "For example, the 100-foot restricted zone around the polling place that the Supreme Court approved in *Burson* as a narrowly tailored restriction to meet the compelling state interest of reducing voter intimidation would have no effect in the election at issue here because members of the bargaining unit could vote from the workplace, from home or from another location over a 20-day period. However, preventing voter intimidation and coercion are as important in a statutory certification election as they were in an election of the type reported in *Burson*."

So, Roggensack asserted, that set up the balancing test of the competing public interests: the general presumption that public records shall be open to the public unless there is an overriding public interest in keeping the record confidential, and a clearly expressed right to vote in certification elections that are free from intimidation and coercion.

In its arguments, Roggensack wrote, the union had contended that because voting was ongoing, those who had not yet voted could not be treated as a firm 'no' vote and, therefore, the lists of those who had voted would not violate the secrecy of the ballot by revealing the votes of anyone.

But that wasn't the problem, Roggensack countered.

"MTI's argument misses the point of why disclosure of the names of those who had voted affects the important public interest that underlies the use of secret ballots," she wrote.

Let us explain, Roggensack continued for the majority.

"Throughout the election, MTI remained free to provide truthful information to all members of the bargaining unit that bore on the advisability of electing MTI as the exclusive representative," she wrote. "However, giving MTI lists of employees who had voted at various dates before the election process was concluded, through simple deletion of voter names from the list of all members of a bargaining unit, also would give MTI names of all who had not voted by those dates. Those non-voting employees could then become individual targets of MTI's most forceful efforts because if they did not vote by the conclusion of the election, MTI may have been unable to secure 'yes' votes from 51 percent of the members in the bargaining unit and thereby fail in its certification efforts."

When elections are conducted over a period of time and voting occurs in many locations, Roggensack continued, there is no physical boundary by which voter intimidation can be regulated as there was in *Burson*.

"Therefore, preventing voter intimidation during elections conducted by phone and email, as occurred here, is challenging," she wrote. "Given MTI's repeated requests for the names of those who voted before the election concluded, it is entirely possible that those employees who had not yet voted would become subject to individualized pressure by MTI of a type that MTI could not exert when speaking to all members of the bargaining unit collectively."

As the history underlying the use of secret ballots teaches, Roggensack contended, a major purpose of secret ballots is to protect "the fundamental right" to cast votes in elections that are "free from the taint of intimidation."

"While *Burson* did not involve a statutory right to vote in certification elections as is presented here, the public interest in certification elections that are free from intimidation and coercion is evidenced by the requirement that those elections be conducted by secret ballot and free from prohibited practices," she wrote.

Without question, Roggensack wrote, intimidation in the WERC certification election was a concern.

"Scott had received detailed and specific complaints of past coercion in other certification elections," the chief justice wrote. "Complaints included: a union representative directing an employee to a computer and coercing her to vote for recertification; another employee being repeatedly asked whether she had voted; and a third employee witnessing employees being similarly pressured to vote."

Each individual voter has a fundamental right to cast his or her vote without intimidation or coercion, the decision stated.

"WERC is charged with conducting fair and accurate annual certification elections, free from the taint of voter intimidation," she wrote. "The public has a significant interest in fair elections, where votes are freely cast without voter intimidation or coercion. Accordingly, the public interest in elections that are free from intimidation and coercion outweighs the public interest in favor of open public records under the circumstances presented in the case before us."

Scott's denial of MTI's requests for voter names during the course of the certification election evidences the lawful balance of public interests presented, Roggensack concluded.

Justice Ann Walsh Bradley wrote a withering and correct dissenting opinion —justice Shirley Abrahamson joined the dissent—saying the majority was merely paying lip service to the public records law when it reaffirmed a presumption of open access to public records.

"Such exaltation seems to be all hat and no cattle," Bradley wrote. "Despite Wisconsin's longstanding public policy favoring transparency, for the third time in three years this court continues to undermine our public records law. Yet again, this court overturns a lower court decision favoring transparency of records to which the public is rightfully entitled."

This time, Bradley wrote, the majority undermined the presumption of open access to public records by imputing an unsupported and nefarious purpose to the records requests based on nonexistent facts.

"Without supportive evidence in the record, it speculates that by providing the requested records to Madison Teachers, Inc. (MTI), employees who had not yet voted in the recertification election 'could then become individual targets of MTI's most forceful efforts,'" she wrote.

And yet, Bradley continued, neither the majority nor the records custodian pointed to any evidence of voter intimidation or coercion by MTI.

"Rather, this concocted concern is based solely on one uninvestigated and unsubstantiated complaint from Racine County, involving a different union, in a different election, in a different year, that did not involve a public records request," she wrote.

Unlike the majority, Bradley said she concluded that Scott failed to overcome the presumption of open access to public records and that the unfounded speculation that the records might be used for improper purposes did not outweigh the strong public interest in opening the records to inspection.

For one thing, Bradley wrote, the majority engaged in selective vision— seeing facts that did not exist while at the same time failing to recognize existing facts of record.

"Left with non-existent facts, the majority instead speculates," she wrote. "It imputes an unsupported and nefarious purpose to the records requests."

But, Bradley wrote, absent from the record was any evidence that fulfilling the request would present a reasonable probability of voter intimidation or coercion.

"There is no evidence in the record that the Wisconsin Employment Relations Commission (WERC) opened an investigation about MTI engaging in such acts here," she wrote. "The record is devoid of any evidence of a verbal or written complaint of voter intimidation or coercion in this recertification election. The majority cannot point to any allegation in the record that MTI has ever acted improperly in this or any other recertification election."

Left with such a void, Bradley continued, the majority instead relied on that unsubstantiated allegation from Racine County that voters there "had been coerced and harassed into voting."

But, Bradley emphasized, those allegations were never investigated or substantiated.

"In short, it is difficult to imagine a scenario where there is less evidence of potential harm in the record than here," she wrote. "One would expect the highest court of this state to rely on more than such unrelated and unsubstantiated allegations for its assertion that the risk of voter intimidation or coercion here was great enough to overcome the strong presumption of open access to public records. It does not."

What's more, Bradley wrote—and this is critical to this book's purpose—in this state a public record that is available to one is available to all. She quoted previous court decisions determining that "[n]either the identity of the requester nor the reasons underlying the request are factors that enter into the balanc[ing test]."

Those guiding principles are rooted in the language of the statutes, Bradley wrote, quoting the statutory language that a records custodian may not refuse to release a public record "because the person making the request is unwilling to be identified or to state the purpose of the request."

"The identity of the requester and the purpose of the request should not matter here," she wrote. "Nevertheless, if the majority is going to erroneously superimpose its own speculative motive upon the requester, it should at least mention existing facts of record that support a contrary conclusion. It fails to do so."

Indeed, Bradley wrote, the majority omitted facts that might provide legitimate reasons for the union to have the list: During MTI's 2015 recertification election, an eligible voter's name was not in the system; a voter was blocked from voting because she was told she had already voted; a voter submitted a ballot but did not receive confirmation that the vote was submitted; a voter's name was missing from the eligible voter list; and a voter needed a new access code to submit a ballot.

"When speculating about the intent behind these records requests, the majority also ignores the record evidence that MTI advised WERC that it 'w[ould] not engage in voter coercion or any other illegal election practices during the upcoming election,'" Bradley wrote. "MTI explained at oral arguments that it made these records requests to ensure WERC properly executed its election-administration duties."

Bradley also pointed to a recent decision in *Erpenbach*, when state Sen. Jon Erpenbach (D-Middleton) withheld names of constituent emails related to 2011 Act 10, ostensibly to protect them from retaliation. The court rejected Erpenbach's reasoning, Bradley observed, saying he did not identify actual threats, harassment, or reprisals against concerned citizens and failed to demonstrate "a reasonable probability" that the email senders "would be subjected to negative repercussions for sharing their views regarding the legislation."

Finally, Bradley challenged the majority's reasoning in drawing a distinction between physical in-person voting and electronic voting.

Bradley pointed to the union's observation that if the election was an in-person paper ballot exercise, MTI would have had no need to request the record but could simply have had representatives observe the election firsthand—a practice allowed under WERC's administrative rules. The bottom line was, Bradley stated, again quoting the union, as a result of WERC's change in the administration of the certification election, what was formerly an open and observable government process was now closed.

"Unlike the majority, I would not permit a technological upgrade in the administration of an election to shield the release of records to which the public is rightfully entitled," she concluded.

Simply put, as Bradley pointed out in her dissent, the law clearly states that "no request ... may be refused because the person making the request is unwilling to be identified or to state the purpose of the request." The only exception is that a requester "may be required to show acceptable identification whenever the requested record is kept at a private residence or whenever security reasons or federal law or regulations so require."

Perhaps the justices could argue that security reasons were involved, but in that case the union only needed to identify itself—which it did—and the records could not be withheld. In this decision, the majority simply decided to strike the provision that "no request ... may be refused because the person making the request is unwilling ... to state the purpose of the request."

Either that, or they inserted into the law a new exception governing union elections. But both of those modifications are legislative responsibilities, not the role of the court. It's hard not to believe the decision wasn't guided by a partisan dislike of unions rather than by a clear reading of the law.

Here again, though, the prevailing view of the importance of open government laws comes into play. Obviously, as Thomas Jefferson warned us, the courts are benched with people, humans, and that means they are no more or less political than anybody else. Jefferson, writing in 1820, put it this way: "Our judges are as honest as other men and not more so. They have with others the same passions for party, for power, and the privilege of their corps."

By the same token, I don't believe our state justices are any more partisan than anyone else. That is, they are honest people who try hard to balance constitutional principle with personal political impulse. They likely try harder the more important the issue at hand is.

That they consider open government a lower echelon principle likely increases the temptation to partisanship because they don't view any fundamental principles to be at stake. But they are badly mistaken.

—

So now, thanks to the courts, there is precedent to consider the motive for requesting a record as a just reason for denying that request. That's potentially fatal to open government statutes. But here's another ruling by the courts that is just as potentially fatal: Thanks to a circuit and appeals court decision, public officials now have every right to refuse to disclose such things as letters of reference and notes used for staff management planning, even if those officials fabricated the notes and letters to undermine the employee.

Not even a judge can review the records to make sure they are real records, and that should be especially disturbing to public employees because it opens the door to the creation of false records about them, which, while not available to the public, could be used against them in such things as employment references.

The courts are living in Crazy Town. Paul Fussell, in "The Great War and Modern Memory," wrote that "every war is ironic because every war is worse than expected. Every war constitutes an irony of situation because its means are so melodramatically disproportionate to its presumed ends."

One might apply that same observation to a case involving, in the first round, Forest County circuit judge Leon Stenz and then the court of appeals in a decision favoring Lakeland Union High School (LUHS) in a *Lakeland Times'* open records complaint against the school district. In the case, an appeals court used the state's open records law—the very law designed to ensure accountability and transparency in government—to subvert transparency and accountability, and it used a provision of that law designed to protect public employees to put every public employee in harm's way.

Talk about a situation in which the outcome is exactly the opposite of what was intended, and melodramatically so. It's quintessential irony.

Specifically, the newspaper had sought two pages of negative comments about an LUHS basketball coach, purportedly compiled from phone conversations with his former employers during the hiring process for the LUHS position. The problem was, the newspaper's own phone calls to a number of the coach's former employers couldn't substantiate any negative comments. With reasonable suspicions about the veracity of the document and with a significant question about whether the administration, which did not prefer the coach and was trying to persuade the school board not to hire him, had unfairly maligned him, *The Times* went to court to seek third-party verification of the document, and its release if it turned out to be a fabrication.

The newspaper only asked the court to verify the administration's own claims. After all, the administration had told the public those were honest comments made by former employers and, when asked to prove their own claims, they refused. Instead, the high school administration opposed release and then made an astounding argument: It didn't matter whether officials made up the comments—it didn't matter whether they lied to a citizens' advisory committee and to the school board—because documents such as letters of reference and notes used for staff management planning, which these undoubtedly were, qualify for a blanket exemption under the open records law.

In other words, get lost, the school said both to *The Times* and to Stenz.

The Times argued that the exemption would apply only if the document was what officials purported it to be, an accurate rendering of former employers' comments. Thus, *The Times* argued, some mechanism of court-protected, confidential discovery was needed to verify the truth of what the high school was asserting.

Both the circuit court and the appeals court disagreed. They concurred with the high school that the document belonged to a class of records exempt from the get-go, whether they were authentic or false, and neither the public nor the employee were entitled to compel proof of their veracity or see them if fraudulent.

Let's take a look at the implications and flawed logic of that decision.

First, there was evidence at least strong enough to credibly raise suspicion about the records, which were presented to LUHS school board members after interviews for the position were held. LUHS had allegedly made phone calls to the coach's former employers, but *The Times* called a number of those former employers, including all of his listed references and four former direct supervisors not listed as references.

Of the four, only one was called by LUHS, and that person told *The Times* he had nothing negative to say about the coach.

The newspaper did not seek public disclosure if the records were what the district said they were; instead, the newspaper wanted proof that the records were authentic—that people actually made the comments the school district wrote down. *The Times* offered multiple ways to authenticate the records and maintain their confidentiality. For example, the newspaper proposed that the court appoint a referee to investigate whether the comments were genuine and report its determination to the court, subject to an appropriate protective order.

LUHS rejected all the proposals, arguing instead that such documents have a statutory blanket exemption. That exemption, the district argued, gave the school district the right to keep them sealed to everybody, even if the school district simply made them up.

According to the appeals court judges, the first decision a records custodian must make after receiving an open records request is whether the record qualifies for release. If the record belongs to a class subject to a blanket exception, then the request is denied and no further questions are to be asked.

With all due respect, though, that's not the first question a records custodian needs to ask. The first question should be, is it a real record? Any document that misrepresents the truth, makes false claims, or otherwise presents a dishonest accounting of government activity should not be considered a legitimate public record worthy of protection under open records law.

To put it another way, while such a document might technically meet the statutory definition of a public record, it should not be a record protected by the exemptions in the public records law, and that statutory clarification needs to be made. Just as false evidence in a criminal trial cannot be used to determine the trial's outcome, so a false record should not be used in an open records determination. Otherwise the public records law can itself be used as a means by which to cover up fraud and dishonesty.

Far from being considered exempt, it should be considered evidence of fraud by public officials. And, if a records custodian doesn't make the correct call, then a court-ordered third party should.

In his one lucid moment at the circuit-court level, judge Leon Stenz thought to ask the right question when he queried the LUHS attorney: "You're saying 'you don't get the records, judge,' and 'trust me,'" Stenz said. "What kind of review do we get then? Where is it implied in the statutes that, if the authorities say it is so, it is so?"

Precisely. Unfortunately, in his later ruling, Stenz concluded that if the authority says it is so, it is indeed so, and so did the appeals court, but Stenz's original question has never been answered.

The implication in the statutes must in fact be the opposite, that is, it cannot be presumed that the authorities are telling the truth. That's why we have an open records law in the first place, and, if we can't presume officials are telling the truth, then we can't presume the records they submit are always honest.

The presumption must be that only legitimate, or genuine, records qualify for withholding. And, logically, that requires the ability to verify a record's authenticity, without sacrificing confidentiality, in those rare instances when authenticity is questioned. Indeed, that is the only way the open records law can work, for if exemptions to the law can be used to protect officials who fabricate records, as well as the fabricated records, then the very mission of the open records law—transparency and accountability—is subverted and stood on its head.

To be sure, the Legislature made no distinction between real and fake records, and that's what the appeals court hung its hat on. But logic and common sense tells us the Legislature probably didn't think it was necessary to make the distinction because it is obvious on its face they are seeking to protect authentic documents. It's absurd to think the Legislature, in constructing a law to further transparency and honesty in government, would insert a provision to encourage and protect fraudulently compiled records.

With the appeals court's decision, however, that distinction evaporated into thin air. The court ruling in effect erected a legal shield behind which government officials can secretly conduct dishonest and malicious activity, and hide it behind an exemption in the open records law.

Now that's irony.

To make this point, consider a situation in which a corporation keeps two sets of books, one the real set of the company's financial activity, and another one a fabricated document for public consumption. Is the latter document legitimate? Is the latter document worthy of legal protection from public scrutiny and even from regulators seeking to ensure accuracy?

The answer, of course, is no, and it was precisely the cooking of books by Enron and others in the late 1990s and early 2000s that caused the nation's financial markets to be ransacked for billions of dollars.

In this case, the appeals judges answered yes to those same questions. They concluded that fabricated documents are not only legitimate records—as legitimate as real ones—but worthy of the same legal protection from public scrutiny, even from court-ordered determinations of their veracity. Such a conclusion renders the open records law useless and meaningless. Or, as Leon Stenz might say, if the authority says it is so, it is so, and so there is no need for an open records law at all.

If anyone should have been disheartened in the wake of that ruling, it should have been public employees. That's because every single one of them is now potentially a victim. There is nothing to prevent an unscrupulous employer who doesn't like an employee from concocting a false record about that employee, without fear of public exposure or even that the employee could defend himself or herself against the allegations.

In effect, the appeals court ruling gave public officials a carte-blanche license to blackball public employees whenever they so choose.

In the case of basketball coach, it didn't succeed. With massive public support, the school board hired him anyway. But what if the negative comments against the coach were fabricated and what if he hadn't gotten the job because of them? The protection of those records would then have allowed the perpetrators of the dishonesty to go unpunished, while the coach would not only have lost a job but be forced to contend with the same smear in the future.

Indeed, he still does. The school district was able to proclaim it has two pages of negative comments about him, but neither the public nor the coach are ever able to see the comments, or to know who reportedly said them or contest their accuracy. Tellingly, in coming to their tortured conclusion, the judges couldn't help but indulge themselves in the very thing they said was irrelevant: the authenticity of the records.

"Even assuming such a standard could be adopted, the result of *Lakeland Times'* proposal would be public disclosure of inaccurate records," the decision stated. "But *Lakeland Times* does not explain the logic of shielding accurate employee records from public scrutiny while authorizing the release of inaccurate or false information."

Instead, the decision stated, it seems the Legislature desired to prohibit the disclosure of all qualifying employee records, regardless of their accuracy or truth. But wouldn't the logic be irrelevant if the accuracy was irrelevant? Since it apparently is relevant—and here the judges inadvertently admitted to the relevance of authentic records—it needs explanation, though it should have been self-evident.

As the Legislature has determined, the protection of accurate but sensitive information protects a public employee's privacy interests when there isn't a compelling public interest in disclosure. To be sure, there's no compelling public interest in publicly impugning a person who got a bad but legitimate reference and who likely didn't get the job anyway.

But, if the reference—or any other such document—isn't legitimate, there becomes a compelling public interest in its release: holding accountable the officials who fabricated it. Dishonest public officials must always be held publicly accountable. The public employee would be likewise served because a bad allegation would be publicly exposed, making it impossible to use against that employee in the future. Employees would not then have to live with the cloud of "negative comments" hanging over their heads.

The release of false documents while protecting accurate ones would only be illogical if the false documents were portrayed as accurate ones when they were released. That, of course, wouldn't be the purpose of compelling their disclosure in the first place—indeed only false documents in that class of records would be released—and the judges knew better.

The court also contended *The Times* failed to propose a workable standard for determining whether a record is truthful and honest.

"Instead, *Lakeland Times* contends the veracity of the quotes in the record lies somewhere on a spectrum between 'verbatim transcript' and 'complete fabrication,'" the decision stated. "What *Lakeland Times* does not tell us is where the line between disclosure and nondisclosure should be drawn on that spectrum."

In short, the judges concluded, *The Lakeland Times* would have the appeals panel remand to the circuit court while giving it virtually no guidance regarding the proper application of the statute.

But again, the guidance should be self-evident. Either the court or a court-ordered third party under a protective order of confidentiality would investigate the claims. Either the person made the comment, as LUHS contends, or the person didn't. Either records are truthful and honest or they are not. How's that for a workable standard for determining whether a record is truthful and honest? How hard can that be?

What became self-evident throughout the decision was the judges' clamor to protect public officials from scrutiny. In so doing, the court made a fundamental error by concluding that a document that falls under a class of excepted records in the open records law is exempt from scrutiny all the time and from everyone.

The court misread the law. To use its own words, it conflates exemption and scrutiny. The law says records are exempt from disclosure; it does not say they are exempt from scrutiny. The two are distinct concepts, and the latter is crucial to determine the applicability of the former.

The school district claimed such an interpretation would lead to endless challenges, but records are rarely exempt, and it is rarer still that significant issues about their authenticity arise. But when they do, as in the LUHS case, then confidential scrutiny by the court is not only warranted but necessary. And if the document is not legitimate, it should fail to qualify for the exception.

Only that interpretation allows for the open records law to work, to both protect the privacy and reputations of public employees while carrying out the statute's commitment to transparency and accountability. The court's decision destroyed the latter and allowed unethical public officials to destroy the former.

In the wake of the Enron scandals more than a decade ago, federal legislation tightened corporate disclosure rules to assure the legitimacy of financial documents. In other words, heightened scrutiny was applied.

In Louisiana, to cite just one example, officials can be sent away for five years for filing false public records, for forging or wrongfully altering documents, or creating documents containing a false statement or false representation of a material fact. Of course, to prove such a crime requires both scrutiny of the records and the disclosure of those found to be false.

Under the appeals court decision in the LUHS case, such accountability is not now possible in Wisconsin because so-called exempted records are exempt any time officials say they are, and no scrutiny or exposure is allowed. The decision should not stand, and public pressure should be brought to bear on the Legislature to fix what is a lethal flaw.

Most of the time we should trust that the records given to requesters are truthful and accurate ones. But, as Ronald Reagan might advise, 'Trust, but verify.'

As Reagan understood, but which the appeals court did not, the ability to verify lies at the heart of open, honest government. That its administrators choose to stand behind a defense that a hiring process must be secret, even if it is corrupt, should scare every citizen.

—

And now, for the most egregious court decision so far, a circuit court decision that would completely redefine what a government meeting actually is, and in such a way that almost any government discussion or action short of a formal vote could take place behind closed doors.

Fortunately, as of this writing, this decision by Oneida County circuit court judge Michael Bloom is still in the appeals court, and the hope is it will not survive closer scrutiny. Let's take a closer look at the walking quorum case filed by Heather Holmes, the general manager of *The Lakeland Times* and *Northwoods River News*, against the city of Rhinelander, the Rhinelander city council, the mayor, and four city council members.

Bear in mind that this case involves open meetings and not open records. Open records complaints are far more common than open meeting violations, as the space devoted to them in this book demonstrates, but it doesn't mean open meetings aren't crucial to transparency. Far from it.

In this case, Holmes appealed a decision by Bloom to dismiss a complaint filed against Rhinelander mayor Chris Frederickson and the four city council members, Andrew Larson, David Holt, Steve Sauer, and Ryan Rossing.

In the complaint, Holmes—and *The Lakeland Times* in a prior complaint—contended that the mayor and council members conducted a series of personal communications, email messages, in-person meetings, and communications leading effectively to the writing and signing of a letter of reprimand to the city council president George Kirby (Kirby has since died), all of which amounted to an illegal walking quorum concerning governmental business without public notice.

Bloom had disagreed, saying Holmes had failed to prove that the contents of the letter referred to "governmental business" or that the letter manifested an agreement among the defendants to take some uniform course of action relative to a proposition that would require a formal vote by the common council, all of which he said was required to prove a walking quorum.

"The subject letter does not discuss or allude to any potential action that would require the vote of the common council to implement," Bloom wrote in his decision.

The lawsuit stemmed from a January 30, 2019, letter signed by Frederickson and the four council members and sent to Kirby. In the letter, the officials questioned Kirby's leadership and promised a forthcoming conversation that "may be uncomfortable." The officials also concluded that Kirby's conduct at a January council meeting did "not reflect the level of leadership" they were looking for from a seasoned, experienced elected official and suggested that he resign "given recent events."

Holmes filed the complaint in circuit court after Oneida County district attorney Michael Schiek declined to prosecute a similar complaint by *The Lakeland Times* and *Northwoods River News* publisher Gregg Walker. Holmes resubmitted the allegation to Schiek as a verified, or notarized, complaint, a statutory necessity to go to court if Schiek again declined to prosecute.

After the district attorney did exactly that, the lawsuit was filed.

After the appeal was announced, Walker said Bloom's decision could not be allowed to stand because it would rewrite the state's open meetings law and destroy a large part of its foundation.

"If allowed to stand, judge Bloom's decision significantly narrows the scope of the law," Walker said. "It legitimizes walking quorums, encourages officials to avoid putting controversial topics on agendas for public discussion, and expands what officials can do when quorums are actually gathered in one place."

Walker said the decision would enable and tempt government officials across the state to use informal communications and sub-quorum-sized meetings to engage in private government actions outside the view of the public.

"Much of what was illegal before is legal now, so long as this decision stands," he said. "Judge Bloom has effectively privatized much of the public's business."

In his decision, Bloom, citing two court cases known as *Conta* and *Showers,* determined that a walking quorum can occur only if it involves a proposition requiring a formal vote before a governmental body, and that the letter the council members sent contemplated no such proposal.

Case law has established two necessary elements for an open meetings violation—there must be a purpose to engage in governmental business, be it discussion, decision, or information gathering; and the number of members present must be sufficient to determine the parent body's course of action regarding the proposal discussed. The standards are even higher for a walking quorum violation, that is, proof is required that a sufficient number of members reached an explicit or tacit agreement to act uniformly relative to some form of "governmental business."

In the decision, Bloom quoted *Showers* to make his point: "When a group of governmental officials gather to engage in formal or informal government business and that group has the potential to determine the outcome of the proposal or proposals being discussed, the public, absent an exception found within the law, has the right to know—fully—the deliberations of that group."

In Bloom's view, that language requires that the proposals being discussed require a formal vote by the governing body.

"Implicit in this reasoning is that the discussions or activity at an alleged 'meeting' or 'series of gatherings'—a 'walking quorum'—must involve some proposition that will ultimately require a formal vote of the governmental body in order to implement," Bloom wrote. "The sufficient numbers prong of the Showers test and the 'walking quorum' test both require that the number of members present at the meeting or involved in the series of gatherings be sufficient to determine the governmental body's course of action on the subject proposition."

In fact, the language Bloom quoted directly contradicted his logic.

That is to say, the *Showers* decision expressly stated that a violation can occur when a majority of the body gathers to engage in either "formal or informal government business" without proper public notice. That begs a question: What can possibly constitute illegal informal government business if the government business being discussed must be formal to be illegal?

Indeed, in Bloom's decision, informal government business doesn't exist, that is to say, Bloom believes that by definition governmental business involves formality, as he makes clear in laying out the questions of the case: "The questions are: 1) whether the suggestion implicates "governmental business" (i.e. some proposition requiring a formal vote by the Common Council to implement); and 2) whether the suggestion manifests an agreement among the defendants to take some uniform course of action relative to such business."

Bloom's belief that a formal vote is an essential element of governmental business would also seem to fly in the face of language in the *Showers* decision that "there must be a purpose to engage in governmental business, be it discussion, decision or information gathering." That language would seem to suggest that mere discussion of governmental matters constitutes governmental business, in addition to formal voting and making a "decision." But in his ruling the judge tried to square that apparent inconsistency by claiming that mere discussion of a government matter only becomes governmental business in certain situations, that is, in situations requiring a formal vote.

"However, Wisconsin's Open Meetings Law does not address officials convening to discuss governmental 'topics,'" Bloom wrote. "Wisconsin's Open Meetings Law does not address officials convening to discuss matters that may be of 'public and governmental interest.' Wisconsin's Open Meetings Law addresses officials convening to discuss governmental business, consistent with the definition of 'meeting' set forth in sec. 19.82(2), Stats. As will be discussed more thoroughly in the next section of this decision, nothing in the subject letter indicates an intention on the part of the signatories to take any formal action ...."

Simply put, in Bloom's view, government officials can gather—either as an outright quorum or in a series of sub-quorum meetings—to discuss any government topic or any matter of public and government interest so long as there is no intention to pursue a formal vote on those matters.

The truth is, Bloom reads more into the *Showers* language than is there because *Showers* never explicitly says that proposals discussed when officials gather must involve a formal vote. Indeed, the logic of the language suggests that when a group of officials gathers to even informally discuss government topics within the governing body's realm of jurisdiction, as well as options for action, "the public, absent an exception found within the law has the right to know—fully—the deliberations of that group."

Bloom's view would seem to suggest that majorities or even entire governing bodies could act in private so long as no formal vote was being considered. For example, could a majority of a county board convene to discuss the future of its highway department—including the possibility of a new facility—so long as no formal vote was proposed, or no specific proposal discussed? Could an entire town board privately compose, sign, and send a letter to Congress, affixing their official titles and districts next to their names —as those signing the Kirby letter did—opposing wolf delisting or the impeachment of the president simply because the members decided to do so without taking the matter to a vote as an official town policy?

The public has the right to know about such deliberations. The public has a right to know when a government body, or a quorum of one, gathers to discuss new buildings, or, say, options for taxation. And the public has the right to know about officially signed letters staking out positions on topics related to the governing body's jurisdiction, whether it is about highway departments, or wolf management, or about the job evaluation of a council president by a majority of the city council and its mayor.

Otherwise, government officials at all levels will be incentivized to not bring important public matters before governing bodies for a vote because, if they withhold doing so, they can gather in private to discuss those matters and even take action. Such cannot possibly be the intent of the open meetings law.

In his decision, Bloom did find language in another court case, known as *Conta,* that referred to the need for a formal vote by a governing body to trigger a violation. Indeed, Bloom targeted the plaintiff's own language in her brief opposing the defendants' motion to dismiss when the brief quoted *Conta* as follows: "[q]uorum gatherings should be presumed to be in violation of the law, due to a quorum's ability to thereafter call, compose and control *by vote* [emphasis added] a formal meeting of a governmental body."

To Bloom, the words "by vote" are critical.

"This necessarily requires that the subject of the alleged meeting or series of discussions involve some form of proposed action that would require a formal vote of the governmental body in order to implement," he wrote.

However, Bloom omitted vital information from his reading of the *Conta* case that rendered his viewpoint null and void. While *Conta* does say that "the appearance of a quorum could be avoided by separate meetings of two or more groups, each less than quorum size, who agree through mutual representatives to act and vote uniformly," it also says that the appearance of a quorum could be avoided in another, less formal way.

According to *Conta*, the deception could also be orchestrated "by a decision by a group of less than quorum size which has the tacit agreement and acquiescence of other members sufficient to reach a quorum."

In that independent clause there is no mention of a vote, only of a decision by a small group (such as two council members and the mayor discussing and editing and signing a letter to Kirby) who then attained the tacit agreement and acquiescence of other members (two other council members acquiescing in signing the letter) sufficient to reach a quorum.

"Such elaborate arrangements, if factually discovered, are an available target for the prosecutor under the simple quorum rule," the *Conta* decision states.

Moreover, Bloom's decision narrowing the scope of "governmental business" only to those proposals requiring a formal vote conflicts with the state Department of Justice's view of public business, which in its training sessions on transparency defines governmental business in much broader terms.

"'Conducting governmental business' is an expansive concept that is not limited to formal or final decision making," the DOJ training states, expressly contradicting Bloom. "'Conducting governmental business' includes: preliminary decisions, discussion, information gathering."

Indeed, Bloom is trying to significantly narrow the scope of the open meetings law contrary to the intent of the Legislature. Until now, as DOJ training makes clear, governmental business applied to informal actions and information gatherings and discussion of any government matter within the jurisdiction of a governing body, not just those matters for which a formal vote is pending, and the DOJ open meetings compliance manual also interprets *Showers's* definition of governmental business as "any formal or informal action, including discussion, decision or information gathering, on matters within the governmental body's realm of authority."

In other words, discussion and information gathering and other actions don't become government business only when they are actually put on an agenda for discussion and possible action but when they involve any matter that is within a governing body's realm of jurisdiction—both broad matters that might conceivably come before the body for discussion and action in more specific form and those that should go before the body for discussion and action.

That was exactly the situation in the walking quorum case—a letter by the council majority and the mayor effectively censuring Kirby's conduct and suggesting he resign should have come before the board. The public had a right to know that a council majority and the mayor was condemning the council president and effectively calling for his resignation. That they decided not to bring their conclusions to the board in public session should not and cannot relieve them of their legal responsibility to do so.

Such a decision rewrites the law. Now, unless an actual vote is looming, Bloom has severed all information gathering and discussion from the open meetings requirements. That cannot possibly comport with the policy of the state that the public is entitled to the fullest and most complete information regarding the affairs of government.

In addition, the newspaper took issue with Bloom's conclusion that the letter did not represent any agreement by the defendants to take any proposed action, or did anything more than ask questions.

"The letter does not specifically request or demand that Kirby do anything," Bloom wrote. "The letter does not threaten Kirby. The letter does not indicate that, unless Kirby does some act desired by the defendants, the defendants will take some stated course of action against Kirby. The letter merely asks Kirby to ponder his role as council president in light of the events at the January 28 meeting. In the court's judgment, provocative though it may be, the suggestion in the letter that Kirby ponder 'not continuing' as council president does not implicate 'governmental business' insofar as it does not get at any proposition that would require a formal vote by the common council to implement."

Bloom also noted that the words 'reprimand and 'censure' never appear in the letter. But the newspaper said Bloom's view was flawed because the letter itself was the uniform action taken.

"The decision implicating government business was the decision to compose, sign, and send the letter in the first place, with all the defendants identifying themselves officially by signing the letter as council members with their district numbers," the newspaper stated.

The newspaper also said the letter did far more than ask questions, as Bloom contended, but rendered a judgment of Kirby's performance as council president, writing that Kirby's conduct "does not reflect the level of leadership we are looking for from a seasoned, experienced elected official, such as yourself."

"The word 'reprimand' does not have to be used for there to be a reprimand, just as one would not have to use the word 'praise' to actually praise someone's work by calling it commendable," the newspaper contended. "Call it a reprimand, censure, or job evaluation, a majority of the council is rebuking the council president, and they go on to suggest he resign. That's a discussion that the public has a right to be involved in. It's a no-brainer."

Not only did the letter contain a discussion that should have been on an agenda, the very decision to send the letter should have been on the agenda. After all, the common council has the ultimate authority over the council president. Thus, the public is entitled to discussions about matters involving their judgment of the council president's conduct. Yet, the defendants admittedly decided to act in private to avoid that public discussion.

And that's an absurd outcome.

To wit, according to the judge, they can't legally pre-determine in private the outcome of a public vote, but if they just refuse to schedule a public vote, they can indeed determine that very same action in private. Somehow, in judge Bloom's mind, they can avoid breaking the open meetings law by breaking the open meetings law.

The cases above, and especially the walking quorum case, is a case study demonstrating both how good-old-boy politics still dominates in the halls of justice and how the state's activist judges are, case by case, rewriting the state's open meetings and open records laws.

But Bloom's decision has to rank as one of the worst ever, a serious blight upon judicial sensibility. It should be said that all of us at the newspaper thought the judge had a conflict of interest in hearing the case, either real or perceived. From the outset, nobody on our side wanted either of Oneida County's judges to hear the case, but we could only substitute one of them. Bloom could have done the honorable thing and recused himself, given his life-long connections to Rhinelander, if not to some of the defendants. We wonder, too, if, as an officer of the court, he interacted in prior cases involving Ryan Rossing, when Rossing worked for the sheriff's department.

Even if no real conflict of interest existed, there was certainly the appearance of one, but Bloom chose not to give up his seat in the good-old-boy lounge. In any event, Bloom took it upon himself to exonerate five men whose admitted aim was to keep a very serious discussion about the future of Rhinelander council president George Kirby out of the public eye—in reality a confession that should have been all Bloom needed to at least deny dismissal of the charges and to let the case proceed to trial.

Remember, the judge dismissed the case rather than let the parties argue the case on its merits. He took it upon himself to short-circuit a comprehensive arguing of why the defendants were guilty, and he did so in a way that could gravely injure the entire open meetings law.

As to the decision itself, first there is the absurd conclusion that government business isn't really government business unless it involves a specific proposal requiring a vote by a governing body. In this larger realm, Bloom is trying to rewrite the substance of the entire open meetings law, expanding by a frontier's reach what government officials can do behind closed doors.

Case law lays out what a meeting under the open meetings law is—there must be a purpose to engage in governmental business, be it discussion, decision or information gathering. Bloom rewrites that to add the requirement of a formal vote, which I put in italics: "There must be a purpose to engage in governmental business, be it discussion, decision or information gathering *that will ultimately require a formal vote of the governmental body in order to implement.*"

The problem is, that's not what the case law says, and it's not what the statute says, either. Here's the statutory definition of a meeting: "'Meeting' means the convening of members of a governmental body for the purpose of exercising the responsibilities, authority, power or duties delegated to or vested in the body."

The word 'vote' isn't in there, and clearly a governmental body can engage in governmental business—exercising its responsibilities, authority, power or duties—in many ways in addition to formally voting.

But don't take my word, or the DOJ's word, for how broad that makes the concept of government business. The Wisconsin Bar Association also defines it broadly: "If a governmental body meets to discuss an issue, make a decision, or gather information about a subject related to a governmental body's realm of authority, the purpose of the gathering is to conduct governmental business."

Note that making information gathering and discussing issues is separate and apart from decision making [discuss an issue [*or*] make a decision *or* gather information], meaning decision making is not required to make a meeting governmental business.

And, finally, there is an attorney general's 1982 opinion that a Senate Special Committee on Reapportionment likely violated the open meetings law in 1981 when it did not post a meeting even though "there was never any intention prior to the gathering to attempt to debate any matter of policy, to reach agreement on differences, to make any decisions on any bill or part thereof, to take any votes, or to resolve substantive differences" and in fact during the meeting none of that occurred.

So even though there was no formal vote and nothing discussed that required a formal vote, a violation likely occurred, according to the attorney general. We could cite other examples but the point is clear: Bloom simply waded into waters far over his head, and issued an opinion of breathtaking incompetence.

It legitimizes walking quorums and encourages officials to avoid putting controversial topics on agendas for public discussion. After all, why put a matter on an agenda, making it formal and thus subjecting officials to open meetings violations if they collude before that meeting, when not putting the matter on an agenda or pursuing a vote relieves those officials of guilt if they collude in private.

Here's how absurd it is: According to Bloom, the Rhinelander defendants would not be guilty of a walking quorum by writing a letter of reprimand because there was no existing proposal requiring a vote to officially reprimand the council president. So a council majority and the mayor can get together, in a series of sub-quorum meetings, and sign a letter of rebuke and call for the council president's resignation, and there's no violation because, in judge Bloom's mind, that's not government business.

But, if they put on an agenda an item for the council to send the same letter to the council president, and then before the meeting a council majority and the mayor get together, in a series of sub-quorum meetings, and agree to vote to send the letter of rebuke, well, then there is a violation because that is government business.

Except for putting the item on an agenda, the facts and the collusion are the same in each scenario. The only difference is that in the first scenario, hiding what you're actually doing from the public protects you—you can avoid breaking the open meetings law by breaking the open meetings law, you get a get-out-of-jail free card.

So why would officials put things on agendas if they can just carry out government business in secrecy?

In Bloom's world, the public is shut off from ever more discussion about government topics that affect them. All this is so much nonsense, and I suspect Bloom knows it. I suspect he just threw a sop to his good-old-boy buddies. Maybe not, but if this is what he really thinks, Oneida County's justice system is a lot scarier than we thought. And it has put the entire open records law in the state in jeopardy.

Chapter 9

Consequences

At the end of the day, the only way to combat the growing resistance to open government is to rewrite, modernize, and strengthen the law, and then make those who intentionally violate the statutes suffer serious legal consequences.

Ideally, the solution would be to substantially increase the penalties for intentional violations, and to criminalize some infractions. Right now, penalties are laughably weak to nonexistent; for instance, an open meetings violation is simply a forfeiture of between $25 and $300.

For records, any authority or legal custodian who arbitrarily and capriciously denies or delays response to a request or charges excessive fees may be required to forfeit not more than $1,000, though I have never heard of such a penalty being levied. In addition, a public records infraction may involve criminal penalties only for destruction, damage, removal, or concealment of public records with intent to injure or defraud, or for altering or falsifying public records.

All other infractions involve civil forfeitures.

Those laws should be amended so that capricious withholding of records or the intentional charging of excessive fees, or intentionally violating the open meetings laws, carry criminal rather than civil penalties, with the most serious infractions automatically classified as felony misconduct in office.

Because that's exactly what it is.

Sadly, there's no chance in today's anti-transparency environment that such amendments to the law will happen. That leaves one other deterrent: you, you, and you—all of us.

That's a glimmer of hope, too, because in the past few years we have seen the citizenry rise up, both locally and statewide, to demand clean and open government. When then Gov. Walker and the Legislature tried to effectively repeal the entire open records law, the public rebelled with such furor that they backed down.

We have seen such avidity on the local level, too, where citizens have engaged to open up and clean up their town governments. To cite just one example, and a model one at that, in Boulder Junction, up in Vilas County, citizens took a stand over several years to change the way their town government worked. Such citizen leaders as Jeff Long, Barbara Boston, Laura Bertch, and others deserve kudos for rallying their fellow citizens for change and openness.

It's a story worth telling—how citizens on the most grassroots level can force their elected leaders to abide by the rules of transparency, and how they can boot them from office if they don't. It's a story every Wisconsin citizen—and especially advocates for open government—should hear. It's a story of how, if our lawmakers won't change the laws that need to be changed, citizens can change the lawmakers.

But it's also a cautionary tale because it demonstrates the lack of mechanisms that aggrieved citizens and taxpayers have even when officials are found to be guilty.

Let's head to the Junction.

—

Ultimately, in a Boulder Junction open meetings case, it was *The Lakeland Times* that filed a complaint in 2017 with the Vilas County district attorney's office concerning what appeared to be an improper payout of almost $9,000 to the town clerk and another smaller payout to a town employee, a decision that was made in violation of the open meetings law.

I write that in the passive tense because, in all honesty, *The Times* really was a passive actor in the case. The actual heroes of the story were a long-time former town chairman of Boulder Junction, Jeff Long—who spent years building a stellar reputation for his town and for town government before stepping down from his position and from the town board—and Barbara Boston, a community activist who had served in various capacities in the town, including sitting on its economic development board.

One day, the husband-and-wife duo showed up at the newspaper with a tale to tell. In their view, there were potential ethics violations and other possible statutory infractions, including misconduct in public office, by the town board concerning two payouts, one to then town clerk Kendra Moraczewski and another, smaller one to another town employee. The board paid Moraczewski $8,700 for accumulated unused sick days and vacation days; it paid the other employee for five unused sick days.

But, Long and Boston argued, by the actual language of the ordinance, Moraczewski had only 41 sick days—77 days short of the days she needed to collect what she did. The ordinance also made no provision of paying out unused vacation days during employment, though it was not clear whether past practice had allowed it.

The board passed a motion to compensate Moraczewski "per policy." The problem is, as Long and Boston explained it and which the newspaper later relayed to the Vilas County district attorney, Martha Milanowski, under the plain language of the town ordinance, Moraczewski would be entitled to no payout, raising the serious issue of whether the town misallocated tax dollars in improper compensation.

Long and Boston had done their homework. They had also argued their case locally and repeatedly at the town level before turning to the newspaper. As they explained it to us, the town's ordinance for clerk/treasurer was perfectly clear: "Sick leave benefits—Sick leave benefits will be the same as those for Town's other full-time employees. The Clerk/Treasurer will be given one sick day per month per year, accumulative to 60 days. Once 60 days have accumulated, any excess of those days can be turned into a cash payment either to an investment plan, or directly to the Clerk/Treasurer, the same as the Town's other full-time employees."

First and foremost, Moraczewski had not accumulated 60 days, Long and Boston demonstrated. At the end of August 2016, she had worked only 41 months, collecting 41 sick days. She thus did not qualify for a payout.

Even so, the town board at the time somehow calculated that Moraczewski had accumulated 58 days, equal to the $8,700 the town paid her, based on her pay rate. However, as the newspaper's complaint to Milanowski pointed out, that still would not qualify for a payout according to the town's ordinance, yet the motion that passed stated the vote was "to compensate clerk/treasurer for paid time off (sick/vacation days) earned but not used as per policy."

And that wasn't all, Long and Boston told us.

"The town added up 58 days by including vacation days as part of the ordinance," the newspaper's complaint stated. "Vacation days are not part of the pay-out language, only sick days are, and nowhere does the ordinance specify a payout for vacation days."

Finally, and perhaps most seriously, the town's calculations and the motion assumed that Moraczewski could cash in all of her unused days. *The Times* even made the same assumption in its calculations in one of its stories, but the assumption wasn't accurate, as Long and Boston pointed out to us, and which we corrected in the complaint to Milanowski.

"The policy clearly allows, once 60 days have been accumulated, a cash out of *'any excess of those days,'*" the complaint stated. "Thus an employee with 65 accumulated sick days could take a cash payment of five days. To be paid for 58 days, as Moraczewski was, would require her to accumulate 118 days, when she in fact had only 41," the newspaper stated.

Even including unused vacation days and using the town's calculations would have left Moraczewski three days short of any payout (and if she had those three days she could only be paid for one) and 60 short of a 58-day payout. So, under the black-and-white language of the town ordinance, Moraczewski was entitled to no payment, much less a 58-day payout, and the same went with the payout to the other employee, the newspaper wrote in the complaint.

Ah, yes, all well and good, but what does this have to do with transparency, readers might be asking. Well, long story short, the town board discussed the payouts in closed session prior to voting on their approval in open session.

"We believe this to be an egregious misuse of taxpayer dollars in violation of the town ordinance, and it is even more egregious that these actions, especially the payout to Moraczewski, was discussed, calculated, and determined in closed session, without any public input or oversight," publisher Gregg Walker wrote in the complaint.

According to a later Vilas County sheriff's office report, board members voted to go into closed session on the morning of September 8, 2016. The purpose of the closed session, per the meeting minutes, was to consider employee compensation. The closed session went on for more than two hours, finally adjourning at 12:25 p.m.

"Upon returning to open session, a motion was made by (Dennis) McGann and seconded by (Dennis) Duke, 'to compensate clerk/treasurer for paid time off (sick/vacation) days earned but not used per policy,'" the complaint stated.

The closed session during which the town board discussed and approved the payout was illegal not least because the open-meetings-law exemption for discussing public-employee compensation does not include elected officials. Specifically, the exemption cited was that which allows governmental entities to convene in closed session to consider "employment promotion, compensation or performance evaluation data of any public employee over which the governmental body has jurisdiction or exercises responsibility."

According to the state's open meetings compliance guide, elected officials such as town clerks are not public employees for purposes of the exemption because the town board does not have jurisdictional powers over them, including the power to hire and fire them.

"The attorney general's office has interpreted this exemption to extend to public officers, such as a police chief, whom the governmental body has jurisdiction to employ," the compliance manual states. "The attorney general's office has also concluded that this exemption is sufficiently broad to authorize convening in closed session to interview and consider applicants for positions of employment."

But a town clerk would not qualify.

"An elected official is not considered a 'public employee over which the governmental body has jurisdiction or exercises responsibility,'" the manual states. "Thus, (the exemption) does not authorize a county board to convene in closed session to consider appointments of county board members to a county board committee."

The compliance manual was referring to a 1987 attorney general's opinion concerning a specific county board issue, but, as that opinion made clear, the reasoning would apply to all elected officials.

What's more, even if Moraczewski had been eligible, the closed session would not have been justified, for the exemption applies only to discussions of compensation based on individual performance and circumstances, not to any general policy related to compensation that would apply to any employee meeting the criteria.

"The apparent purpose of the exemption is to protect individual employees from having their actions and abilities discussed in public and to protect governmental bodies 'from potential lawsuits resulting from open discussion of sensitive information,'" the compliance manual states. "It is not the purpose of the exemption to protect a governmental body when it discusses general policies that do not involve identifying specific employees."

As such, discussing compensation of an employee based on that employee's job performance and capabilities could be held in closed session, while a discussion of whether an employee had met the terms of a general payout policy, such as in Boulder Junction—a policy that is the same for all employees and not based on individual actions and abilities—should presumably be held in open session.

Indeed, the compliance manual states, closed sessions should be held only rarely.

"The policy of the open meetings law dictates that the exemption be invoked sparingly and only where necessary to protect the public interest," the manual states. "If there is any doubt as to whether closure is permitted under a given exemption, the governmental body should hold the meeting in open session."

Finally, compensation for town elected officials is set by electors at the annual town meeting, an open session by its very definition. Under state law, town electors can delegate that responsibility to the town board, but it would be counterintuitive for the board to be able to set that compensation in closed session when the delegating authority could not. Still, in this case, the closed session was called not to set compensation but to apply it to a particular public employee—an elected official who did not qualify for the exemption.

The board also met in closed session on August 30, 2016, to approve payment to the other employee for five sick days not taken, and, the newspaper stated in its complaint, while that employee would be a public employee for purposes of the exemption, the board was still only discussing whether he met the established criteria for a payout—the amount of accumulated days—not any of his capabilities or job performance. Such a discussion should have been held in open session, the newspaper argued.

To her credit, Milanowski filed a formal complaint after the Vilas County sheriff's department investigated the matter, and, after initially indicating they would like to have their day in court, the town supervisors who had been charged admitted their guilt.

According to the court order in the case, signed by Vilas County circuit court judge Neal A. Nielsen, because the vote approving the compensation "per policy" was based on illegal deliberations in closed session, the vote was deemed to be void. Town chairman Dennis Reuss and then supervisors Denny McGann and Dennis Duke acknowledged in a stipulation they had broken the law.

But here's the thing. The stipulation and order did not include any forfeitures for violating the law, though Milanowski had asked for forfeitures in her formal complaint. According to the court order, it was too legally complicated.

"In light of the context of the actions and the complicated statutory/ordinance/regulatory framework in which the actions were taken, no forfeiture will be levied against the individual defendants," the stipulation states.

That framework includes a 1996 ordinance to "establish and define the position and duties of the office of Boulder Junction town clerk/treasurer" and an earlier vote by town electors to combine the positions of clerk and treasurer. The ordinance also required the position to perform, in addition to statutory duties, "office administration and service to the public, which are ones that must be coordinated and communicated with the Town Board's involvement."

According to the stipulation, the town board members maintained they had no intention to violate the open meetings law. Of the three, two continued to serve on the town board. So no punishment for the violators. But what about the money paid to Moraczewski?

Turns out, there was no mechanism to get that repaid, either.

In her complaint, Milanowski asked for a nullification of the compensation vote—the approval of the payout—on the grounds that the public interest in voiding the action outweighed the public interest in sustaining it. Specifically, the complaint alleged that the action taken posed a fiscal impact to the citizens of Boulder Junction.

But, while the order and stipulation voided the board's vote to approve the payout to Moraczewski, as Milanowski had urged, it made no mention about the repayment of the money. Ultimately, the money was repaid through paycheck deductions.

And there was one other thing. In her complaint, Milanowski had also asked for public disclosure of the discussion and decision made in closed session.

"Plaintiff also requests that the court award equitable relief, pursuant to (state statutes), by ordering that the discussions and decisions made on September 8, 2016, in closed session that violated the open meetings law be disclosed to the public," the complaint urged.

Such a disclosure, Milanowski stated, would best fulfill the open meetings law's purpose of fostering an informed electorate where the public is entitled to the fullest and most complete information regarding the affairs of government.

"In the present case, the public should have access to the board's discussions and decisions made in this closed session since it would have otherwise been entitled to hear them if the board had properly followed Wisconsin's open meetings law," the complaint states.

However, in the end, such disclosure was not mentioned in the stipulation and order. So let's sum up.

One, the Boulder Junction town board broke the open meetings law when it convened a closed session to consider the compensation of an elected official, namely, the town's clerk/treasurer, and decided to pay her $8,700 that she wasn't entitled to.

Two, because they made that decision based on illegal closed session deliberations, the vote to pay her was deemed null and void.

Three, the town board members who broke the law suffered no consequences for doing so, and there was no apparent legal mechanism to compel the recapture of illegally disbursed funds. That latter fact is a major concern, though one not relevant to the open meetings discussion. As it was,

$8,700 in taxpayer money was removed illegally from the town treasury, and that should have been a prosecutable offense.

At the newspaper, we wondered why Milanowski did not insist that the defendants stipulate to repaying or retrieving the money for the town as a consequence of the illegal disbursement. We believe that should have been part of the deal, and we believe there should have been consequences and fines if they failed to do so or were unable to reclaim or repay the money.

In the context of open government, though, the town board members should have had to pay forfeitures for the open meetings infraction itself, though Milanowski let them off the hook. We believed forfeitures were warranted because there were aggravating circumstances surrounding the entire incident.

For instance, the public was asked to believe that the supervisors were simply ignorant of the law because of a complicated ordinance framework. 'No, no,' they proclaim, 'we didn't mean to violate the law.' Yet we are taught from early on that ignorance of the law is no excuse, and especially that should be the case for elected officials. And it is especially incumbent upon government officials to know the open meetings law, and to suffer consequences when they violate it.

In addition, not only was the closed session (and thus the vote) illegal but the board members failed to amend the town budget to accommodate the payment, something they would have been obliged to do even if a payout had been legitimately forthcoming and the vote had been legal.

What's more, Moraczewski was not even entitled to any payout because she had not accumulated the needed days (60) to qualify, and, not only that, but according to the plain language of the ordinance, she would have had to accumulate 60 more days than she had to get the payout of $8,700 that she received. In all this, the public was asked to believe that the board members were incapable of reading the clear black-and-white language of the law when they agreed to such an unconscionable payout. Perhaps, but I believe it smacked of official misconduct of the highest order. Sadly, the court let these officials off without consequences and without even an overt stipulation to return the illegal disbursement.

What it all boils down to is, the lack of consequences screams out to other towns and officials to go ahead and break the law. Without any consequences, officials may continue to act in the same brazen fashion as in the past, and, even worse, officials in other towns are also encouraged to break the law, too, if no one is going to be held accountable.

After all, what's the worse that can happen? A little bad press?

As I have written, the Legislature's hatred of transparency makes passing laws to provide for serious consequences all but impossible, but what's very possible is to form a grassroots movement to demand commitment to openness as an almost-litmus test of support, if you will. If the lawmakers won't change the law, the people must change the lawmakers.

Again, Boulder Junction is instructive, for that is just what they did. They cleaned house and got rid of the worst offenders in subsequent elections. The people of Boulder Junction did not let the court decree become a hollow victory, an infraction in name only that allowed those officials to continue to behave in the same way and to serve in official capacities.

In Boulder Junction, the legal system found those supervisors guilty, but it did not hold them accountable. That was left to the people of the town, and they came through, a role model for the state.

Now it's up to the people of the state to do the same thing in the Legislature.

It won't be an easy task, to be sure. With a few notable exceptions, state lawmakers are hostile to reforming the open government laws. Meanwhile their opponents in the next election, no matter which party, shout from the rafters how committed to open government they are. If they happen to be elected, history tells us they will be just as anti-transparent as their predecessors, and perhaps more so.

Rinse and repeat. It goes on and on. Little wonder that most voters just chuck transparency as a campaign issue because it has proven totally unreliable as a gauge of where a person really stands on openness. For one thing, candidates for office aren't afraid to lie about their open government positions because they figure voters don't give a rip in the first place. And, to use a hypothetical example, asking an anti-union stalwart to vote for Tony Evers because Scott Walker wasn't a friend of open records would never work as a strategy.

There's not an easy way out of this bramble, but once again Boulder Junction points the way. It's not that open government needs to be a litmus test issue, it just needs to be one of the central issues on the table to consider, rescued from its second-class status. And it doesn't mean transparency candidates have to be victorious overnight.

In Boulder Junction, transparency was just one issue in a larger complex of issues, including fiscal responsibility, the organization of government, and town priorities and future direction. The difference was, it was an important issue, rewoven into the fabric of core electoral considerations.

Boston and Long, too, worked for years without winning on every point right away. Their own frustrations, in fact, led them to the newspaper. And Boston herself was defeated in a run for town board, before reform candidates in the next election secured victory.

Clearing your way out of a bramble requires exactly two things: Knowing which of the vines are the important ones to always keep, and which to cut away, and perseverance. Barbara Boston and Jeff Long and their fellow citizens demonstrated both those qualities, with a touch of tenacity thrown in.

—

Once the Legislature is recombobulated, and lawmakers enact exacting penalties for breaking the law, an entirely new component is needed to ensure that there are indeed consequences for doing so.

That component would be a new administrative process by which citizens can pursue open records and open meetings complaints outside of taking the complaint to the local district attorney. The problem with filing complaints with district attorneys is that they are notoriously deficient in pursuing the prosecution of those complaints. Most often they refuse to prosecute, and, even when they do, they offer nothing more than a slap on the wrist, or no penalty at all besides bad press, as the case in Boulder Junction demonstrates. With heavier penalties and less discretion in the law, the likeliest outcome without a new administrative process is even fewer prosecutions.

Yes, citizens can already take their complaints to the state attorney general if the district attorney provides no satisfaction, but the odds there are like winning a million dollars in a slot machine. All of which begs the question: Why don't district attorneys prosecute these cases, many of which are rather serious?

Part of the answer is that they are simply overworked, and open records and open meetings complaints aren't high on their priority list. They should be, but they are not. Another reason, and one that I find to be much more common, is that district attorneys are traditionally part of a county's good-old-boy network, which runs especially deep in the local courthouse.

In Oneida County (the county I am most familiar with, but believe me there are stories like these in most counties) a long line of district attorneys—it's so unfair to all of them to single out any one of them—have so distorted the law to exempt the county's good old boys from their provisions that they have all but transformed it into a funhouse mirror.

There have been some real laughers. One time, the DA covered for a good-old-boy supervisor who apparently destroyed public records and otherwise wouldn't give requested records up because he said they were available elsewhere. The district attorney thought that was pretty good reasoning and concluded that an official didn't have to release requested records if you could get them by asking somebody else for them. So, if more than one official had a record, every official could just say it was available elsewhere, and nobody would ever have to turn any records over.

Brilliant! It takes a very special district attorney to think that way.

Then there was the time the Oneida County district attorney's office arrested a person twice—not once but twice—for a crime the person did not commit, due to an error by an assistant district attorney. That wasn't about open records, but it was buffoonery of the highest order, and so the DA properly rewarded the prosecutor who wrongly charged the person more than $1,500 in bonus pay shortly after the assistant mistakenly filed the erroneous charges for the second time.

Settle back with hot cocoa and get ready for more. Another time *The Lakeland Times* filed an open meetings complaint against members of the county's Labor Relations & Employee Services Committee for improperly discussing routine benefits issues in closed session, and for discussing an open records request made by *The Times* without putting that discussion on the agenda.

After *The Lakeland Times* filed the open meetings complaint, the Oneida County district attorney found that the committee had indeed violated the law. Pretty neat, eh? Except that the committee chairman only had to pay a forfeiture of $25. Beyond that, the DA ordered all county board members to attend a training seminar on compliance with the state's open meetings laws.

As *The Times* reported at the time, the minutes of the closed session held during the meeting of the committee indicated that the committee engaged in routine leave-of-absence and policy discussions. It sounds pretty minor, and no doubt it was, but the problem with allowing such infractions to go nearly unpunished is that it encourages future infractions and routine violations. It just becomes second nature to go into closed session and discuss anything, and that leads to more serious infractions.

Yeah, but someone might say, at least the district attorney ordered everybody to undergo training and for all county supervisors, not just those on the committee. Right?

Well, yeah, but about that training ....

According to the settlement, the training seminar would be provided by a third party at the county's designation. That was a mistake, maybe one of those mistakes that were "accidentally on purpose," for it allowed the good old boys of Oneida County to choreograph a game of theatrics, staged to show the public just how open and transparent they were, or wanted to be.

Since they could hire whomever they wanted, the county hired attorney Lori Lubinsky, a lawyer who was a partner with Axley Brynelson. The problem was, Lubinsky was a well known defender of local governments and a well known opponent of transparency. Lubinksy represented municipal corporations and school districts on a variety of legal issues, including open records cases, according to the firm's website. She was a lead attorney for the county in a *Times'* case against the Oneida County sheriff's department, as *The Times* fought to obtain the investigatory files of a former deputy. The county lost that case and agreed to pay total costs and fees of $52,645.38.

In the case, the newspaper repeatedly warned the county it would lose, but the county dug in its heels, based on advice from corporation counsel Brian Desmond and the outside legal team, of which Lubinsky was a lead member. They did lose, of course, but their case was really doomed after they changed their minds about some of the records they had denied, and decided they were public records after all. They toasted their own case with an admission that robbed all the records of any serious legal exemption.

Lubinsky also defended the county in 2004 in an open records case filed by *The Times* against then corporation counsel Larry Heath. *The Times* settled that case out of court, with the county agreeing to pay more than $6,000 in legal fees to the newspaper.

Because of Lubinsky's career pattern and her history in Oneida County, *Lakeland Times* publisher Gregg Walker asked the district attorney to reject Lubinsky's role in the training. However, the district attorney said he had no authority to do so.

"I reviewed the agreement after I got off the phone, the agreement provides that the training will be provided by a third party at the county's designation," he wrote to Walker. "Ms. Lubinsky was designated to give the training. I am unable to renegotiate that agreement."

The district attorney said he understood Walker's concerns and was told by Lubinsky that the prepared materials had been reviewed and approved by attorney Phil Freeburg with the UW Extension Local Government Center.

But hiring Lubinsky was like hiring the fox to guard the henhouse.

"The same attorney has been around for more than a decade representing the interests of closed government, and more than once in Oneida County," Walker pointed out. "And now they are going to teach the county board about openness? It's a sham. Oneida County should be embarrassed, and voters should be outraged."

At the training, county board chairman Dave Hintz sounded completely authentic. He went on about how Lubinsky had raised the board's awareness, and pledged that better awareness and a right attitude would help Oneida County in the future.

Lubinsky sounded pretty good, too. But, as it turned out, her "training" guide was about as sound as the advice she and her team of lawyers gave the sheriff's department. In other words, the Titanic could float better than that boat: Lubinsky was sailing a ship full of supervisors right to the bottom of the open meetings sea. When it came to defining a meeting, for example, Lubinsky correctly noted that you need to have a majority of members of a governmental body present to have a noticeable meeting, and that it still wasn't really a government meeting unless you conducted government business.

Shades of Michael Bloom there, but let's keep going. So that means a majority of a committee can hang out together in a bar, or have lunch, and they don't have to post the meeting; they just have to not discuss any public business. OK. But she completely left out the part where those social gatherings are by law presumed to be official meetings subject to posting requirements. And it's on the shoulders of those government officials to prove no public business or discussion went on if someone challenged their little social gathering at the Good Old Boys Pub.

Without warning supervisors of that legal presumption, Lubinsky led county officials down yet another primrose path, almost encouraging them to socialize without worry of telling the public. That could have opened the board to legal challenges and violations.

It's even worse advice if you are an open government advocate. Just how long do you think it will take the good old boys to realize—if they don't have to post social gatherings—that they can start holding social gatherings that are really designed to conduct secret government business? The problem is not the occasional lunch between two board members or attending a wedding; stuff like that is always going to happen. The problem comes with contrived social gatherings—holiday parties, periodic social lunches, weekly drinks at the pub —routine "social gatherings" by a government body that become an excuse to conduct business.

Who isn't going to start talking about things if such periodic meetings are held? And, despite what Lubinsky said, that honest officials will say, 'Hey, we can't talk about this,' talking is the very reason those social gatherings would be held. They shouldn't be held, at least not routinely, and, if they are, they should be posted to keep government officials honest.

Lubinsky also advised only posting the statute number and language for the reason a government body can convene in closed session, though often that simply will not give the public any meaningful information about what is being discussed.

Incredibly, during the same meeting Lubinsky was playing pretend, the county board scheduled a possible closed session for "Section 19.85(1)(g), Conferring with legal counsel concerning strategy to be adopted by the governmental body with respect to litigation in which it is or is likely to become involved." Now, is that enough information to know what is really being discussed? No, but if the county had followed Lubinsky's advice, that's all the information there would have been.

Fortunately, the county, to its credit, went further and listed the case and the issue at hand: Oneida County Case No. 16-CV-21; Child Support Legal Procedures-Stipulations and Orders.

Lubinsky had a handout for the board, but, for my money, the county board should have just tossed the handouts and distributed as required reading the state Department of Justice compliance manual. I wonder why Lubinksy didn't do that herself, unless there were things in there she didn't want supervisors to see. The bottom line is, when the LRES committee violated the law, the district attorney allowed the county to stage an anti-open government demonstration camouflaged as training.

And that's not all.

In another remarkable case, only a month after Lubinksy's training session, this time involving generic meeting agenda items, the district attorney again allowed open government infractions to go unpunished. He once again allowed government officials to evade accountability. In this case, the district attorney added a twist. The county board broke the law, he said, but not in a way that would require any consequences—that's par for the course—but, on top of that, he concluded that they didn't really break the law, after all.

Say what?

Well, first, there's the issue of the basic violation, an illegal generic agenda item on the county board's March agenda called 'other business,' without any specific topics mentioned, which the attorney general has said is not specific enough by itself to satisfy the notice requirements of the law.

No problem here; the district attorney agreed that it was "inherently insufficient" under the state's open meetings law. But, of course, he added, there's no reason to fine anybody because a county ordinance forced them to put the generic 'other business' item on the agenda, and they had done so since 2008.

That is, except for the April meeting following the aforementioned March session. The board dispensed with the item in April because supervisors were getting ready to change the county ordinance to get rid of what was now viewed as a legally insufficient posting requirement. The only problem was, in April they had yet to delete the requirement from the ordinance. So they had put 'other business' on agendas for years to obey the county ordinance, but suddenly they took it off agendas before they actually changed the county's ordinance.

There are multiple problems with this sort of thinking.

First, the county could have satisfied both the ordinance requirement to put the item on the agenda and the state requirement to specify what topics would be discussed by including the item 'other business' and then listing the topics to be discussed below it. If there was no other business, they could explain that on the agenda, too.

All laws would be satisfied. The board didn't have to break state law to satisfy county law.

What's more, that they had broken the open meetings law since 2008 by putting the item on the agenda shouldn't have been a reason for not fining them, it should have been a reason for fining them. Who should get the stiffer punishment, a guy who committed nine house robberies or someone who committed one? Habitual lawlessness is not usually an argument for a get-out-of-jail-free card.

As for correcting their ways by refraining from putting the item on one meeting agenda, at a time when the press was looking over their shoulders and the DA was investigating, that hardly assured that the county board, so acclimated to breaking the open meetings law, had really changed its ways. Maybe they had, but a stiff fine to show them the consequences of future violations would send a stronger message than assuming they had reformed.

At this point, the district attorney decided to address two arguments the newspaper made in its complaint, namely, that the generic item allowed the board "to discuss two pieces of business" that were not listed on the agenda, and a charge that items such as 'other business' allow supervisors to evade the law by discussing matters of public business that they don't identify or specify.

Here, the district attorney managed to miss the point of the newspaper's arguments and hopelessly mangled legal definitions. He asserted that the matters discussed under that item were innocuous and so were not public "business" at all, meaning statements made for the purpose of exercising the responsibilities, authority, power, or duties delegated to or vested in the board.

He was wrong—shades of Michael Bloom again—and he misread the statutes in being wrong. The language he was referring to comes from the definition of a "meeting" that must be posted: A meeting, he says, means the convening of members of a governmental body for the purpose of exercising responsibilities, authority, power, or duties delegated to or vested in the body. That's true enough, but the district attorney then read that to mean that any statement made by officials during a meeting that is not "for the purpose of exercising responsibilities, authority, power, or duties delegated to or vested in the body" is somehow not part of the meeting.

Did that mean that a 10-minute stretch of the meeting transcript or recording that happened to be innocuous should be deleted and is not part of the record? Who would decide what was innocuous and what was not?

Of course clerks can't erase whole stretches of meetings. The district attorney's whole notion was absurd. While a meeting is indeed a gathering convened for governmental purposes, every part of the subsequent meeting is presumed to be public business that must be noticed precisely because the officials are presumably there only to conduct public business.

Now, it is true that some non-posted matters or statements might be made that do not rise to the level of an infraction, impromptu birthday greetings, for example, and it is also true that that was the case with the comments made during the 'Other Business' session at the March county board meeting—a fact this newspaper conceded when the complaint was made.

But that's where the district attorney missed the larger point. Our issue was not with the comments made—they could have been made at any time and place during the agenda and indeed did not require posting—it was with the agenda item itself. Put simply, the mere listing of 'other business' by itself with no topics or with no explanation that there would be no other business is illegal, and the board would have been in violation even if supervisors had made no comments. It was illegal because it provided a formalized platform for supervisors to insert business they didn't have to or want to post. That comments were made shows how tempting it is for supervisors to do so.

As we observed in our complaint, the comments were innocuous and no harm was done, but they could have been important and public harm could have been done, and that's why the agenda item is illegal. And that's why county supervisors should have been fined, and especially so since the board was advised at the very meeting before that one that such items were not legally allowed. In her infamous training session, Lubinksy had informed the board that "it is a no-no," and they couldn't get away with it.

Thanks to the district attorney, they did get away with it.

Let's imagine you are driving down a highway, tooling along at 85 in a 55-mph speed zone. Suddenly a state trooper appears and stops you. You can imagine the conversation.

"Is there any reason why you are going 30 mph over the speed limit," the trooper asks you.

"I can only say I didn't know any better, Ms. Trooper," you say. "I won't do it again. I didn't know what the speed limit was."

Ms. Trooper is in a good mood, or she already has her quota, so she decides to give you a warning. But, she cautions solemnly, "driving 85 in a 55 is a no-no. You can't get away with that."

And with that you're on your way. Only, a few weeks later you are driving down the same highway and once again you are doing 85 in a 55. This time a different trooper stops you but sees you have just been recently warned.

Now what do you think this trooper will do? Will he give you a ticket or merely say, "Well, you didn't smash up any cars or kill anybody, so I guess you were wrong but since it was harmless I'm just going to look the other way."

No, you are likely going to get a ticket. And, if you don't, you are likely going to keep driving 85 in a 55-mph speed zone. The same thing happened in Oneida County. In this case, Trooper Lori Lubinsky had the entire county board pulled over for a session on obeying the open meetings law because the board had already been busted for speeding past it. She warned them they couldn't keep getting away with it, and then they kept on speeding. Then they were caught again, and along comes Trooper district attorney, who lets them off again. That means they are likely to keep on speeding, i.e., breaking the open meetings law, and the message it sends to other local governments is that they can get away with it, too.

We do offer thanks to the district attorney for one thing. Though we disagree with him in the end, he did pursue the matter diligently. He dutifully handed the case for investigation to the county sheriff's department, which passed it to Langlade County to avoid any potential conflicts of interest, and they looked into it. At least they have taken the open meetings laws seriously enough to devote resources to ensure compliance. Our only advice to the district attorney is, when he finds a violation, he should apply the penalties the Legislature provided for violating that law. They put those penalties there for a reason.

The reason is deterrence. It's a good one.

—

In another case, *The Times* filed complaints against Lakeland Union High School in Minocqua. One involved a closed session by the school board in which an item not on the agenda was discussed.

In his findings, the district attorney said he found evidence that the school board did violate the open meetings statute, though he said it was arguable. In any case, he said it didn't matter because he was convinced the board did not knowingly do so, if they did. So, no citation. On the DA's planet, if you don't know you're breaking the law, it doesn't matter that you're breaking the law, and we'll let the whole thing go. In his mind, it's the knowledge, not the act, that's important, at least when it comes to good old boys. Tell that to their victims.

It's buffoonery at its finest, but there are problems with this thinking in the real world. First, there's the old adage that ignorance of the law is no excuse. That's especially true when it comes to elected officials, whom as lawmakers and policy makers must be held to a higher standard. It's not the same as a person on an unfamiliar highway who may not know the speed limit and goes too fast. It is not the same because it is elected officials' job to know the open meetings law. It is part and parcel of the territory of holding public office, and so ignorance of what's allowed in closed session is not ignorance only, it is malfeasance, and it should be punished.

In another complaint against LUHS, *The Times* alleged that the high school improperly deleted emails before the records' retention period expired. The DA did find a violation, but what was the consequence? No citation needed, just tell us you've taken steps to make sure it never happens again.

Again when a prosecutor loudly announces that he doesn't consider open meetings or open records violations serious enough to cite or serious enough to impose the statutory penalty for those violations, he is announcing to the world that it is okay for them to break that law. Any law for which there is no consequence for breaking is in effect no law at all. As I said earlier, it's a mirage, always seemingly there in the distance, teasing you with thirst-quenching protection, but never quite materializing when you need it.

While there is such a thing as prosecutorial discretion, that discretion should err on the side of the people, not in favor of the good old boys. Refusing to exact consequences for transparency violations leaves public officials to act as they please with no accountability—either to being knowledgeable about the laws they are sworn to obey or to assuming responsibility for protecting public records—and it leaves the public vulnerable to mischief.

The only way to stop open records and open meetings violations is to get tough about prosecuting infractions. It is not so much how large the fine is, but the certainty that a fine will have to be paid, along with the cost of bad publicity, that is important.

Lest anyone think I'm picking on poor old Oneida County, the county is not alone. If this much is happening in a county where there is a watchdog newspaper, just imagine what is happening in communities where there is no effective oversight by the media. Indeed, a startling survey in 2014 by USA TODAY Gannett found that only seven open meetings citations had been imposed in Wisconsin in the previous five years, and none for public records cases, according to the newspaper company's analysis of court records. Prosecutors said that's because public officials generally follow the law, and, when there were violations, they were minor. There's nothing to see here, in other words.

But, as demonstrated in Boulder Junction, there can be plenty to see if prosecutors would only look, and Gannett found significant cases, too. One woman found multiple open meetings violations preceding a $500,000 outlay for wind turbines, Gannett reported, and went to court with a verified complaint after the Sheboygan County DA never answered her. She succeeded, but she also spent thousands of dollars pursuing the litigation. Again, violations are rampant, and they beg for an administrative procedure by which citizens avoid spending money they don't have to contest infractions in court.

According to Gannett, which hired Court Data Technologies to perform the analysis, the seven citations since 2009 stemmed from just three meetings. Five of the seven cases yielded fines, Gannett reported: three board members in Red Cedar paid $200.50 each; two board members in Smelser paid $154.50; two board members in Pence had to perform 25 hours of community service.

The Gannett analysis found dismissals in 17 other cases, of which nine were dismissed outright while the other eight involved one-year deferred prosecution agreements in which the charges were dropped if no other infractions occurred. The deferred prosecution agreements might have deterred those involved in the eight cases, but the overall dismissal of open government infractions likely encourage exponentially more officials to break the law.

The encouragement should stop by making the consequences real.

Chapter 10

And in the end

This is where we sing.

If we prefer not to sing, and that's probably a good idea, let's at least agree to get together and really discuss the future of open government in Wisconsin. There's obviously a lot of problems. There's a lot of problems I haven't had space to touch upon, and no doubt many more I haven't thought to address. Maybe, just maybe, I am wrong about some things.

So it's time for people to talk.

I'll cite just briefly two examples of issues I haven't had time to address: the status under the open government laws of quasi-government corporations such as economic development corporations, and the status of powerful groups like the Wisconsin Counties Association and the Wisconsin Towns Association.

In particular, the status of economic development corporations, which are generally exempt from the open records and open meetings laws, should be revisited. Now some economic development corporations do just fine in complying with open government requirements, but others, such as in Oneida County, don't, even though they rake in thousands and thousands of tax dollars. Ironically, these organizations use a state Supreme Court decision, *State of Wisconsin v. Beaver Dam Area Development Corporation,* that declared such corporations can be covered by the open government laws—consideration must be made case by case—as a tool to evade the law.

Beaver Dam was a lawsuit brought by the state against the Beaver Dam Area Development Corporation (BDADC), and, after analysis, the court found the BDADC to be a "quasi-governmental corporation" subject to transparency laws because it resembled a governmental corporation in "function, effect, and status." In other words, in considering the "totality of circumstances," the court decided the BDADC was enough of a government entity using enough public monies that its operations needed to be open to the public.

Unfortunately, other economic development corporations have used that case-by-case approach to declare that, in their case, the totality of circumstances does not demand openness.

Here's how attorney Christa Westerberg, who advocates often for open government, put it in a Wisconsin Freedom of Information Council column: "The court's decision did not create a bright-line test for whether a corporation is quasi-governmental, stating instead that the determination must be made on a case-by-case basis. Factors in *Beaver Dam* that swayed the court's analysis provide guidance for determining when a corporation is quasi-governmental. A primary consideration in *Beaver Dam* was funding, because the BDADC was supported exclusively by city tax dollars and interest earned on tax dollars and because the city provided the BDADC with office space, supplies, and clerical support. This holding is consistent with prior case law emphasizing the importance of openness when public tax dollars are concerned."

Through the years, the court's interpretation has been manipulated, so that now the court decision is sometimes read as meaning that an economic development corporation is only under the law if its funding is exclusively from the public sector.

In Oneida County, for example, the Oneida County Economic Development Corporation (OCEDC) receives huge inflows of public dollars but says, hey, we're private because it's not all from the government. Still, in 2018, the OCEDC captured $212,742 in revenues, of which $133,450, or 63 percent, came from taxpayers. So, why shouldn't taxpayers know what they are doing?

Westerberg cited other factors that can be considered on that case-by-case basis: whether the private corporation serves a public function and, if so, whether it also has other, private functions; whether the private corporation appears in its public presentations to be a governmental entity; the extent to which the private corporation is subject to governmental control; and the degree of access that government bodies have to the private corporation's records.

It's a long list, and the longer the list, the easier it is to manipulate and find reasons why the open government laws don't apply.

Westerberg said it had been suggested that the Legislature might intervene on the question, but of course it didn't. It should, though, and declare statutorily that any organization receiving significant public funds for its general fund or operations should come under the open records laws. It's important to stress that that would not include the multitude of organizations that receive government grants or dollars for specific programs. In those cases, only the use of those dollars and those programs should be accessible. But for corporations that pretend to be private organizations but that use boatloads of tax dollars to pursue their general operations—sometimes a majority of their funding—the public records laws should apply.

All of which brings me to four organizations that should not even exist, but, if they are going to, must be brought under our open government laws: Wisconsin Counties Association, Wisconsin Towns Association, Wisconsin League of Municipalities, and Wisconsin Association of School Boards.

These are interest groups formed by those various government entities to lobby the state for them, and that's problematic. For one thing, towns, villages, cities, and counties are all creatures of the state; their existence depends on laws enacted by the state. There are some home rule powers for cities and villages, but the main job of these units of government is to provide services and serve as administrative arms of the state.

So why do they need to form an interest group to lobby the state? As a creature and subordinate of the state, they should not be lobbying it for anything, and, in doing so, they are in fact lobbying against the public interest. It's appalling that we elect local representatives who should be advocating on our behalf but who instead form associations to lobby state government on their behalf, and especially on behalf of the bureaucracies they preside over.

And what have they been lobbying for? Well, for one thing, more secretive government. These groups have all put great time and effort into various bids to end the requirement that public notices be published in newspapers, for example. That is a decision they should decidedly not have a hand in.

On the federal level lobbying by government agencies is outlawed; these units of government are essentially state agencies by virtue of their relationship to state government, and they shouldn't be lobbying, either. When they do, they are almost certain not to lobby for the people so much as for the public officials themselves. That's why they formed an interest group for themselves, and that means they'll be lobbying for ever more secrecy, as they did with the public-notice legislation.

A few years back, the Wisconsin Counties Association held a meeting to "educate" elected officials about various aspects of mining. Only, until they were called out on it, they wanted to exclude the public from the session, which was attended by a quorum of multiple government committees, making the whole thing an open meeting.

These organizations do not have the public interest at stake; they are a club of elected officials devoted to furthering their own agendas and longevity. It is high time these groups be called out for the special interests they are. What's worse, the WCA has successfully challenged in court that open records laws do not even apply to such entities as the WTA and the WCA.

That is preposterous. As the lobbying and educational arms of government interests, these organizations are by definition conducting public business when they lobby for legislation supported by those local governments. Any other interpretation renders the very notion of public business superfluous and meaningless.

What's more, if they are indeed private entities working in secret to advance private agendas, then they are admitting they are special interests, no different from such groups as the Wisconsin Manufacturers & Commerce (WMC), to cite an example, and that their client members are not representing the public but themselves.

If local governments funneled money to the WMC to lobby for various pieces of legislation, the heavens would sing in protest.

These groups are no different, and the heavens should be singing.

—

So it's time to say goodbye, but before doing so let's close with a list of recommendations for making the Dark State just a bit brighter again. The list certainly isn't exhaustive or infallible, and many of the suggestions are no-brainers, while others have floated about in the air for a long time. The hope is they can be a starting point for a much needed dialogue in state government. It's a dialogue that should take place sooner rather than later.

In closing, as I look out upon the transparency landscape in Wisconsin, this is simultaneously one of the most discouraging times and one of the best times.

To say it another way, at the end of the day there's a lot of bad things happening out there in the arena of transparency, as this book demonstrates, but, in one sense, there is also that glimmer of hope I mentioned. It is always the darkest before the dawn, and that may well be the case here.

I conclude with two final points that I think citizens need to grasp.

The first is a re-emphasis of a point I made earlier, and it is that citizen participation and engagement in this state is alive and well. Voter turnout is one barometer—and it's good in Wisconsin—but I think a better gauge is the number of people who attend local and county government meetings, and I can tell you, I have seen a lot of packed houses. To be sure, when there is nothing on an agenda, the seats may be empty, but, when there is a hot-button issue, our people are there and ready to fight in the flesh for the things that define and shape their daily lives. A lot more so than in other places I've seen.

Of course, that brings up a vital point about open government: People have to know about hot-button issues before the fact to be able to influence outcomes, and so transparency about what government is doing—and about what it intends to do—is of the utmost importance. That's why agenda specificity, open meetings reform, and adequate notice in places the public is likely to see are vital.

The second point is, it doesn't take very long to grasp why these are dark days in a dark state. Read this book and look at who is the worst of the worst—the governor of the state, the entire Legislature as a body, and activist judges hell-bent on rewriting open government laws.

Elected officials, in other words. It is a puzzling phenomenon. You would think that bureaucrats with little tolerance for public opinion would be far worse on these matters than politicians who must win elections and who routinely promise transparency. But that's not the case.

That's right, the elected governor and the elected Legislature—the people who make our laws and enforce them—are the biggest proponents of the Dark

State, the biggest enemies of openness, and the elected judiciary has pulled up along side them as they round the turn for home, vying for the lead.

Why this is so I do not know. It's certainly not that bureaucrats have any more love for openness than elected officials do, but it seems their transparency sins these days are on the whole less egregious than those of elected officials. And to the extent that they are just as bad or worse, it is elected officials who enable them to be so bad—the examples they set with their own violations, the weak laws they refuse to strengthen, the strong laws they seek to weaken, and the precedents they set with their secrecy-sealing decisions.

That's the bad news. The good news is, elected officials are easier to replace than unelected bureaucrats. We don't have to scale the walls of the administrative state to achieve transparency; we can do it at the ballot box if we only engage. And in Wisconsin, as I just noted, we have an electorate that is ready to engage when they realize just how important an issue is.

To help people realize that, the centrality of transparency laws must be the core mission of advocates of open government these days.

Through it all, though, there is that glimmer of hope. There are all those activists out there—citizens and professionals alike who work tirelessly for transparency. In 2015, we saw the people rise up en masse when the entire canon of open government law was about to be jettisoned. Now, we need to show them it's important to fight in the trenches—day by day and township by township—to prevent the same thing from happening piecemeal.

That very recently law enforcement has stepped up to the plate and joined that fight makes me believe we are closer to a new and brighter day than we know.

We are a Dark State, yes, but there are those glimmers of light. So, on that positive ending, here are some recommendations to consider for an open government platform, or at least to engage a discussion. Except for the first, I proceed from the more minimally important to the most important.

Convene a stakeholders' group to reform the open government laws

This idea has been floated time and time again: A diverse stakeholders group needs to be established to comprehensively revisit the open government laws and update them.

Former Gov. Scott Walker promoted the idea during his first campaign for governor but never followed through. In 2015, then attorney general Brad Schimel hosted an open-government summit to address the law's inadequacies, acknowledging that many in the public and media viewed the state's open meetings and public records laws as outdated.

Such a gathering could hash out and resolve disagreements, and even lead to new reform ideas. Forming yet another stakeholders' group is not a panacea, but it could be a starting point for reform, if only the actors in charge would undertake it. Such a group would include state and local elected officials, executive branch and judicial system representatives, as well as broadcasters and newspapers, and non-media groups that advocate for open government, such as the Wisconsin Freedom of Information Council, Wisconsin Institute for Law & Liberty on the right, and the Wisconsin Democracy Campaign on the left.

A movement to apply pressure to recalcitrant politicians sometimes needs a boost to get off the ground, and a committed, activist, and diverse group of stakeholders could be that launch pad.

Budget transparency

No discussion of transparency would be complete without some discussion of the state budget process, another example of excessive legislative secrecy. Late-night and last-minute budget proposals that receive no public notice and no debate—often dealing with major policies—have long been a staple of the state's Joint Finance Committee.

It was just such a last-minute late-night budget motion in 2015 that nearly repealed the entire public records law.

Back in 2017, a pair of Republican lawmakers, Rep. Scott Allen (R-Waukesha) and Sen. Steve Nass (R-Whitewater), introduced the Budget Transparency Act that would have ended such shenanigans forever, and they gained support among some liberal Democrats in their effort.

Naturally, though, thanks to the leadership of both parties, the legislation never went anywhere, and, also naturally, the media didn't pay much attention to it. But it was important legislation, and it should be brought back and this time passed and enacted. Specifically, the legislation would have restricted activities of the budget-writing Joint Finance Committee by creating a 48-hour budget review provision that would apply to all JFC actions.

According to an analysis by the Legislative Reference Bureau, the bill provided that the JFC could not consider or take executive action on any motion relating to the biennial budget bill unless the motion had been distributed to all members of the JFC at least 48 hours before the committee considered or took executive action.

In addition, the motion would have to be posted on the Legislative Fiscal Bureau's website at least 48 hours before the JFC considered or took executive action.

The provisions of the bill would not have applied to a motion that related to an emergency, as determined by three-fourths of the members of the JFC, or to a motion that contained minor substantive differences from a motion that had met the bill's requirements, the LRB stated.

That legislation would have mostly dispensed with the committee's habit of putting last-minute proposals into the state budget bill without debate or prior notice, in what is known as a motion 999.

The last-minute 999 motions have become a growing problem, according to numbers published by Gannett's Larry Gallup. According to Gallup, the 999 motion, which was intended as a technical fix for budget language, averaged five pages and 15 motions in the five budget bills before 2011 but grew to 11 pages and 54 proposals with the 2011-13 bill and to 24 pages and 81 proposals in the 2015-17 budget bill.

In 2019, the wrap-up motion worked as it was supposed to, a bill limited to mostly technical changes, but one outlying example should not be an excuse to make sure lawmakers don't revert to their past bad habits in the future.

Whistleblower protections

To preserve accountability, whistleblower protections need to be substantially strengthened.

On the federal level, Wisconsin Sen. Ron Johnson worked with fellow Sen. Joni Ernst (R-Iowa) and others a few years ago to increase whistleblower protections—a major initiative given the attacks on federal whistleblowers during the Obama years. Obama used the U.S. Espionage Act to prosecute whistleblowers eight times, more than all other administrations combined.

A VA scandal in Tomah, Wisconsin, prompted the initiative by Johnson, then chairman of the Senate Homeland Security and Governmental Affairs Committee, and Ernst, a combat veteran. They subsequently introduced the Dr. Chris Kirkpatrick Whistleblower Protection Act, named for a whistleblower from the Department of Veterans Affairs Medical Center in Tomah, who committed suicide after being fired for questioning excessive prescription practices at the facility.

The matter came to light, Johnson and Ernst say, after Kirkpatrick's brother, Sean, testified at a Homeland Security and Governmental Affairs Committee hearing in September 2015 about the retaliation his brother faced after blowing the whistle on the Tomah facility. Johnson and Ernst say the legislation implemented a number of suggestions made at the hearing to improve whistleblower protections throughout the VA.

The legislation strengthened penalties for those who retaliate against whistleblowers, added protections for probationary period employees, and ensured that federal employees have a greater knowledge of whistleblower protections. The Senate Homeland Security and Governmental Affairs Committee first approved the bill unanimously in May 2016.

But, as Dee Hall, an investigative reporter with the Wisconsin Center for Investigative Journalism (WCIJ), has urged, whistleblower protections need to be strengthened at the state level, too.

In 2017, Hall, a cofounder and managing editor of the WCIJ, reported on the state's curious whistleblower law, which, she wrote, prohibits retaliation against state employees who disclose "information about violation of any state or federal law, rule or regulation, mismanagement or abuse of authority in state or local government, substantial waste of public funds or a danger to public health or safety."

Unfortunately, Hall reported, while those employees "may disclose information to any other person," that "any other person" must be an attorney, union representative, or a member of the Legislature. Otherwise, the employee has to report the information in writing to the employer's supervisor or "an appropriate governmental unit designated by the Equal Rights Division," before going elsewhere.

That is a little confining.

Hall cited the case of former Department of Justice special agent Dan Bethards, whom she reported lost his case because he blew the whistle to the head of the DOJ human resources department at the same time but not after he notified his superiors of his allegations.

He was fired.

Bethards told Hall that he believes a whistleblower is precisely a person "who goes outside the company or agency chain of command in order to alert press, public and politicians about a wrongdoing" rather than forcing the employee to self-disclose internally.

He is right, and forcing employees to blow the whistle to the agency or people they are directly blowing the whistle on is akin to an invitation to attend one's own funeral. The law should be changed.

Strengthen laws, penalties regarding the use of digital formats

Despite what should be obvious, public officials still use various technologies to try and circumvent the law.

One of increasing prevalence is the use of text messages or chat apps to communicate with fellow members of a government body during a meeting. This is a no-brainer of a violation, but the practice must be clearly prohibited. Since most government officials already are aware that such communications are a violation but just feel they can get away with it, harsh penalties—perhaps a felony—should accompany the prohibition, so that those who do get caught will pay the price.

Similarly, officials increasingly use personal email and text accounts to communicate and conduct government business. It's well known that, no matter where the communications come from, those records are public. But again, officials continue to use private accounts and devices to end run the law because they think they can get away with it. And they are usually right because only in extraordinary and likely criminal cases would an official's private device be searched, and even then it would require a warrant.

It's not practical or efficient or even desirable to ban the use of private accounts and personal devices for official use, but it should be required, by statute, that officials must deliver a copy of all such communications to an official government account. Again, the penalty for violating that law should be harsh.

Mission statement and privacy

The public records law should state clearly that application of the public records law does not turn on whom the public record is from or who owns a computer from which a public record is transmitted.

It should also reinforce that citizens do not have to reveal their identities or motives when seeking records, thereby overturning the disastrous decision in Madison Teachers, Inc.

Clarify legislative immunity

As this book reports, in 2013, then state Sen. Leah Vukmir (R-Wauwatosa) argued that lawmakers are immune from being sued for a violation when they are caught with records and don't turn them over. That's because, she argued, the state constitution prevents a legislator from being served with a civil summons while the Legislature is in session, and—giggle, giggle—the Legislature is almost always in session, with "the session" running for two years from when lawmakers are sworn in until the next Legislature is sworn in.

The constitution does provide relief from civil lawsuits, which is the blood thread of open government litigation: "Members of the legislature shall in all cases, except treason, felony and breach of the peace, be privileged from arrest; nor shall they be subject to any civil process, during the session of the legislature, nor for fifteen days next before the commencement and after the termination of each session."

The best fix would be to toughen up penalties for open government violations by making most of them criminal charges, either felonies or misdemeanors, and define all open government violations as a criminal breach of the peace. With that, legislative immunity for many open government violations disappears.

Still, for many it does not, and the law should void legislative immunity for lawsuits brought under the open records law.

End certain judicial and law enforcement system exemptions

Wisconsin Freedom of Information Council president Bill Lueders has called for an end to the exemption for prosecutor records. As Lueders has pointed out, a 1991 Wisconsin Supreme Court ruling declared prosecution files exempt from the public records law, and, in 2005, then-Gov. Jim Doyle announced his support for ending this exemption.

Indeed, there's no good reason for the exemption, but it lives on.

Likewise, certain law enforcement records, including police body camera video, must be open to the public, as well as law enforcement training videos. An entire suite of issues exists when it comes to exemptions in the law enforcement and judicial systems, and a comprehensive task force needs to address them.

Bill drafts and internal legislative investigations

State statutes should be amended to make clear that legislative drafting files are public records from the very moment they are created—or at the least from the very moment a bill is formally introduced—and that no attorney-client privilege can be claimed between bill drafters and lawmakers.

State law should also require certain best practices for those drafting files. Among other things, the law should mandate the inclusion of all drafters' notes and make clear they do not fall within the open records exemptions for document drafts. After all, it is a drafting file. Emails, legal opinions, constitutional assessments, communications with lobbyists and special interest groups pertaining to the proposed legislation must be open, and, as in the past, drafters should be required to note if "the person who requested the draft is different from the person for whom the request is to be drafted. If the person who requested the draft is a lobbyist, note the organization that the lobbyist represents."

What's more, again as in the past, drafters should be required to "place any written drafting instructions received from or on behalf of the requester and a description of any oral drafting instructions provided by or on behalf of the requester" in the file, while questions about a bill's constitutionality should be memorialized in a written memorandum or drafter's note.

As Mary Bottari has argued in calling out the dangers of moving away from those earlier policies in the state's drafting manual, winnowing the drafting files of critical information obstructs the public's ability to see who has influence in writing various pieces of legislation. Having complete and open drafting files is the only real way to ensure that the people of the state know exactly who is writing the legislation that lawmakers consider and pass. Mandating the inclusion of critical information in drafting files, and guaranteeing public access to them, represents the perfect marriage between freedom of information and open data.

Likewise, state statutes must declare that the internal probes of possible misconduct by lawmakers are as open as those of other state investigatory files, that is to say, they should be released when the investigations are closed. And any redactions made to those records should be decided by the records' custodians, not by any subjects of the records. Public records should be public records, period, and either exempt under the law or not. That law should wear a blindfold when it comes to the subjects of the record.

And while redactions are necessary to protect the identity of victims, the law must be clear that the names of accused lawmakers and the names of potential legislative witnesses to that misconduct be revealed and not redacted. That's crucial to the public's right to know what lawmakers are doing or not doing; but it's also necessary to be fair to those who might be wrongly accused.

The Erpenbach Exception

Many times, public officials will try to redact publicly identifying information from emails and other correspondence, especially from constituents, for a variety of specious reasons—the chilling effect it would have on constituents wanting to correspond with lawmakers, for instance, or the possibility of opening up citizens to reprisals.

As this book has discussed, that issue came to a head in *MacIver v. Erpenbach*, in which state Sen. Jon Erpenbach (D-Middleton) tried to hide the identities of more than 25,000 email senders who contacted him during the state's 2011 Act 10 controversy.

He lost. The MacIver Institute successfully argued that it was critical for the public to know who was communicating to lawmakers on matters of public policy, not to mention where those communications came from, and the court agreed.

"Public awareness of 'who' is attempting to influence public policy is essential for effective oversight of our government," the decision stated. "For example, if a person or group of persons who has played a significant role in an elected official's election—by way of campaign contributions or other support —contacts a lawmaker in favor of or opposed to proposed legislation, knowledge of that information is in the public interest; perhaps even more so if the person or group also stands to benefit from or is at risk of being harmed by the legislation."

The "where" aspect was important, too, the court found.

"It is also of public interest to know from 'where' the sender is attempting to influence public policy," the decision stated. "Whether a communication is sent to a public official from a source that appears associated with a particular unit of government (such as Milwaukee County or Waukesha School District), a private entity (such as Northwestern Mutual Life or Marquette University), or a nonprofit organization (such as American Red Cross or Clean Wisconsin, Inc.), or from individuals who may be associated with a specific interest or particular area of the state, from 'where' a communication is sent further assists the public in understanding who is attempting to influence public policy and why. Thus, the redacted information identifying 'who' sent emails attempting to influence public policy and from 'where' the emails were sent is not 'purely personal,' and the public has a strong interest in disclosure of such information."

In the end, the court stated, application of the public records law does not turn on whom the public record is from or who owned the computer from which the public record was transmitted. The bottom line was, the court determined, the public has a right under the law to know who is attempting to influence its public officials.

Because of the ongoing possibilities and even opportunities for mischief, state statutes such clearly codify the court's decision—that personally identifying information, including the computers used to send correspondence, not to mention other metadata—is public information unless release of the information would violate a critical right to privacy or falls under an explicit exemption in the law.

The right to privacy

When it comes to the right of privacy, most who use it to deny records are sending out red herrings. We have thoroughly explored the attempt to use the fig leaf of privacy to shoot down access to online court records. But, as this book has also discussed, there are gray areas where privacy and open government issues collide, particularly when it comes to constituent correspondence to lawmakers.

Most of that correspondence should be absolutely open—particularly when constituents are merely expressing opinions about matters of public policy—but the intimate details of a family's personal life should indeed be off limits. The public does not need to know about someone's BadgerCare or chemotherapy treatments. The public does need to know, however, how a lawmaker intervenes or does not intervene on behalf of a constituent's request. Again, though, redactions of identifying information resolve most of those issues.

There are times when they don't, though. There appears to be no statutory protection for redacting the identities or the actual health or financial scenarios of people, and HIPPA laws do not protect those conversations with a lawmaker. Likewise, the open records law, when it comes to health, provides certain exemptions for health information but those pertain only to official health care records prepared by or under the supervision of a health care provider.

As such, as a subsection of the open records law, the state should create a right to privacy statute that states—much as the Florida constitution does—that every person has the right to be let alone and free from government intrusion into their private life.

First and foremost, that right would extend HIPPA protections to the open records law, as well as personal finances and other family matters. It should also declare that such discussions between citizens and public officials do not represent any express or implied consent to a waiver of the right to privacy but must be subject to a balancing test.

But the law should also specifically emphasize that any such information deemed to be exempt should be redacted while the rest of the correspondence remains open. And, to prevent judicial activism and "reinterpretation" of legislative intent, the law should declare explicitly that no right of privacy exists for any record category for which there is no enacted statutory exemption.

As such, the details of a person's *private* life would be exempt from the open records law, except when criminal conduct is involved, or when such conduct relates to public employment, or otherwise is not subject to any reasonable right to protection.

Open data v. freedom of information

Inclusion must be a foundational principle of open government, and it should be reflected in state statutes. Interestingly, Wisconsin's statutory language already makes this a part of its governmental policy: "Further, providing persons with such information is declared to be an essential function of a representative government and an integral part of the routine duties of officers and employees whose responsibility it is to provide such information."

That's pretty inclusionary but because the declaration is so often ignored it should be strengthened by adding an "inclusionary" requirement that would mandate that governments, in providing that information and in fulfilling its essential function, shall make every effort to provide the most expansive and inclusionary means to access.

However it is written precisely, government must be required not simply to provide minimum access but to provide as much access, in as many venues and formats as it possibly can, with the right of citizens to appeal instances where the government has fallen short. In sum, such a standard would automatically rule out limiting court records to public inspection at a courthouse. A public record is a public record and an inclusionary approach to providing access to those records requires their online availability.

To use another more recent example, during the Covid-19 pandemic, many governments at all levels have begun providing access to their meetings via phone teleconference or Zoom or other platforms. The question is, why haven't they been doing so all along? What would prevent them from continuing these means of access? Holding an in-person meeting should always be a required standard, but just holding such a meeting when existing technology allows much larger participation by the public is an example of an exclusionary approach to government, and is a signature of the Dark State.

(As an aside to that, however, members of a governmental body should be required to attend meetings personally and not be permitted to vote or collect per diems for remote participation; they are, after all, elected to show up and face their constituents, body language and all.)

Open government, to be truly open, is about being proactive rather than passive. It is about including people—not merely about breaking down barriers to participation but actually pursuing ever wider engagement.

As talked about, freedom of information has lagged in investment. At the very least, governments should be required to spend at least as much on freedom of information as they do on open data. Data portals are important but so are online tools that promote transparency in every-day government decision making and accountability.

The state should build a Freedom of Information website that would allow state agencies to accept open records requests and that allows the public to track those requests and the responses to them. And, as Rick Blum suggested, it should not be simply a series of links to agency request forms, or a single form that is sent to any agency of one's choosing, but a request-to-response processing and tracking tool where agencies and requesters can manage requests and responses.

Lastly, the state should codify the open government best practices put in place by Gov. Scott Walker via executive order but that have been abandoned under Tony Evers. First, state agencies should identify those areas of records the public consistently and routinely asks for and to make those records publicly available online without a records request.

Agency Performance Dashboards should include public records metrics that track how many public records requests each state agency receives, as well as the average time to fulfill a request, and the state should maintain a better public notice website than it has with the goal of providing a centralized location for citizens to find all state government public notices and meeting minutes.

Fix the Woznicki fix

The bottom line is, the Woznicki fix needs to be fixed. Just as any citizen should be able to ask for and receive a public record regardless of motive, so should a citizen be able to ask for and receive a public record without having to seek the permission of the subject of the record. A public record should be a public record, and releasable. Period.

These days, Woznicki gives most public employees a right to challenge disclosure if the records pertain to disciplinary investigations and records obtained by a subpoena or search warrant. But, as this book and others have pointed out, it is precisely those records that are the most important for the public to have—disciplinary records that examine what one does on the job.

There is simply no reason that public employees should have a right to notice, which has become a right to obstruct and delay. Public records should be public records, period, and either exempt under the law or not. That law should wear a blindfold when it comes to the subject of the record.

Put an end to location and other excessive fees

Under the law, Wisconsin officials can't charge copying fees greater than their actual cost, but there's a loophole (the charge can be higher "if established by law") and the statute is often ignored anyway, while authorities sometimes charge exorbitant fees for simply locating public records.

In the first instance, the statutory loophole should be eliminated, and citizens should be able to administratively appeal excessive fees. As the DOJ recommends, authorities should annually evaluate their copying costs, based on the actual costs of a copy machine or contract, and the actual cost of paper. Those itemized costs should be publicly posted as a per page cost of copying.

As for location costs, how about doing away with them completely, as the DNR consultant Helen Flores long ago advocated? After all, location costs are much lower in the digital age than they were years ago when paper files had to be physically searched. These days location times are minimal, and, in any case, should be seen as a cost of doing the people's work, already paid for as a core function of government by taxpayers.

Online court records and expungement

This one is pretty simple. The state's online court records must remain intact and the records need to be complete. That means all arrest records need to be posted, and the disposition of those arrests as well. There should be no deletions because charges are dismissed or because they are watered down to misdemeanors. Plea bargaining shapes the outcome of final charges—sometime multiple felonies can be reduced to one or none—and citizens should be able to see an entire record to have full context. There should be no time limits, and what you can get at the courthouse, you should be able to get online.

As for expungement, the FOIC's Bill Lueders suggestions are on point, make it more lenient to have a record expunged—end the requirement that expungement be sought only at the time of sentencing, make it available for anyone, not just those under 25, and stress that an expunged case cannot be considered a conviction for employment purposes.

By all means, Lueders has written, expunge convictions for small time pot conviction and other minor offenses. But, he quickly follows, make sure the records, including the expungement, stay in the system, including the online records system. Just because a conviction is removed doesn't mean it never happened.

People, Lueders reasons, can understand the context of a conviction and why it went away. So this guy was busted for possessing a small amount of pot when we were hanging people for any possession, and times have changed. People understand that.

But people can understand other contexts as well. As Lueders wrote in a 2019 column in *Isthmus*, lawmakers were pushing to have records expunged for "first-time drunk drivers who do all the right things for a period of time— because God forbid that the guy applying to drive your kids' school bus should have *that* hanging over his head."

As he pointed out, though, employers can refuse to hire people convicted of crimes substantially related to a given job, if they know about them, and they won't know about them if they are not only expunged but erased.

More lenient criteria for expungement are good and proper and just; erasing history is not.

Attorney-client privilege

Though case law makes clear that not all communications between government attorneys and their clients are privileged, government actors continue to cherry pick the case-law language to assert a blanket privilege for all such communications. And they get away with it all too often because even attorneys who advocate for open government are scared, for obvious reasons, to tackle the issue.

But case law is clear, and it should be codified to clarify the privilege: When it comes to open records, the privilege applies only to confidential communications from the client to the lawyer, and it does not protect communications from the lawyer to the client unless disclosure of the lawyer-to-client communications would directly or indirectly reveal the substance of the client's confidential communications to the lawyer.

Likewise, for purposes of the open records law, the privilege must be narrowly construed, and should only protect legal advice that is sought by the client. As such the privilege does not apply to general policy discussions. A blanket exemption for all communications between government attorneys and their clients should be ruled out explicitly.

The statutes should also clarify that the burden of proof lies with the government actors, who should be required to demonstrate that withheld records actually merit the privilege, as the court of appeals ruled in *Wisconsin Professional Police Association v. Marquette County.*

Finally, the statutes should require that any denial or redaction of records based on attorney-client privilege must state the general subject matter of the privileged advice being given. After all, when government bodies go into closed session to consult with their attorneys under the public records law, they must cite not just the exemption but enough of "the subject matter of the contemplated closed meeting to enable the members of the governmental body to intelligently vote on the motion to close the meeting," as the state open meetings compliance guide states.

For example, if the requested documents are denied because they represent advice the client sought about litigation the government body was facing, or was likely to face, the subject matter of that litigation should be disclosed, just as it would have to be to convene into a closed session to discuss it with the attorney. So the government body should not be able to deny the record by simply claiming attorney-client privilege, or by saying it is privileged because it contains advice pertaining to litigation it is facing. Instead, the authority should have to say the record is being denied because it represents legal advice sought by the government body with respect to its lawsuit related to illegal pier X, or to public health directive Y, or to wrongful termination allegation in Department Z.

Open meetings reform

An ongoing problem, especially in local government, involves abuse and misuse of the open meetings laws—walking quorums, as we see in Rhinelander, or illegal closed sessions, as was the case in Boulder Junction. Officials also routinely fail to be specific enough when it comes to agendas, or to provide substantive minutes that are adequate to inform the public.

Many of these types of violations are very subjective, and probably cannot be remedied by statute. Just how specific must an agenda be? How likely is it that a local government is going to be sued over a matter, the likelihood of which gives the local government an excuse to go into closed session? Has the governmental body been threatened with a lawsuit, or is it just a remote possibility, and does the latter qualify for an exemption that allows for a closed session? Are the minutes substantive enough to pass muster, and where is the line drawn?

No amount of legislative reformulation is going to resolve such case-by-case questions. Still, there is a way forward toward transparency. Allowing challenges to be made before an administrative review board would allow many more of these routine transgressions to be challenged, and would serve as a deterrent.

More specifically for open meetings, there are some elements that can be codified to strengthen public participation and awareness. For example, increase the 24-hour notice requirement of a public meeting to at least 48 hours, and better yet to 72 hours, and require that substantive meeting minutes effectively summarize discussions on agenda topics.

One more thing: Require closed sessions to be recorded and retained for future inspection, allowing for judicial review if their legality is challenged. Illinois and Iowa have similar statutes. Not surprisingly, the League of Wisconsin Municipalities advises local governments not to record their closed sessions. Recordings can leak, of course, and they may be subject to release in an open records request under the right circumstances, especially because there is no specific exemption for records created during a closed session. That understandably makes local government officials and groups like the LWM nervous.

Still, it's important to note that closed session records are not closed forever. Once the underlying purpose for a closed session ceases to exist, the records of the meeting are open and must be provided to any person requesting access.

Thus requiring recordings of such meetings to be made and retained—for the standard seven years, no less—serves two purposes. As stated, if the legality of the meeting is challenged, a full record is available for judicial review. Second, after an issue is put to rest and the records of the meeting become accessible, they will provide tremendous insight into how decisions concerning the issue were made, and how public policy was fashioned.

That brings up one last point. Most local governments rush into closed session anytime they can hang their hat on a statutory exemption, no matter how flimsy the foundation may be. The truth is, even when there are solid grounds for a closed session, state law does not mandate that a closed session be held. Especially for policy-oriented matters, while a closed session might be legal, it is not required, and local governments can choose to hold those discussions in public.

That's a dirty little secret the Dark State doesn't want you to know, but, in 2008, the state Supreme Court, in *Sands v Whitnall School District*, pointed it out.

"Furthermore, the closed session exemptions to the open meetings law are limited in scope, confined to those specific contexts listed in Wis. Stat. § 19.85(1)(a)-(j)," the court decision stated. "Even in those contexts, the statute only permits, but does not require, meetings to convene in closed session, i.e., with members of the public not allowed to attend."

In the case, Sands had filed a lawsuit against the school district and was seeking through discovery to access the records of a closed session discussion about her contract renewal. The school district said closed session discussions were privileged under the law, but the high court ruled that discussions at a closed meeting did not acquire the status of confidential communications that are privileged from any other use.

"Our conclusion is also based on the fact that if these communications were privileged solely because they occurred during a closed session, a private litigant would be left without the ability to challenge the validity of the public body's actions during a closed session," the court stated. "To determine whether a public body, in a closed session, has acted outside of its authority, a private litigant must have access to those communications by means of a legitimate discovery request. To conclude otherwise would, in essence, immunize a public body from any challenge relating to the propriety of its closed session."

So the ability to access closed session records could be critical in a litigative context, but that is equally important when public policy is involved, the justices observed.

The bottom line was, the justices wrote, the language of the statutes does not describe the contents of closed meetings as either secret or exempt from discovery.

"We will not infer a mandatory discovery privilege for closed session contents when the closed session statute itself speaks in permissive terms, not requiring any meeting to be closed in the first place," the ruling stated.

Finally, and this should be a no-brainer, but make the Legislature subject to the state's open meetings law.

In related matters, the statutes should clarify that the draft minutes of meetings are public records the minute they are completely drafted, not when they are approved, and that exemptions for materials prepared for an originator's personal use specifically exclude any material whose final form will ultimately be made public.

Lastly, the statutes need to make clear that periodic social gatherings in which a majority of a government body may attend—regularly scheduled luncheons, or drinks at the pub—need to be noticed, even though no discussion of government business is planned.

Statutorily overturn egregious court decisions

In recent years, the state Legislature has become increasingly less shy when it comes to passing new statutes that effectively overturn various court decisions interpreting existing law.

That's not necessarily a bad thing. If a court interprets a law in a way that the Legislature finds conflicted with the legislation's original intent, or even if it is an accurate interpretation and lawmakers feel the new parameters are outdated or wrong, they should be able to change them if they can, so long as they stay within constitutional boundaries.

Here's a recent example. In 2017, the state Supreme Court determined that Trempealeau County had the authority to deny a conditional use permit to a mining company even though the company met or agreed to meet all permit standards. The *AllEnergy Corp. v Trempealeau County* case was related to a proposed frac sand mind in which the county adopted 37 conditions for a permit. When AllEnergy agreed to meet them all, the county voted to deny the conditional use permit anyway.

It was a divided issue, but the high court acknowledged the discretionary power of boards in such cases, even when code standards were complied with.

Supporters of the mine were outraged at the ability of a local government to look beyond the written standards of law and apply their subjective judgment, and, later that year, the Legislature passed—and Gov. Scott Walker signed—new legislation that overturned the decision, essentially relegating subjective judgments in conditional use permit decisions to the dustbin.

Under the new law, if a project meets all requirements and conditions within the municipality's conditional use permit ordinance, the permit must be issued, and any decision that a permit does not meet the standards must be accompanied by substantial rather than subjective evidence why that is the case.

To be sure, statutory fixes of bad court decisions should not be common occurrences. However, lawmakers must feel compelled to enact similar fixes when court decisions threaten the very fabric of open government laws. This book has cited three of them just in the past several years. There are certainly more. Repairing them statutorily could well deter an activist court from rewriting transparency laws in the future, but in any event it is the right thing to do.

Immediately, the Legislature should state and/or restate in no uncertain terms that the motive for seeking records cannot be considered under any circumstances; that forged and fake "records" are not considered protected records under the law; and that government business does not require any formal or informal action but occurs whenever a quorum—traditional, walking, or otherwise—of a governmental body gathers information, discusses, gathers facts, or otherwise engages in any way matters that fall under the realm of its jurisdiction.

Last and not least, state statutes should declare that no category of exempt records is foreclosed from judicial review. The very idea that executive agencies can declare records to belong to an exempt category and thus are exempt from even judicial review to see if they are real or in fact do belong to such a category is either insane or heinous. Take your pick.

Criminal penalties

Ideally, the solution would be to substantially increase the penalties for intentional violations, and to criminalize some infractions. Right now, penalties are laughably weak to nonexistent; for instance, an open meetings violation is simply a forfeiture of between $25 and $300.

For records, any authority or legal custodian who arbitrarily and capriciously denies or delays response to a request or charges excessive fees may be required to forfeit not more than $1,000, though I have never heard of such a penalty being levied. In addition, a public records infraction may involve criminal penalties only for destruction, damage, removal, or concealment of public records with intent to injure or defraud, or for altering or falsifying public records.

All other infractions involve civil forfeitures.

Those laws should be amended so that capricious withholding of records or the intentional charging of excessive fees, or intentionally violating the open meetings laws, carry criminal rather than civil penalties, with the most serious infractions automatically classified as felony misconduct in office.

Establish strict statutory deadlines for responding to records requests

Wisconsin's records laws are simply too vague when it comes to the time given to respond to a records request, allowing government officials to drag their feet and substantially delay the production of records.

To wit, as the DOJ's compliance manual points out, the law does not require a response within any specific date and time, such as "two weeks" or "48 hours," only that a response must be provided "as soon as practicable and without delay."

That said, DOJ policy is that "10 working days generally is a reasonable time for responding to a simple request for a limited number of easily identifiable records. For requests that are broader in scope, or that require location, review, or redaction of many documents, a reasonable time for responding may be longer."

Obviously, that's all subjective. Let's take a page from other states and add time specificity, with a mechanism for allowing agencies reasonable time for fulfilling complex requests.

Here's one proposal, as suggested earlier: The state could impose a five business day deadline for an initial response, giving the body five days to provide the records, deny the records request with reasons, or to request more time. If more time was needed, the government body could invoke a 10-day automatic extension, which would be unappealable. Or the government body could say it needs even more time and advise the requester of the time it needs. That last action would be appealable administratively, and, if the extended time was granted, the agency would relinquish any claim to costs.

Under that proposal, no agency could delay fulfilling an open records request beyond three weeks without risking an immediate administrative appeal with possible penalties. While this proposal is just one of many, the important point is that, as much as is humanly possible, subjectivity needs to be taken out of the time agencies have to fulfill requests, to be replaced with specificity.

Establish an administrative appeals process for citizens

When the open government laws were overhauled in the early 1980s, a critical piece of reform was proposed but deleted from the bill: the establishment of an Ethics and Open Records Board to provide oversight and accountability.

For average citizens who do not have the time or money to contest records denials or other open government violations by government agencies and officials, this is a crucial reform.

Among other things, the board should be able to review denial of access to a record, especially in an age when most district attorneys simply will not seriously prosecute transparency violations, and requesters are compelled to pursue expensive and burdensome litigation if they want their records.

It's important that some legal groups, such as the Wisconsin Institute for Law & Liberty and the Wisconsin Transparency Project, now exist to undertake those efforts on behalf of citizens, but it's not nearly enough. It would be better still if citizens didn't have to go to court in the first place.

To further those goals, state law should establish an administrative appeals process that must be responded to within a limited amount of time prior to filing litigation, that could review and overturn records denials, as well as review proposed costs for fulfilling records requests, among other things.

The membership of the board should be split between those appointed by elected officials—the governor, the attorney general, the Assembly, the Senate —and members appointed by various ideologically balanced stakeholder groups, such as broadcasters and newspapers, and non-media groups that advocate for open government, such as the Wisconsin Freedom of Information Council, Wisconsin Institute for Law & Liberty on the right, and the Wisconsin Democracy Campaign on the left.

Put the Legislature under the records retention law

This is the biggest no-brainer of all. As reported previously, in the 2019-20 legislative session, Democratic state Sen. Chris Larson (D-Milwaukee) circulated a bill to end the Legislature's exemption of itself from the state's open records retention law. It went nowhere; it should be enacted.

This book has reported on this exemption almost ad nauseam, but I'll make a final point. This is the most important open government step that advocates of transparency can take. The Legislature is the central elected body of our state government, its heart and soul. If that body does not take open government seriously, if it defiantly sets itself above the laws others must follow, then we simply cannot expect to have a broadly open government, not in state agencies, not in the governor's office, and not in local governments.

A person with a terminally poisoned heart doesn't live very long, and neither will an opaque system of government. The people of Wisconsin need to demand this reform, and demand it now, in every legislative session and in every campaign. If not a litmus test, this issue should be a core consideration for support of a candidacy.

There is only one reason to allow the destruction of records memorializing government activity, and that is to prevent the activity's memorialization. And the only reason to do that is to keep the people from knowing what you have done, from knowing what you are doing, and from knowing what you plan to do.

Enough said.

Establish a constitutional right to know

One of the unique problems an issue like open government runs into is that it is seen as neither partisan nor fundamental. Partisans get fired up about partisan issues, of course, and transparency most often runs across the political spectrum.

If you ask someone if open government is fundamental, they will naturally answer in the affirmative, but it only runs tongue deep. It seems to be a no-brainer, on the one hand, but most people don't view it as essential as, say, the First Amendment, or freedom of religion. Sure, it's essential, people say, but it's not like it's one of the big Ten Amendments.

That's one of the problems. It can and is reasonably argued that open government and transparency are implicit in the First Amendment, as both freedom of speech and freedom of association are implicated. The right to petition the government for a redress of grievances is especially implicated.

As such, open government is most often subsumed as an implied subunit of the First Amendment. It's there, to be sure, but it doesn't get its own seat at the table like religion and the press.

The media plays a major role in undermining the important nature of transparency, too. In part, that's because a closed session violation just isn't as sexy as issues like guns and abortion. In part it's also because, as Denise Young of the Future Earth Media Lab has written, the media is unable "to handle issues which are complex, cross-cutting and more to do with processes than outcomes."

All true, and yet the importance of open government has been contemplated since the founding of the nation. James Madison allowed that democracy without information was "but prologue to a farce or a tragedy." Patrick Henry allowed, "The liberties of a people never were, nor ever will be, secure when the transactions of their rulers may be concealed from them."

So why, then, no inclusion of open government in the Bill of Rights? For one thing, the constitutional convention itself was held in secret, behind literally closed doors and windows, with George Washington admonishing anyone who spoke out of turn outside of the hall. Certainly no provision for open meetings was going to be written into a document that itself was being written in closed session. Even Madison accepted the secrecy, opining that no "constitution would ever have been adopted by the convention if the debates had been public."

As today, the delegates feared what the press might do with an open session. Delegate George Mason, foreshadowing today's debates about the openness of bill drafts, proclaimed secrecy to be "a necessary precaution to prevent misrepresentations or mistakes; there being a material difference between the appearance of a subject in its first crude and undigested shape, and after it shall have been properly matured and arranged."

So there you have it, today's patrons of the Dark State might say, the country was actually founded in secrecy, and the constitution written and rolled in its wrappers. But not so fast. The issue is a lot more complex than that.

For one thing, there was a lot of criticism of the secrecy by major players, and the secrecy rule, as it was called, became a lot more controversial in the year of ratification after the convention, as John Kaminski wrote in an excellent 2005 paper for the Center for the Study of the American Constitution.

Thomas Jefferson, who wasn't at the convention because he was serving in Paris as the French ambassador, made his displeasure known in a letter to John Adams: "I am sorry they began their deliberations by so abominable a precedent as that of tying up the tongues of their members. Nothing can justify this example but the innocence of their intentions, and ignorance of the value of public discussions."

After the convention, it became increasingly clear that secrecy could not be sustained and that the public would not tolerate it. All of the state ratification conventions were open to the public, Kaminski observed, and the new constitution did require both chambers of Congress to keep a journal of proceedings, with certain exemptions for secrecy. The march for openness was on.

That march today should continue, and why not crown Jefferson's sentiments by finally—at the state level—giving open government a seat at the constitutional table with a constitutional amendment.

That's exactly what Florida did way back in 1992. The Florida state constitution gives "every person the right to inspect or copy any public record made or received in connection with the official business of any public body, officer, or employee of the state, or persons acting on their behalf, except with respect to records exempted pursuant to this section or specifically made confidential by this Constitution."

The provision applies to the legislative, executive, and judicial branches of government and to every agency or department created by the three branches, as well as to counties, municipalities, and districts; and to each constitutional officer, board, and commission, or entity created pursuant to law or the constitution.

Likewise, all meetings of any public body of the executive branch or of any public body of a county, municipality, school district, or special district, at which official acts are to be taken or at which public business is to be transacted or discussed, must be open, and meetings of the Legislature must be open and noticed.

The Florida constitution allows for exemptions but those must be passed by a two-thirds vote of each house of the Legislature and signed into law, "provided that such law shall state with specificity the public necessity justifying the exemption and shall be no broader than necessary to accomplish the stated purpose of the law."

Take note that the constitutional provision applies both the records law and the meetings law to the Legislature, and that "government business" (please acknowledge, Michael Bloom!) takes place at any meeting in which "official acts are to be taken *or* at which public business of such body is to be transacted *or discussed.*"

It's time for some courageous lawmakers to propose such a constitutional amendment for Wisconsin. The sooner, the better.

The truth is, in Wisconsin, voters pass constitutional amendments from time to time, some questionable, like Marsy's Law, and some of them called for, such as a reaffirmation of our right to hunt.

I can't imagine what could be less questionable or more called for than a constitutional right to know.

Epilogue

The Public Health-Big Pharma Syndicate

This book—finished during the Covid-19 pandemic—must address the sweeping implications for government transparency that policies related to the pandemic have brought to bear, and not just brought to bear but exposed, for this subterfuge has been ongoing for many years.

The truth is, the nation's and the world's civil liberties are under sharp attack, and, while there are many fronts to this war, two front lines in particular have formed that are leading efforts to rob us of our civil liberties, free speech, and government transparency.

Before I get to them, though, it's important to understand the nexus between free speech and open government. To be sure, free speech is the key to all our other civil liberties. The ability to freely assemble and worship, to petition our government, to advocate for causes and candidates and to try and persuade others—freedom of speech is the foundational principle of democratic governance. Without it, transparency fails for lack of voice and standing.

Similarly, government transparency—open government, open records, open meetings—is the functional imperative of free speech. Without open government, without full access to information regarding the functioning of government, citizens have no meaningful way to judge and debate government actions, or to hold officials accountable. When government operates in secrecy, withholds its proceedings, and chokes off information needed for informed opinion- and decision-making, meaningful democratic participation becomes impossible, and freedom of speech is rendered a hollow shell of a right, a mere talking point for campaign sloganeering.

While this book has documented the shut down of government transparency in one state—which readers everywhere should know is simply a mirror of what is happening in most states—the past year has seen a parallel and often intertwined effort to attack civil liberties directly. If the shut down of open government is a back-door attack on the First Amendment, the direct assault on free speech through censorship is a front-end attack, a loud knock on our constitutional front door.

Those two front lines I mentioned are in our faces. One is Big Tech's censorship of speech it does not like on platforms such as Twitter and Facebook, and its banning of free-speech platforms and apps by Amazon, Apple, and Google. This represents a dangerous turn of events, for these few companies dominate and control the vast majority of our social and political communications. One may argue that these are private companies that may do as they wish, but one can also argue that they are monopolies that have subverted and imperiled a free market in communications, thus subverting and imperiling markets for free expression.

We hear much in the headlines about the censorship of conservatives, but they are not the only ones impacted. Those who question vaccine safety are censored, and that's an especially important concern now that Covid-19 vaccines are being distributed. Those who challenge the human rights abuses and oppressive acts of dictators are censored. Those who question the activities of favored international corporations are censored. And all with government protection.

Big Tech is beyond the scope of this book, but the other major force of censorship this year is not, and that is the brazen actions of the world's powerful public health syndicates to suppress information, destroy civil liberties, and shut down open government during the Covid-19 pandemic.

While Big Tech may be as dangerous, the threat from Big Public Health is more immediate. Simply put, a coalition, or cartel, of public health agencies, acting in concert with major pharmaceutical companies and their institutional allies, has undertaken a breath-taking grab of power in the name of its own interest and profits in what amounts to a gutting of the constitution.

It cannot be allowed to stand if we are to preserve civil liberties and government transparency.

It would be a mistake to believe, however, that this has happened overnight. Public health's long-term plans to transfer power has been on a fast track since at least the 1990s, the present pandemic only being the penultimate trigger, and it has been in the long-term works for decades more.

This chapter takes a brief look at that pre-pandemic history, a look at how an attempted public-health power grab played out in Wisconsin (perhaps the quintessential and premier example in the United States), and finally how local health departments have thwarted government transparency to conceal their real activities.

—

The belief in a strong public health doctrine in western societies has long put civil liberties in the crosshairs, or at least potentially so.

In pre-revolutionary Europe, the power of monarchs was resolute and absolute, and those monarchies sought to project images of a healthy and fit population by requiring certain public health practices. They were unevenly applied, and poorer classes were ignored and/or punished, but the police power of the state to enforce public health regulations was considered to be not only absolute but benevolent.

That same "given" took hold in pre-revolutionary and post-revolutionary America. As Jorge E. Galva of the University of Iowa wrote in "Public Health Strategy and the Police Powers of the State," in 2005, state police power was validated for the first time a few years following the Revolutionary War, when Philadelphia was threatened by an outbreak of yellow fever.

"By the time the federal Constitution was drafted, quarantine was already a well established form of public health regulation, and was considered proper exercise of the police power of the states; the Supreme Court, in its affirmation of this power, noted that the state had the power to quarantine 'to provide for the health of the citizens,'" Galva wrote.

The uncontrollable nature of epidemic diseases moved the Supreme Court to uphold such extreme measures on the basis of defending the common good,

Galva wrote, and the communitarian doctrine held all the way through the latter part of the 20th century.

Thinking changed in the 1950s, and the view of public health changed with it.

"The latter part of the 20th century, however, brought legal, social, and ideological transformations that substantially limited such [police] powers," he wrote. "The main forces that restricted public health police powers were: (*1*) the advent of civil rights jurisprudence; (*2*) the rise of patient autonomy and the rapid expansion of state personal health services expenditures; and (*3*) federal encroachment on state authority."

Mine is a superficial swipe at a complex history, to be sure, but the point is, by the time the nation headed into the last decades of the 20th century, the institutional power of public health had been constrained. And so had the bureaucratic leaders who led those agencies. The result was a national and state public health authority that was seen as, at best, neutered of power, and, at its worst, weak and complacent.

But beginning in the 1970s and 1980s, two nascent but powerful social and economic forces began to intersect that would begin to change things again in the 1990s. One was the rise of a powerful new social reform movement that demanded that public health reassert its proper role and function in society, which included, in this view, political engagement. One of the first calls to action came in the early 1970s, as described in "The Exodus of Public Health," by Dr. Amy Fairchild of Columbia University.

"This critique was made perhaps most memorably by Paul Cornely in a 1970 address to the American Public Health Association," Fairchild wrote. "Newly elected as the group's first African American president, Cornely leveled a blistering attack on what he saw as the complacency of his profession. It had been 'a mere bystander' to the profound changes in the health care system that had taken place in the 1960s; its members wasted their time on 'piddling resolutions and their wordings.' Public health, he charged, remained 'outside the power structure.' Cornely's address was a clarion call for more aggressive action against a host of health problems integral to modern industrial society."

Implicit in this call to action was a challenge to corporate special interests who were seen as contaminating America in various ways, and rightly so. But then the second force asserted itself, and, quite frankly, that was a counter assertion of power over public health institutions by some of those corporate malefactors themselves, primarily major pharmaceutical companies.

To wit, Big Pharma and public health agencies such as the World Health Organization, the Centers for Disease Control (CDC) and the Food and Drug Administration (FDA) have become deeply intertwined—they have formed a syndicate that at its heart is about powering the institutional interests of the public health bureaucracies and simultaneously furthering the interests and profits of major pharmaceutical companies.

As Children's Health Defense (CHD), a group whose mission is to eradicate chronic and increasing childhood epidemics around the world, puts it, the pharmaceutical industry enforces policy discipline through agency budgets— mind you, the budgets of the very agencies that regulate them.

"The World Health Organization (WHO) gets roughly half its budget from private sources, including Pharma and its allied foundations," CHD states. "And CDC, frankly, is a vaccine company; it owns 56 vaccine patents and buys and distributes $4.6 billion in vaccines annually through the Vaccines for Children program, which is over 40 percent of its total budget."

Further, CHD states, Pharma directly funds, populates, and controls dozens of CDC programs through the CDC foundation.

Or take the Food and Drug Administration. As Drs. Leslie E. Sekerka of Menlo College and Lauren Benishek of Johns Hopkins University wrote in 2018 (*Emory Corporate Governance and Accountability Review*, "Thick as Thieves: Big Pharma Wields its Power with the Help of Government Regulation"), even though the FDA is responsible for approving pharmaceutical products for marketing in the U.S., as well as having the statutory authority to regulate prescription drug labeling and advertising, the pharmaceutical industry contributes heavily to its annual budget.

Since 1992, the authors reported, pharmaceutical companies contributed $7.67 billion to the federal agency's coffers.

"This creates an interconnectedness between the two entities: a marriage between Big Pharma and the government can potentially blur the intent of government regulation and the role that it plays in protecting citizens," they wrote.

The result has been a international and national public health syndicate, comprised on the one hand of a bureaucracy that increasingly pursued its mission politically, while simultaneously doing the bidding of the biggest of the big special interests, Big Pharma. In other words, within the public bureaucracies the reformist push to engage remained, but much of the content was subverted by big money and special interests.

—

A self-interested public health authority on the one hand and its Big Pharma sponsors on the other—little wonder that the current pandemic has led to an unprecedented assertion of power by public health, with consequent lockdowns, mask mandates, and other abuses of civil liberties, and, of course, coming down the home stretch with the widespread distribution of a Big Pharma vaccine that has not passed standard protocols of testing but that will ensure big profits.

It raises the specter of ever less transparency and more requirements—vaccine passports?—along the way. In a way, trying to force compliance with lockdowns and other abuses of power could be seen as a trial run to gain compliance with vaccine mandates down the road, an all too predictable endgame.

But, as I said, the planning for this past year's assertions of power are a long time coming. They were not just hatched yesterday. For that we have to go back to the 1990s and the push for states to pass what is known as the Model Emergency Health Powers Act (MEHPA), which called for empowering states to quarantine, isolate, or fine anyone who refused to take untested drugs and vaccines and for suspending "the provisions of any regulatory statute prescribing procedures for conducting state business, or the orders, rules and regulations of any state agency."

As Paul Cornely had urged in 1970, public health by the early 1990s had become way more activist, and by then they were determined not to sit outside the power structure, as Cornely put it. Indeed, they were determined to be at the center of it. All the while, their efforts, as we have seen above, were being funded by big pharmaceutical companies.

So let's take a look at what that formula looked like by the early 1990s, as presented in the MEHPA, which was funded by the CDC and written by Dr. Larry Gostin, a veteran of the Clinton administration's health care wars and co-director of the Center for Law and the Public Health at Georgetown and Johns Hopkins Universities.

On its face, the MEHPA was simply a draft act that states were encouraged to adopt, ostensibly to increase state powers to respond to bioterrorism or other outbreaks of disease. The draft came on the heels of the September 11, 2001, terrorist attacks at the World Trade Center.

Under the proposal, governors and state public health authorities could declare public health emergencies that would greatly expand the state's police powers. Among other things, governors and public health officials would be empowered to preempt state laws and rules; control roads and public areas, including ingress and egress and the movement of people, not to mention to occupy premises in "threatened" areas; to track and share an individual's personal health information and to compel health examinations; to identify and interview potentially infected persons, based on "reliable information"; to force persons to be vaccinated, treated, or quarantined for infectious diseases; and to isolate and quarantine any persons deemed necessary for the protection of public health.

Also under the plan the state could control public and private property during a public health emergency, including pharmaceutical manufacturing plants, nursing homes, other health care facilities, and communications devices.

Sounds real familiar, doesn't it?

In fact, it sounds like a script for what many state governments have tried to do during the coronavirus pandemic. Back then, though, both the left and the right howled in protest. On the right, Sue Blevins, then a Heritage Foundation analyst, put it this way: "We can and must find a better way to defend citizens against bioterrorism while protecting our precious individual freedoms—the very freedoms that this current war on terror is being waged to defend. As a gentleman reminded me recently, 'You can't defend freedom by eliminating it.' I believe—and believe it should be evident to you—that this model plan, if enacted throughout the states, would indeed do just that: eliminate our freedom to choose our medical care and health treatment and potentially eliminate a broader range of our basic civil liberties."

On the left, the ACLU warned that the act failed to include basic checks and balances, went well beyond bioterrorism, and lacked privacy protections.

"Although extraordinary measures may be required during an emergency, the Model Act is replete with civil liberties problems," the ACLU remarked in a gigantic understatement of the day.

Against this backdrop there are two competing philosophies—one is that a lethal pandemic is so serious as to warrant and indeed necessitate the suspension of constitutional rights to protect the public, meaning, in effect, that the government must protect the public from itself; the second is that constitutional rights and open government are even more important in a crisis precisely because public and informed decision making is vital to a proper response to a real pandemic and because of the potential for bad actors to manipulate or manufacture a crisis for anti-democratic purposes.

Unless one is a bureaucrat or pharmaceutical executive, the second is the only reasonable position. But I admit it requires walking a fine line. A pandemic may require extraordinary measures, but to fit within constitutional parameters those measures must, at the very least, be temporary and of defined and limited duration; they must have a legitimate purpose, that is, transparency is required to assure that measures are indeed supported by sound scientific science and that power is checked by other branches of government; and, last but of equal importance, they can never contravene fundamental constitutional rights—they can regulate but not foreclose.

One important point to make is that the model act was announced as a response to the 9/11 attacks, but in reality the drafting was well under way before the terrorist attacks happened.

"It is also significant that two articles related to this proposal were published or prepared well before the Trade Center attacks," Blevins wrote. "In January 1999, in a *Columbia Law Review* article, a plan was presented for changing public health laws. A similar plan appeared in an *American Journal of Public Health* article, published coincidentally in September 2001, but accepted for publication in March 2001. It appears that this model legislation—formulated long before the terrorism of last fall—actually represents the promotion and expansion of a long-standing agenda. As these proposals come before the individual states, our elected officials should be aware of this history and examine carefully all proposals submitted to them."

So how did that model legislation work out?

As of 2011, most states had adopted some form of the laws granting governors greater emergency powers. It is also important to note that Wisconsin rejected one form of the law in 1992-93, but, with its progressive tradition, it had already given the governor and state and local public health authorities expansive authority a long time before. Because Wisconsin statutes seemingly gave them unbridled authority to act, Wisconsin did not take up the model plan per se. That might have been their undoing. When the time came to act, Wisconsin's governor and his public health secretary acted precisely according to the act's script, confining all residents to their homes, prohibiting all private gatherings, broadly restricting travel, and closing all businesses deemed nonessential.

The problem is, while the act authorized a long list of specific police powers the state could unilaterally take, in Wisconsin, their powers were laid out in a broad statutory grant ("[t]he department may authorize and implement all emergency measures necessary to control communicable diseases"), except for certain specific enumerations, and that ultimately complicated the plan. Let's take a look.

After Gov. Tony Evers declared a public health emergency, and, acting within that broad statutory grant of power to the executive, Andrea Palm, Evers's designated but unconfirmed secretary of the Department of Health Services, began taking the aforementioned unilateral actions.

That prompted a legislative lawsuit, with the Legislature arguing that Palm's order exceeded the department's authority, and was arbitrary and capricious. More important, it claimed that to take those specific actions, Palm would have had to undertake emergency rule making to specifically implement a vague statute, and she did not do so.

In describing the lawsuit, the Legislature's petition laid out clearly what was at stake for the citizens of Wisconsin, and what is at stake for the citizens of the United States.

"Purporting to act under color of state law, an unelected, unconfirmed cabinet secretary has laid claim to a suite of czar-like powers—unlimited in scope and indefinite in duration—over the people of Wisconsin," the petition stated. "Per her decree, everyone in the state must stay home and most businesses must remain shuttered (with exceptions for activities and companies arbitrarily deemed essential). These restrictions apply not only to metropolitan areas with more Covid-19 cases but also to rural counties with few or no known cases."

And Palm's order was even more shocking than the governor's: Palm claimed that her shutdown authority had no expiration date, meaning it was even greater than Evers's emergency powers, which could last only 60 days unless extended by the Legislature. In other words, the state's public health authority was running the state with the powers of a dictator, and no one, she argued, not even the governor, could stop her.

It was just what the doctor had ordered—or hoped to have ordered—under the Model Emergency Health Powers Act. Note, however, how her self-proclaimed authority violated the constitutional limits of emergency powers talked about above—by not undertaking emergency rule making, which could have swiftly put her measures in place, she avoided having to show supporting science or having the Legislature oversee her decisions to make sure they were legitimate; and they were not time-limited, a critical failure for any emergency measure.

Not that the governor didn't support her. He did. Ironically, though, it is likely that Wisconsin's failure to adopt the specific planks of the MEHPA was ultimately its undoing, for that act included all the specific actions, and more. They would have thus been embedded in the statutes and no rule-making would have been required, which the Supreme Court ruled had to be done.

In court, Palm and the administration argued that any legislative oversight must be general and limited and that the statute gave her the right to "issue orders." In this world view, the Legislature did not have the authority to "second-guess" (as one Supreme Court justice put it) whether agency rules were faithfully implementing legislative intent or were actually subverting it.

Implicit in this whole notion was that the Legislature had delegated legislative powers to the executive agencies as is explicitly done in the MEHPA. Many scholars have long contested the ability of one branch to delegate core powers to the other branch.

The majority did indeed hold that the power was so unchecked as to violate the separation of powers between the branches, as surely as the grant of unchecked power does in the model act. In Wisconsin, the court concluded, constitutional safeguards included adherence to administrative procedures that

Palm had ignored. To be constitutional, the statute delegating authority must contain standards to constrain the exercise of power, they majority found.

"Core powers, however, are not for sharing," justice Daniel Kelly wrote in a concurring opinion. "The importance of constitutional limitations, chief justice Marshall once said, is that they compel restraint when restraint is not desired."

Neither can laws, even in an emergency, trump the constitution, Wisconsin justice Rebecca Bradley asserted, and that was true especially in a time of emergency. And she quoted Chief Justice Charles Evans Hughes in a 1934 decision: "The Constitution was adopted in a period of grave emergency. Its grants of power to the federal government and its limitations of the power of the states were determined in the light of emergency, and they are not altered by emergency."

But that is what happened in Wisconsin, Bradley argued.

"In issuing her order, she [Palm] arrogated unto herself the power to make the law and the power to execute it, excluding the people from the lawmaking process altogether," she wrote. "The separation of powers embodied in our constitution does not permit this. Statutory law being subordinate to the constitution, not even the people's representatives in the legislature may consolidate such power in one person."

The thing is, that executive arrogation of power to make the law and to execute it didn't just happen in Wisconsin. The assertion of powers during the Covid-19 pandemic brought us to the brink of a constitutional crisis, a crisis occurring in state after state across the nation, and, again, it is a crisis that is 30 years in the making, as a powerful Big Pharma-public health alliance was conceived, born, and grew out of all proportion.

In other words, this was not some singular overreaction to a rightfully concerning pandemic; it was a predictable and planned response that the actors involved had been salivating for decades. It is institutional in nature, and it calls for an institutional response.

None of which is to say that the pandemic isn't real or serious or even that extraordinary measures weren't required, so long as those measures were constitutional and democratic, meaning justified and transparent. But it is to say that the pandemic also represented an opportunity to put into play a plan that had been incubating for more than 30 years. In the end, the government response to the pandemic turned out to be more about the latter than about the former.

To put it another way, under her emergency public health authority, the DHS secretary might well isolate an individual reasonably presumed to be infected— with due process of course—but nowhere does the statute give her any authority to isolate every citizen without any reasonable evidence that it is necessary, and without any due process, nor do the statutes even contemplate such authority in passing.

Institutional exercises of extreme power are by their very nature arbitrary, and that Palm's actions during this pandemic had so little to do with public health is evidenced in how arbitrary and capricious the orders were. Take business closures. It's as if the list of favored essential businesses and of disfavored nonessential businesses was made with the flip of a coin.

You could buy furniture in a hardware store or a Walmart but not in a furniture store. Car dealers with heavy foot traffic were open—hey why not? — but jewelry and other retail stores with far less traffic were not. Stores that supplied schools with supplies were open, but schools were not.

In Wisconsin, a liquor store was essential but a church wasn't. In Michigan you could kayak but not use a motor boat. You couldn't invite your neighbor over for dinner but you could golf with him or her shoulder to shoulder in the morning. It went on and on.

It has all been inherently unfair and discriminatory.

So if the orders weren't about the logic of public health, what were they about?

They were about power and politics, pure and simple. What else would the answer be? They were an effort to corral into a few corners all the seats of corporate and government power. To do that, as Robert F. Kennedy, Jr., the founder of Children's Health Defense, has observed, they have to take away our freedoms.

"If you're a Republican or a Democrat, stop talking about that," Kennedy said in a November message. "Stop identifying yourself. The enemy is Big Tech, Big Data, Big Oil, Big Pharma, the medical cartel, the government totalitarian elements that are trying to oppress us, to rob us of our liberties, of our democracy, of our freedom of thought, of our freedom of expression, of our freedom of assembly, and all the freedoms that give dignity to humanity."

To fight that enemy, civil liberties must be protected, Kennedy said, and transparency is crucial.

"And the first civil right that they begin with is freedom of speech," he said. "They need to clamp down, censorship, because [freedom from] censorship is the most important right. In our country we put it number one, the First Amendment of the Constitution, because all the other rights depend on it. If a government can hide what it's doing, it can get away with anything it wants. If a corporation can lie and conceal information, if there's no transparency in a democracy, you do not have a democracy."

—

Back in the trenches, public health officials have sometimes gotten away with unconstitutional orders—or, in the case of Wisconsin, tried to get away with them—precisely by obliterating that transparency. Their sweeping judgments are to be taken as sacrosanct, without the need to bother with justifying scientific evidence or oversight because they are just too busy saving the world, and they have not just failed to offer that scientific evidence but often enough during the pandemic they have actively sought to suppress requests for the records of their activities leading to such decisions.

This past summer, Dr. Alain Braillon, a member of France's High Council of Public Health, the expert body of the Ministry of Health for the French government, complained about the worldwide lack of transparency during the Covid-19 pandemic, which he called "a major issue that has been overlooked in scholarly journals."

First, he wrote, health care professionals have faced bullying when speaking out in the media about their real-life experiences of the Covid-19 crisis when they faced basic resources shortages or bureaucratic barriers. Even worse, he wrote, in Europe there are no protections for whistleblowers as there are in the U.S., and, he wrote, "[t]he motto seems to be 'Silence is golden.'"

"This issue also extends to scientific committees advising governments," he wrote. "In Great Britain, the government deliberately kept secret the list of participants in its committee of scientific experts. In France, the High Council of Public Health, the expert body of the Ministry of Health for the French government, issued four dozen reports about Covid-19. As a member, when recruited, I had to sign a form swearing I would respect the 'duty of reserve' regarding the content of meetings. This issue is not a theoretical one: I was forced to resign in 2018 from Public Health France's scientific committee after a written threat of being sued for such a breach if I refused to resign because whistleblowing by a civil servant is a specific criminal offense in France."

Transparency was critical but lacking, Braillon wrote.

"Setting transparent and fair rules is a mandatory prerequisite for confidence and effectiveness," he wrote. "Old democracies are deliberately breaching their most basic principle. The crisis is before us."

The crisis is before us no less in the United States and Wisconsin, as directive after directive is pushed forward without any apparent logic or underlying science. In *Wired*, for example, contributor Roxanne Khamsi wrote that she and other New Yorkers puzzled over a statewide rule that bars, restaurants, and gyms had to close at 10 p.m.

"Was this based on some brand-new evidence that the virus mutates like a gremlin, getting worse at night?" she wrote. "You wouldn't know it from Gov. Andrew Cuomo's announcement, which did not cite any research whatsoever that might justify this policy."

Since the start of the pandemic, Khamsi wrote, time and again new "science-based" Covid-19 measures were prescribed, but the science in support of it was either vague or missing altogether. What had been a 14-day quarantine had become an eight-day quarantine combined with a test, Khamsi wrote, but some people who arrived from out of state were allowed to quarantine for just four days.

How did that come to be? Khamsi asked. Well, she was told, the state and Gov. Andrew Cuomo "worked with global health experts" on the plan.

"A formal guidance from the state health department gave no research citations, either, but it did find space to boast about New York's record of 'strict adherence to data-driven, evidence-based protocols,'" she wrote.

The same was true in other states and in the World Health Organization, Khamsi wrote. Back in the spring, when she asked for the science behind WHO's proclamation that the virus wasn't airborne, Khamsi said the organization omitted and/or ignored existing research to the contrary.

"Hiding the scientific basis for pandemic policies makes it harder for the public to evaluate what's being done," she wrote. "That means there's no good way to audit measures that may be poorly crafted or even dangerous. The risks could be even deeper, though. When health authorities present one rule after another without clear, science-based substantiation, their advice ends up seeming arbitrary and capricious."

There's those words again. From the World Health Organization to the federal government to the states to the local level—the battle cry from the public health syndicate is truly 'silence is golden,' leading to arbitrary and capricious directives.

And not only are they refusing to share scientific data, they are concealing the daily activities that lead directly to decision making at every level of government.

Once again, Oneida County provides a perfect example. In May 2020, we requested the work emails for the first three months of the pandemic from Oneida County public health director Linda Conlon. The reason was simple. We wanted to know how she was leading the local response to the pandemic. What internal decisions was she making? How was she making them? Who was she involving in decision making on the local level? What were their priorities? Who was she consulting with on the state and federal levels?

As of this writing, in early January, 2021, more than two-thirds of those emails had not been received, and *The Lakeland Times* has filed an open records complaint against Conlon. The case represents a typically extreme effort by the public health director to conceal what she and her department have done to deal with a crisis of public health, which is, of course, of tantamount importance to the public.

If it's life or death for everybody, as the public health authorities tell us, it is our right to know what they are doing.

Conlon doesn't want us to know. Way back on October 27, 2020, for example, she asked that the scope of the request be narrowed. Conlon indicated that the request was too broad and that it could be argued that it lacked a subject matter as required by the law since the request was for all emails in a three-month period. Accordingly, she asked for 'specific areas of concern,' though she did say the request was not being denied and that she would work to review the emails 'expeditiously' and 'as soon as practicable and without delay.'

Conlon also cited the 'growing pandemic' and her response to it as her 'top priority.' But that request and response failed on multiple levels.

The first is, the public records law contains no requirement that a records request contain both a subject matter and a time limit, as this book has already shown. The clear language of the law is that a sufficient request must contain a time limit *or* a subject matter.

Even so, we explained in a response to Conlon, what she was doing during the first three months of the pandemic was the specific area of concern and was the subject matter.

"The public cannot judge how the county's public health department was responding, or know what decisions Ms. Conlon was making, without all of her email correspondence from that time; separating out narrow portions of her work would enable her to hide certain areas of activity and decision making, about which the public has a right to know," publisher Gregg Walker wrote in the open records complaint.

Second, we believe, the public health department has no authority to suspend the state's public records law because of the pandemic. There simply has been no state legislative or executive or judicial action to do so, and no local order, regulation, or county action to do so. The constitutionality and legality of any such actions would be challenged, of course, but so far they do not even exist, and the county health department and the county are obligated to follow the law. We do not believe they did.

What's more, a heavy workload is no excuse for breaking the law, and withholding thousands of records for seven months and more withers the claim of processing the request "as soon as practicable and without delay" to a veritable pile of insincere and illegal dust.

Third, so far as the newspaper understands, the review of records was taking place by the corporation counsel, and that is where the records were. If that was the case and the records were no longer in the health department, then blaming the delay on the workload caused by the pandemic was preposterous.

The bottom line is, the records request remained unfulfilled more than seven months after the original request was sent, and that is as far from the statutory requirement to fill a request 'as soon as practicable and without delay' as the county could get. It was a de facto denial.

It should be said, even if the records were being reviewed outside her office, it was Conlon's responsibility as the custodian under the public records law to deliver the releasable records in a timely fashion.

Again, contrary to the notion that open records requests should be less of a priority during a pandemic, transparency is especially important for the public at a time when governments are making decisions not only affecting public health but about lockdowns, school and business operations, and other public policy matters that impact our citizens' livelihoods, education, freedoms, and more. The public must be allowed to oversee this decision making and having full access to the data and the communications of officials is vital to that end.

A couple of final points. One of the reasons health officials have said these requests take so long is that there are just too many records to produce, and then it takes oh so much time to review and redact them. In this day and age, though, producing thousands of emails takes very little time. A couple of search words or date ranges, and the records are produced in minutes. This amazing technology is called the 21st century.

In response to open records requests, we have received thousands of emails from lawmakers, county officials, and town officials in several hours and at the most several days. Why couldn't Conlon do what others with equally important jobs have done? What was the difference?

Well, one difference was, the officials who released voluminous amounts of emails weren't trying to hide anything. Conlon apparently was.

I'm not saying that she did anything wrong other than withhold the records impermissibly (which is seriously wrong in and of itself) or that she was trying to cover up iniquitous goings-on. She simply might want to protect her policy-making process. But, whatever the reason, noble or nefarious, seven months going on eight months is beyond the pale, and it was a direct violation of the law to withhold public information so long.

As for all that screening that needs to be done, the truth is, that is a smokescreen used by government hacks and their shills for not fulfilling records requests. These days, both government and private companies use automated redaction software that is highly accurate and that reduces redaction times to a fraction of the time that manual removal takes, actually saving taxpayers money.

If Oneida County and other governments aren't using this software, they should be. In the meantime, no one should let any government official get away with the malarkey about how much time the review takes.

Once again—and this is an all-important point—transparency is not less but more important during a crisis such as the Covid-19 pandemic. None other than the World Health Organization (WHO) puts it this way: "As research on SARS in Toronto has shown, in times of uncertainty and crisis, the notion of accountability is more important, not less so. Without it, public trust is diminished and it is difficult to restore."

What's more, as WHO also acknowledged, public health departments are staffed by humans, and humans are notoriously resistant to releasing information that sometimes is vital for the public to have to participate in decision-making and crisis response.

Shutting the public out to let the experts work in secrecy has produced disastrous results time and again, and it is frankly an outmoded way of thinking, as even WHO acknowledged. It's time to stop it. We don't doubt that the public health department was inundated "with life and death issues," but it is crucial that the public be actively engaged in discussing, planning, and responding to such vital issues, especially because it is the public's lives at stake.

Only with openness will we know whether policies that they tell us save lives are actually saving lives, or whether they are politically driven actions called for by the Big Pharma-Public Health Syndicate.

Not least in considering all this is the absolute hypocrisy of public health officials who want every citizen to follow the directives of the state and the county and their agencies but who are not willing to follow the laws themselves.

When public health organizations take action to obstruct and delay the release of information, when they aggressively subvert transparency, they are engaging in a censorship every bit as oppressive as that practiced in the old Soviet Union, and which has reared its ugly head in the United States.

Let us say it clearly: Government attempts to block the transparency of their actions and decision making is just another form of censorship, for we cannot speak freely in self-government if we do not have the knowledge of events we need to do so.

It is often said that information is the currency of democracy, and with it we can control our destiny.

"Whenever the people are well informed, they can be trusted with their own government; that whenever things get so far wrong as to attract their notice, they may be relied on to set them to rights," Thomas Jefferson wrote.

When government goes dark, though, we the people cannot see our way back to the path of freedom and sound public policy from which we have strayed. The darkness becomes a cell in which we are condemned to wander back and forth without direction or hope.

Make no mistake, the Dark State is a prison. It's time we set ourselves free.

About the Author

Richard Moore's writing and essays have appeared in more than two dozen national and regional publications, including *The New York Times Sunday Magazine*, *The New York Times* travel section, *The Washington Post*, *Charleston Magazine*, *The St. Petersburg Times*, the *Atlanta Journal-Constitution*, and many more.

Richard is the author of *Journeys of Lightheartedness; January Thaw; The Clarity of Clay; How the DNR Stole Wisconsin; Prologue: My Dinners with Dusty;* and the forthcoming books, *Mapping the Close Years* and *How to Write What You Want to Read.*

Journeys of Lightheartedness is a Kirkus Reviews recommended book and also received a five-star Readers' Review rating from Jack Magnus, who called his reading of the book "a remarkable and illuminating experience."

In addition, Richard is the senior investigative reporter for, and former editor of, *The Lakeland Times* in Minocqua, Wisconsin. Most recently, he won the 2017 and 2019 Wisconsin Newspaper Association's (WNA) first-place award for open government and Freedom of Information Act reporting; the 2017 WNA first-place award in enterprise journalism for his series, "Autism and Education"; the 2019 WNA first-place award for investigative journalism for investigating open-government issues at the state Department of Justice; and the 2019 first-place award for editorial writing.

His writing has also appeared in college texts (Social Problems, edited by Stanley Eitzen, Allyn & Bacon, Inc.). He was a contributor to *The Reform of State Legislatures* (University Press of America), which *The Wall Street Journal* called "powerful evidence for those who wish to return to the citizen legislatures envisioned by the Founding Fathers."

www.ingramcontent.com/pod-product-compliance
Lightning Source LLC
Chambersburg PA
CBHW031425270326
41930CB00007B/574